Harrogate College Library
(01423) 878213
This book is due for return on or before the last date shown below.

Contemporary Theatre Studies
A series of books edited by Franc Chamberlain, Nene College,
Northampton, UK

Please see the back of this book for other titles in the Contemporary Theatre Studies series.

ART
INTO
THEATRE
PERFORMANCE INTERVIEWS
AND
DOCUMENTS

Nick Kaye
University of Warwick, UK

harwood academic publishers
Australia • Canada • China • France • Germany • India • Japan
Luxembourg • Malaysia • The Netherlands • Russia • Singapore
Switzerland • Thailand

First published 1996
Second printing 1998

Amsteldijk 166
1st Floor
1079 LH Amsterdam
The Netherlands

British Library Cataloguing in Publication Data

Kaye Nick
    Art into Theatre: Performance Interviews and Documents.
    – (Contemporary Theatre Studies, ISSN 1049-6513; Vol. 16)
    I. Title II. Series
    792.028

ISBN 3-7186-5789-9 (Softcover)

Cover photo: Stuart Brisley, *Moments of Decision/Indecision*, Teatr Galery,
Pałac Kultury i Nauki, Warsaw, Poland, 1975. Photo: Leslie D. Haslam

CONTENTS

INTRODUCTION TO THE SERIES

Contemporary Theatre Studies is a book series of special interest to everyone involved in theatre. It consists of monographs on influential figures, studies of movements and ideas in theatre, as well as primary material consisting of theatre-related documents, performing editions of plays in English, and English translations of plays from various vital theatre traditions worldwide.

Franc Chamberlain

LIST OF PLATES

LIST OF QUOTED TEXTS

ACKNOWLEDGEMENTS

A book such as this has many debts. First and foremost, I wish to express my gratitude to the artists included here. Not only does this volume very obviously rest on their time and interest, but many of these texts have benefited from their invaluable help with source materials, documentation and references. As the project has developed toward publication, I have also had very generous help with illustrations and textual extracts. During this process, many of the interview texts themselves have been substantially revised or developed through further exchanges and correspondence.

Underlying the history of these conversations, too, is their importance to the wider development of my own research and teaching and I have a personal debt, in this respect, both to these particular artists and to the various funding bodies and organizations that have made these meetings possible.

The very first of these interviews, with Marina Abramovic and Ulay in Amsterdam in 1983, occurred during a period of travel and study in continental Europe as a graduate student, made possible by financial support from the University of Manchester. My contact with John Cage arose from a period of time spent in New York during 1985, made possible through the generous support of both the University of Manchester and Vassar College, New York. Subsequent periods of research in New York, firstly in 1990 in support of an earlier book, and in 1993 directly in connection with this publication, would not have been possible without financial support from the British Academy, the University of Warwick and the School of Theatre Studies of the University of Warwick. A final series of interviews within the UK were conducted during a sabbatical term in the Spring of 1994 with the support of a travel grant from the University of Warwick. This period of leave also allowed me to bring the manuscript near to completion.

The majority of interview texts included here have not been published before. However, I am pleased to acknowledge that the conversation with Richard Foreman was originally published as 'Bouncing Back the Impulse: An Interview with Richard Foreman' in *Performance* 61

(1990), while the interview with Richard Schechner was published as 'Theory and Practice of the Indeterminate Theatre' in *New Theatre Quarterly* 20 (1989). An earlier version of the discussion with Joan Jonas was published as 'Myth, Ritual and Narrative: An Interview with Joan Jonas' in *Performance* 65–66 (1992).

Nick Kaye

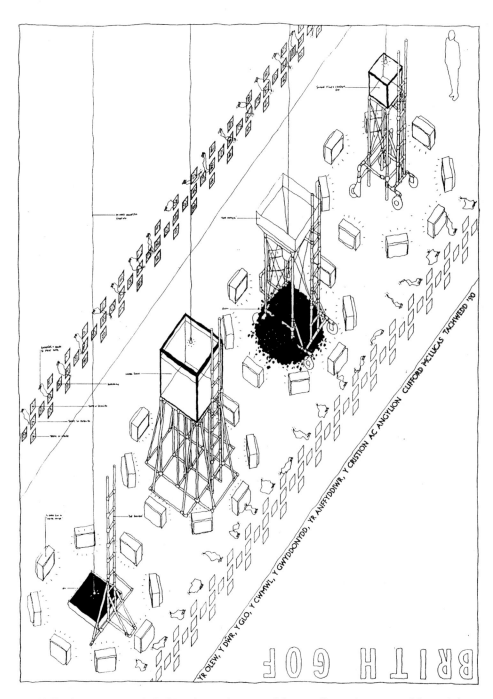

Clifford McLucas, Brith Gof *Pax* (1991–2) proposal for installation (courtesy of the artist).

INTRODUCTION: ART INTO THEATRE

This book is concerned with moves *toward performance* and practices *in performance* which effect an intersection between disciplines or media. Recorded and developed principally between 1990 and 1994, but including interviews from 1983, 1985 and 1988, these texts and documents address concepts of performance and performance practices which mark out a wide range of inter-disciplinary exchanges and engagements in art and theatre occurring between 1952 and 1994. In ranging from John Cage to Forced Entertainment Theatre Co-operative, from Dennis Oppenheim to Richard Schechner, from the Wooster Group to Brith Gof, from Michael Kirby's 'Structuralist Workshop' to Marina Abramovic, these discussions not only engage with many of the principal contexts in which, during the 1960s and 1970s, overtly 'non-theatrical' practices derived from painting, sculpture, music, and site-related art gave rise to radically new and still challenging entries into performance, but also explorations of video, cinema, process, and site in contemporary performance operating in the wake of these earlier moves from art and into theatre.

Yet while *Art into Theatre* is organised and edited in relation to notions of 'inter-disciplinarity', these interviews and documents exemplify an innate tension between any such critical project and the practices it would circumscribe. While the choices that give *Art into Theatre* its form, and effect its exclusions, reflect a critical concern with an inter-disciplinary turn in art *realised* as performance, and for strategies in contemporary theatre which can be read against these challenges to the fixity of the terms and parameters of the work in art, the material presented here inevitably pulls away from any single, critical centre. Thus, what *Art into Theatre* offers is explicitly partial, as it stages a series of discussions whose relationship is left unresolved by any single, overbearing narrative voice. Just as these texts offer a range of debates around moves from art practice and into performance, so they also trace various histories of work.

In this context, this introduction offers an account of the emergence of performance in art and of inter-disciplinary practices in contemporary theatre which set certain parameters for *Art into Theatre*. Rather than pretend to a neutrality the process of editing sometimes hides behind, these remarks offer a critical reflection upon the developing logics of these discussions, setting out, in relation to the work presented here, ideas of inter-disciplinarity against which these dialogues, and many of their parallels and exchanges, might be usefully read. Quotations in this essay for which sources are not given are drawn directly from the discussions that follow.

Raiding the real

Evidently, the entry of performance into art does not, in itself, indicate a turning by artists toward theatre forms or conventions. Indeed, performance in art or performance by artists has invariably arisen in a resistance to the very containment and fixities through which not only the conventional work in art but much theatre and performance would establish itself. In this context, the implications of the turn toward performance through visual arts practices are often at their clearest where the practice of performance is read not in terms of 'theatre', but as an address to the terms and assumptions surrounding the 'art object' itself.

In the 1950s and early 1960s, John Cage's innovations in musical composition signalled a broad reconception of the work of art in American and European art and performance. In its explicit challenge to the conventional distinctions between the viewer's act of perception and the identity of the work, Cage's radical presentations sought to provoke a recognition of the centrality of *performance* to the work of art's definition, whatever its medium or form might ostensibly be. In setting out this concept of the work, Cage's practice had a profound influence on the intersection of painting, sculpture and performance in the late 1950s and early 1960s, while touching on sets of concerns that have animated various moves by artists toward performance since the 1960s.

Key to Cage's concept of the work is the notion of 'silence', through which he characterises occurrences and contents the conventional work of art cannot embody. In particular, through his series of 'silent' pieces, initiated with 4'33" in 1952, Cage proposed that in music:

> *nothing takes place but sounds: those that are notated and those that are not. Those that are not notated appear in the written music as silences, opening the doors of the music to the sounds that happen to be in the environment… There is no such thing as an empty space or an empty time. There is always something to see, something to hear…. (Cage 1968: 8)*

Cage's score for 4'33" consists simply of an indication of a performance in three parts, where each part is designated 'TACET', or silent. Thus, it is a 'musical' performance of a specific duration and structure in which no musical instrument is to be played. In his original presentation of the piece at Woodstock, New York, in 1952, the pianist David Tudor made clear this turning away from notated sound through his closing of the piano's keyboard lid for the duration of each of its three timed 'movements'.

Arguing that 'through the way I place my intention I create the experience that I have', Cage understood the move toward self-containment, in which the work of art is equated with a self-determining *object*, to effect not only a distortion of the notated elements of the work, but, in the work's claim to its own integrity and identity, a suppression of the actual process by which the viewer or listener brings the work into being. In opposition to the pre-determined composition's assertion of its own identity and value as music, Cage defined 'silence' as that which is always in occurrence beyond what would be the pre-determined parameters of the work.

It follows from this, then, that, for Cage, the musical work can only claim to be in possession of its own identity as music, and to define its own limits, by opposing the viewer's attention to 'silence'. Within Cage's terms, however, such a work not only impoverishes music's possible vocabulary, but presents itself as blind to the very conditions under which it acquires identity and meaning. Indeed, it is in direct opposition to this claim to self-definition, that Cage refuses in 4'33" to set out any of the conventional elements of a 'musical work', offering instead an event to be defined by the listener in her listening.

Cage's rigorous opposition to self-containment and fixity in the work of art was rooted directly in a notion of the 'real' as process. In opposition to the 'object' in art, Cage defined the 'real' as a state of continual 'becoming', which the work of art is subject to, but which, *as an object*, it can neither embody nor represent. He writes that:

> You say: the real, the world as it is. But it is not, it becomes! It doesn't wait for us to change... It is more mobile than you can imagine. You are getting closer to reality when you say that it 'presents itself'; that means it is not there, existing as an object. The world, the real, is not an object. It is a process. (Cage and Charles 1981: 180)

In this context, these concerns for 'silence' and 'process' bear not only upon the inherited vocabulary of art, but the conventional opposition between the 'object' in fine art and time-based processes and strategies associated with the performing arts. By the 'object' Cage does not mean the fixed, material object, but any 'work' which attempts to resolve itself into a fixed form, and so which claims to have established its own limits. Furthermore, this claim may be constructed both by way of the work's composition and reception. Even with regard to his own procedures and processes, Cage emphasised that:

Any one of my indeterminate pieces, if recorded, becomes an object the moment you listen to it knowing you can listen to it again. You listen to it again and the object breaks forth. (Cage and Charles 1981: 79)

Where 'art should introduce us to life' (Cage and Charles 1981: 52) as process, it follows, the 'work of art' must open itself to 'silence' and so to an unravelling of its own formal integrity, as an object, even a breaking down of the very boundaries that give it its identity and authority as a discrete work. It is precisely in these circumstances, Cage supposes, where the distinction between what might and might not be 'art' becomes confused, that the viewer or listener might be implicated, in their own eyes, in the definition of *what will be the work*. In these circumstances, too, it becomes clear that if music is defined by the act of listening, then visual art is defined by the act of looking, while 'theatre is something that engages both the eye and the ear.' Cage continues, 'the reason I want to make my definition of theatre that simple is so one could view everyday life itself as theatre' (Kirby and Schechner 1986: 79).

This unravelling of the work of art as a discrete entity is exemplified, in Cage's practice, in the series of 'silent pieces' after *4'33"* and the *Variations* series initiated in 1958. While *0'00" (4'33" No. 2)* (1962) [Figure 1] strips away the three-part structure and concert-hall circumstances of *4'33"*, reducing the work to a disciplined act of attention on behalf of the listener, the *Variations*, at their most fluid, become means of generating occasions for listening which call into question, even at the level of the score, their containment as discrete 'works', and so their possible resolution *as objects*.

The score for *Variations IV* (1963) [Figure 2], a work 'for any number of players, any sounds or combination of sounds produced by any means', consists simply of two sheets of transparent plastic, one with circles, another with dots, providing a means of dividing a given space into particular areas and points at which sounds or activities occur. As Cage's stipulations make clear, each realisation of *Variations IV* is itself a variation, as the 'score' no longer offers an accurate description of any particular performance. On the basis of the score, 'the work' is difficult to locate, except as a procedure which will produce radically differing events, none of which will exhaust the 'scheme' Cage sets out or be entirely repeatable. Cage's own preferred realisation extends this dispersion into performance itself. Recalling its realisation at a found site, he notes that 'I enjoy *Variations IV* best when it is done in a large space, in fact a space that can be defined roughly by how far one can hear.' Bounded only by the limits of what can be seen and heard, such a variation of *Variations IV* offers an extreme dispersal of elements and so a situation which is resistant to the onlooker's desire to unify. At the same time, the conflation of the 'limits' of the work with the viewer's idiosyncratic engagement serves to corrupt the distinctions between the perceiver and what might be the 'work'. Here, where it is the viewer who *performs* the work, in the sense of attempting to define its limits, and so carry it through to completion, there might arise, Cage suggests, 'a confusion as to what is 'art' and what isn't' and so, it follows, what 'is' the piece and what is being found through it. In this context, this realisation of *Variations IV* might best be understood as a staging of a work's *coming into being*, a making visible to the viewer of her own engagement in the process of looking 'for' and so 'through' a work that will never be resolved as a fixed and so 'objectified' composition.

This notion of the performance of the work by the viewer, irrespective of conventional medium or discipline, is a key to the emergence of performance in art practice, and arises across a wide variety of modes of work. Indeed, underlying this elaboration of what, after Duchamp, might be characterised as the viewer's completion of the work (Duchamp 1983), is a fundamental sense that the work in art is perpetually in the process of *being performed*.

In contrast to Cage's attempts to dissolve what would be the elements of the work into that which literally surrounds it, Barry Le Va deals explicitly with the materials and forms of sculpture. Yet Le Va's distributional sculpture, initiated in the late 1960s, presents materials in such a way as to not only refer back to the 'event' of their arrangement, but, through the complexity of the traces which remain, to provoke the onlooker's awareness of her own implication in the construction of these histories.

Le Va's address to the intersection of the various events that would define the work have taken forms ranging from the distribution around specific rooms of simple materials, such as glass, dowelling or flour, to the *Velocity Piece* (1969) [Figures 7–8], an installation tracing through sound Le Va's earlier occupation of a gallery space. In reducing the material of the 'sculpture' to 'the residue of the event that's happened to it', Le Va provokes an uncertain relationship between the presence of materials, the fact of the event their presence recalls, and the viewer's speculations over the 'event-structure' which defined their form and placement. Le Va's own strategies, which include the deliberate subversion of one intention with another, serve to deepen the viewer's self-reflexive engagement. In undertaking the procedures of making the work, he notes, and while the trace itself *is* produced by a specific event, this trace is such that it calls into question:

> any sense of correct judgment, any sense of stableness. It doesn't produce confusion, but it does set up a situation where one has to question one's own thought processes... All of a sudden things are being subverted and you realise the work wasn't about that at all.

By presenting the 'residue' of an event, Le Va invites the viewer to position 'the work' between a performance which is now over and its material trace. Yet, as this implies, the very uncertainty of the relationship between 'performance' and 'trace' serves to draw the viewer into her own moulding of its terms, her own *performance* of the work, and, at this moment, an awareness of this process. It follows that rather than constituting the work itself, the materials which Le Va presents act as points of intersection between performances past and present, and so as the fulcrum of a 'work' which, for the viewer, is always in the process of being 'completed'.

While Le Va's work draws the viewers' attention to the process of their looking through the presentation of material as 'trace' or 'residue', other kinds of sculpture have evidently given rise to notions of performance despite, or even through, an apparent claim to autonomy.

In the context of Minimal Art, this particular departure is quite evident. The pervasive influence of Minimal and Systemic Art on the emergence of performance practice in the late 1960s and early 1970s is founded both on the procedures of Systemic Art and the Minimal object's very resistance to being 'read' by the viewer. Typically, the 'Minimal' objects presented by artists such as Robert Morris, Donald Judd and Frank Stella from around 1965 and 1966, rejected two or three-dimensional representation in favour of a non-representative object, often in the form of a unitary geometrical shape. Placed flatly within the gallery space, such objects seem to offer themselves as simple, irreducible 'facts', offering nothing more than their own sheer physical presence.

For the Body Artist Vito Acconci, however, the Minimal object's very resistance to the viewer's effort to 'read' its terms served only to force what would be 'the work' back toward the viewer, prompting his own engagement with performance. Minimalism, he suggests:

> was the art that made it necessary to recognise the space you were in. Up until that time I had probably assumed the notion of a frame, I would ignore the wall around it. Finally, then, with minimal art, I had to recognise I was in a certain floor… I was in a certain condition, I had a headache, for example. I had a certain history, I had a certain bias… what minimal art did for me was to confirm for myself the fact that art obviously had to be this relation between whatever it was that started off the art and the viewer. (Acconci 1982)

Cage, similarly, read this refusal to provide a content, or even a relationship between parts, as creating an opportunity for 'silence' to enter into the work, and so to reach beyond the conventional boundaries of the object in sculpture. He remarks that, 'Many of those works in Minimal Art are, so to speak, 'silent'… if you don't pay attention to… what isn't 'art', you don't have anything to look at'. Like Cage's refusal to provide conventional 'musical' content in *4'33"*, the Minimal object Acconci describes throws the viewer's attention back upon itself, forcing an awareness of the 'literal' space in which the viewer acts.

Despite their obvious differences in method and form, Cage's giving over of the work to process, Le Va's use of 'trace' and 'residue', and the consequences of the Minimal object's acute self-containment, look toward a very specific space for performance. Performance, here, occurs *before* the object, as a making visible of 'that which is done' around and through 'the work' by the artist and viewer. More precisely, it is an address to that which happens but cannot be fixed or figured *within* the work. It is in this context that the entry into performance is invariably put forward by artists themselves as an opening up to *the real*, an entry into that which surrounds and enacts the work but which is not synonymous with that which can be fixed and presented as the work.

In Le Va's practice, then, the concern with 'events', is a concern with 'real time', 'real space'. Rather than 'figuring' and 're-presenting' a 'virtual' space *within* the work, the turn toward 'event-structure' is a turning toward processes and contexts through which the limits of the work are yet to be defined. For the viewer, this means that rather than be witness to the work's self-containment, to its separation of itself from the 'literal' circumstances in which 'it' stands, she finds herself 'within the boundaries of the performance', a situation which Le Va sees as being made explicit in performance-installations such as Vito Acconci's *Seedbed* (1972) [Figure 10].

For Dennis Oppenheim, working directly from within the contexts of sculpture, the entry into Body Art in the late 1960s meant precisely such an entry into the 'real'. Thus, he notes, the expanded field of Body Art, occurring in the wake of the 'de-materialised' object, 'invaded one's home. It took in one's family'. Emphasising that 'one of the most catalytic aspects of Body Art... was this connection with the real world', Oppenheim recounts that in trying 'to get a configuration that represented fear' for *Rocked Circle — Fear* (1971) [Figures 11–12], 'it was very important that it was not seen as 'drama' in the traditional sense of acting. It wanted to be *real* in the simple sense of the word.' In entering into Body Art, Oppenheim plainly does not simply enter into the medium of theatre. Rather than offer the work as a performance to an audience, *Rocked Circle — Fear* is met as the trace of an act undertaken once only, a document which points to, but nevertheless pointedly resists embodying, that which the 'work' is evidently 'about'. Again, the work is concerned with that which has occurred and is occurring at the periphery of the object or document. Oppenheim emphasises that:

in spirit, in spirit, *there was a feeling that these activities were charges to activate the periphery of things. There was a tendency to see even discrete performances and works as being charges that opened up doors that were not going to be found on the paper that you presented the work to.*

In this context, danger and risk, because of their very resistance to being embodied by the object, become keys to the work. Without risk, Oppenheim notes, 'the results often had certain problems of authenticity, certain problems of the calibre of the pursuit', yet, he suggests, 'with that element of danger, one's work, in every way, became more substantial. It seemed to satisfy the urges within this whole programme to raise the work and raid the real'.

For artists such as Carolee Schneemann and the British artist Stuart Brisley, the act of performance itself is a direct intervention into the 'real', as it challenges and politicises the exchanges through which the performance is constituted. Schneemann's work, like Joan Jonas' early performance, explicitly places the audience 'in the space of the piece'. In this context, Schneemann's engagement with the 'sacred erotic' serves to challenge that 'voyeuristic space of audience to performer... [which] has to be assaulted, aggressed upon'. Here, she meets the spectator's construction of the work, and her place within it, with 'keys' to 'what's missing, suppressed, diverted' in the culture. Brisley's performances, while deriving from a sense that the object in art failed to give volume to the *real*, offer actions which interrogate the circumstances of the event itself. Seeking an intersection between the act of performance and its immediate contexts, Brisley's work is developed *in situ* as responses to and activations of specific places, times and social contexts. The result are actions which frequently become integrated into and even indistinguishable from events they provoke and give way to. Indeed, finally, Brisley's performance can be seen as blurring into an engagement with a social action and process which defeats the formal integrity of 'the work' in the name of political efficacy.

As it arises out of and around the object, this 'performance' evades the fixities and boundaries of the conventional art-work. Performance, here, is not so much an 'act', something 'done' in order 'to be seen', as a revelation of the *performativity* of the work in art, its constitution by unstable processes and exchanges, and the interrogation, aesthetically, socially, and politically, of what occurs when the object is forced to give way. In this context, one might go on to consider Linda Montano's signalling of everyday activity as performance, her announcement of 'art/life' actions which cannot be seen, because, in being seen, they are transformed. Equally, Ulay's definition of performance as 'a moment of great behaviour or concentration', and Marina Abramovic's revelation of a discipline of life in moments before an audience, question art's inevitable separation from the time and experience of the everyday. Such 'performance' deals not only with that which is seen and done as *performance*, but redraws and disrupts the terms of the work in art in order that processes and occurrences this work cannot fix and contain may be seen and addressed.

Performing the object

It is evident here, too, though, that such entries into the'real' are not simply tied to an overcoming or dissolution of the object. In contrast to Cage's attempt to transcend the limits of the object through a blurring of the boundaries between the 'made' and the 'found', the Minimal object can be read as provoking an awareness of the space in which the viewer acts precisely through its very self-containment *as an object*. Indeed, one can argue that while Cage's indeterminate processes and events deliberately stand in tension with the viewer's effort to unify, other performance, especially that which engages with theatre convention in the wake of Minimal Art, pursues an analogous end by entering directly into dialogue with the elements of the object itself.

For Richard Foreman, working from 1968, the 'clearing of the decks' that Minimalism offered served to clarify his efforts to 'begin from the basic building block elements, to reground my theatre and learn a new language'. He notes that:

> *Minimalism and a very superficial encounter with some of the ideas of Alchemy... were really at the centre of the way I began... how the stuff was mixed and remixed or boiled and reboiled. And the repetition of that activity again and again and again...*

For Foreman, not only did 'Systemic' art provide a clarification of means, but the Minimal object's resistance to the viewer's 'reading' of the work seemed to define the effect his early performance procedures might have. At the time of *Pandering to the Masses: A Misrepresentation* (1975), he suggests:

> *whatever intelligence and whatever interest was in the text I wanted to wipe out with the brute fact of — presence. As if to say whatever intellectual construct you make of it and whatever intellectual construct you make in your life, it's so contingent.*

As Foreman's attitude toward 'the text' suggests, rather than assert the self-containment and authority of the 'object', he sought to stage the 'relation between whatever it is that starts off the work and the viewer'. In this way, and while drawing on the conventional means of theatre, in his early work Foreman pursued precisely the kind of rebuttal of the viewer's attention that the Minimal object most obviously effects. Thus he adopted the strategy of 'crossing out', of wrong-footing or displacing the very elements which would appear to move the 'play' or performance toward coherence — signs of character, emotion, narrative. While Foreman's attack is on 'inherited form', his 'subject-matter' is produced by these procedures, by the effect of his continual and repeated disarming of conventional figures. The result is that rather than attempt to reject or transcend the object, Foreman seeks to stage the *possibility* of its coming into being, making visible the promise its elements make just as he wrong-foots them, and, as he does so, provoking an awareness on behalf of the viewer of her reading *toward* fixity. Yet to stage such a promise is not to *present* the object so much as its *dissolution*. Foreman emphasises that:

> I do think that some sort of dissolving *of the object — which is invariably dishonest in its need to convince, is desirable. But what seems most interesting to me is to dissolve the art-work as self-consciously as possible... I'd like to build it into the object... in such a way that my actual making of the work is a* being-there *with the dissolving process. (Foreman 1985: 199)*

Analogous tensions can be read in Kirby and Howell's work, too. Michael Kirby's founding of the `Structuralist Workshop' in 1975 and his concern with 'Structuralist Theatre' was an extension of his engagement as a visual artist with 'Systemic' and 'Minimal' art. Anthony Howell, of the Theatre of Mistakes, similarly drew on the artist Sol LeWitt's procedures for the production of sculpture in developing performance practices from 1973 and 1974. For both Kirby and Howell, work by 'postmodern' choreographers, such as Yvonne Rainer, who sought to account for her own dance work through a translation of the critical terms surrounding the Minimalist object, also provided a bridge between Minimal art and performance.

Kirby, in particular, equates his plays with the procedures and aesthetic of Minimal art. Arguing that 'I'm trying to do something that's a work of art like the visual artists do... not... a theatre piece like the theatre people do', Kirby emphasises his attempt to construct, through a focus on form and structure, a performance in the manner of an object. Formally, however, he distinguishes between the nature and function of form in this performance and the conventional functions of form in art. A piece such as *First Signs of Decadence* (1985) [pp. 123–25], despite its obvious formalism, he notes, is 'not non-objective — it's not form for its own sake. And the form is not supporting the content'.

In fact, and like Foreman, Kirby's work addresses the viewer's act of reading by calling into question the transparency and efficacy of those elements of which it consists. In *First Signs of Decadence*, Kirby presents a play written in a realistic style, yet whose patterns of blocking, lighting, action, interaction, as well as the order and sequence of emotional response, have been determined through entirely arbitrary rules. Once 'justified' through Kirby's writing and by the performer, the 'realism' of the piece is offered through, and despite, this obvious formal patterning. The result, Kirby suggests, is 'a tension between the representational aspects and the completely non-representational aspects' through which the play is 'torn apart', as it works 'with and against common expectations'. Here, as the two schemes by which the performance operates come to inhabit and displace one another, the viewer is presented with twin 'objects' of performance, which, despite their formal integration, cannot be reconciled. Again, then, the viewer finds her attention reflecting back upon itself, as her focus is caught *between* rather than *within* either of these interdependent possibilities.

In contrast to Kirby, in *Going* (1977) [pp. 135–36, Figures 26–31], the Theatre of Mistakes perform a sequence of 'functional' actions, variations on a theme of leaving, in which, act by act, the accumulating sequence of behaviours of each performer is copied as precisely as possible by the next performer to enter the space. As the increasingly self-reflexive and complicated sequence unfolds, the performance effectively rotates on a central axis, and the audience is shown each aspect of the arrangement from each of its four sides as it builds in complexity. Where a 'mistake' occurs, and an action is missed or copied incorrectly, the performance goes into reverse, and the correct sequence is then played again, with the effect of refining the spectator's view of the generating system or structure. What *Going* offers, however, is not an 'object', as Cage describes it, but the process of performing, of *attempting* to fix an 'object' in time. Furthermore, it is a performance that uses inconsistency, the 'mistake', and so the disruption of the object, to establish and clarify the structure which would be presented as fixed and self-contained. Here, the Theatre of Mistakes, like Foreman, enter into the paradox of revealing the object's *coming into being* and so, implicitly, undermine its stability *in process*.

The sensibility that underlies such an address to performance convention is evident in a wide range of approaches to theatre by artists. Joan Jonas, who trained in sculpture and then dance in the late 1960s with Yvonne Rainer and Trisha Brown, among others, makes an analogous approach to narrative. In pieces such as *Upside Down and Backwards* (1979) and *Volcano Saga* (1985) [pp. 94–7, Figures 21–23], Jonas' complex iconographies are played though narrative lines which are collaged one against the other in such a way that while the promise of unity is clearly present, the work itself resists final narrative closure. The Wooster Group, too, who have at various points collaborated with Foreman, Kirby and Jonas, construct their work through radical juxtapositions and reframings of diverse narrative and performance elements, yet their work strongly resists narrative closure or even a reading through a single set of terms. Furthermore, through this very resistance, their performance tends to echo Foreman's pursuit of 'the brute fact of *presence*', but focused here, specifically, on the presence of the individual performer.

The hybrid

In the context of recent British performance and 'live art', the concerns of these moves between art and theatre, and the strategies they have produced, have been reflected in notions of the 'hybrid'. The hybrid might be understood as a work functioning *between* recognisable forms or schemes. It might involve a playing of one set of formally distinct terms through another, or, as part of this, the disarming of the very terms by which a performance presents or would establish itself. Just as the hybrid might signal a re-conceiving of object-based presentations through performance, so it might be associated with performances shaped overtly by terms uprooted from sculpture, object-related processes or film-production. Inevitably, the hybrid offers itself through unsteady or dissonant relationships between terms, and invariably has the effect of foregrounding the viewer's reading of meaning and purpose.

Of course, one could readily draw such a frame around many of the moves between art and theatre which this book considers. Cage's conception of the work as an event defined in looking sets out a situation in which the formal identity of the work cannot finally be fixed. In so far as it is concerned with a *performance* of its terms by the viewer, Le Va's distributional sculpture prompts a recognition that the work is *durational* despite being object-based. Here, then, while Cage's concern with the event of definition confuses the very notion of aesthetic category, Le Va's work positions itself *between* sculpture and performance. Oppenheim pursues a similar point *between* forms in *Rocked Circle — Fear*, and in doing so signals Body Art's broader challenge to the limits of sculpture. Invariably presented *as an act*, Body Art by Vito Acconci and Oppenheim frequently took recourse to the terms and processes of sculpture for legitimacy, despite the fact that the highly formal terms of Systemic and Minimal object-work are unable to fully articulate the implications for the viewer of such actions upon the body. Here, after Oppenheim's earlier Earth Art, information and terms are uprooted from one area of practice and applied to another, leaving the viewer to negotiate between the terms the artist offers and that which remains conspicuously unaccounted for.

Within American theatre practice, one might associate the hybrid with aspects of Richard Schechner's work, where a performance comes to operate 'by several schemes at once'. Ping Chong's 'bricolage' performances or the Wooster Group's multi-media theatre might be set against the figure of the hybrid not only in their articulation of the work through various channels of address, but in their explicit exchanges with the aesthetics and practices of film.

In the same way, one can readily extend the notion of 'hybrid' to the more recent British performance considered here. Since their first performance, *Natural Disasters* in 1981, work by the English performance company Station House Opera has operated self-consciously between theatre and art practices. *Cuckoo* (1987) [Figure 48] presents performers, objects, furniture, and even the fabric of the set itself, suspended in mid-air and made interdependent in an elaborate construction animated by its own instability. As the piece's procedures are played through, so the viewer's attention is caught between the performance's overtly sculptural aesthetic and the invitation to read role, interaction, and narrative promise. In their large-scale site-specific performances, the Welsh company Brith Gof have engaged self-consciously with notions of 'hybridisation' within their work in response to the contemporary Welsh bi-lingual culture on which they draw. Operating through many channels of address simultaneously, the company's highly politicised sited performances draw significance from their integration into specific places. As part of their dialogue with the history and politics of site, however, this very integration of elements serves to call into question the formal limits and parameters of the performance. Since 1984, the English company Forced Entertainment Theatre Co-operative have drawn explicitly on film, as well as television, video and visual art, in work where concerns with media and mediation have found their way into the fabric of the performance itself. Through their self-conscious construction and manipulation of disparate fictional fragments and contexts within a single performance, Forced Entertainment draw the spectator into a reading and re-reading of worlds where there is no escape from the mediated act. Foregrounding 'the inability of the performers to fully inhabit the gestures and texts which they perform', Forced Entertainment take delight in always seeming to be in the process of deferring to some other point, some other source for reason and purpose.

At one level, this contemporary British theatre could not be more removed from that earlier engagement with performance which served to challenge the limits of the object in art. Yet in catching the viewer between readings, in calling into question the limits and boundaries of the work through its integration into site, or in deferring to some absent point for explanation or legitimacy, this theatre operates in relation to earlier challenges to and shifts between disciplines. Significantly, too, it is precisely to a privileging of perceptual process, and to the implication of the viewer within the terms of the work, that Forced Entertainment's director, Tim Etchells, calls on in his own discussion of the meaning of a performance such as *Club of No Regrets* (1993) [pp. 240–49, Figure 68]. In accounting for such a performance, he argues, to refer to character and what happens on stage 'describes the piece without telling you anything about it' as 'the piece is obviously about you as a watcher'. In this respect, he notes, the distinctive characteristic of the work lies in the fact that it 'foregrounds your seeing, your experience of constructing things as they happen'.

Like the turning from object toward process, the 'hybrid', as it might be read through this work, entails a turning away from self-sufficiency and self-containment. In its presentation of a mis-fitting of elements or practices, such 'hybrid' performance inevitably resists the attempt by the viewer to read and resolve the work *in its own terms*. It follows that it is at this point, then, where concerns over process, and the construction of the work in looking, begin to bring together such radically diverse forms of work, that this introduction should reach a natural close, and quite rightly give way to the discussions themselves.

JOHN CAGE

John Cage's compositions, writings and personality had a profound influence on the sensibility and practices arising through the exchanges between music, painting and dance in the late 1950s and 1960s. Following studies with Schoenberg in 1934, Cage composed for percussion, leading him in 1940 to the introduction of the 'prepared piano' in the composition *Bacchanale*. By inserting wood, screws, rubber and other materials into a conventional piano, Cage not only turned its sound toward percussion, but called into question the conventional function of notation. In 1946 he began studies with the Zen teacher D. T. Suzuki and, as a consequence, introduced chance into his method of composition from 1950. In 1952, the year in which he composed the *Music of Changes* using chance procedures drawn from the *I Ching: Book of Changes*, Cage collaborated with David Tudor, M. C. Richards, Charles Olsen, Robert Rauschenberg and Merce Cunningham in an untitled 'mixed media' performance event which prefigured the emergence of Happenings from 1959. In the Autumn of 1952 the first of his silent pieces, 4'33", was performed by David Tudor at Woodstock, New York. From 1956 to 1958 Cage taught classes in composition attended by, among others, the Fluxus artists George Brecht and Dick Higgins, the 'Happeners' Allan Kaprow and Al Hansen, the artist Jackson Mac Low, as well as the choreographer Robert Dunn, whose own series of classes in experimental dance from 1960 to 1962 gave rise to the Judson Church Dance Theatre. Cage's prolific work and influence extended from music and theatre into writing and visual art, as well as directly into dance through his long-time collaboration with Merce Cunningham, with whom he worked from 1942 until his death in 1992. This interview was recorded in London in May 1985.

*   *   *

It seems to me that the silent pieces, and particularly 4'33" (1952), stand outside of the rest of your work, as if to articulate something fundamental about your position. Was 4'33" conceived of in such a way?

It's simply a very obvious turning of the mind away from intention and toward non-intention. It should be clear to anyone from nothing being done that there are no intentions. When I did the *Music of Changes* (1952), for instance, Henry Cowell said that you could perceive my taste in it. But in the silent piece my taste is not present. I wanted to make it perfectly clear. And there was no other way to make it clear (laughs).

Richard Kostalanetz suggests that you thought of the piece in the late 1940s.
    I did. But I didn't think that I had the right to do it. I knew that many people would not take it seriously, they would think I was playing tricks or something. One very dear friend thought I had gone too far and she momentarily broke friendship. Since then we've repaired that, but she thought that it was not a proper step for an artist to take.

Despite their realisations as public performances, 4'33" and 0'00" both seem open to being read as prompts to more private experiences. Might not 4'33" be realised simply through an act of listening undertaken as an end in itself?
    It could be one or the other. You could do it in front of an audience or you could view life itself, really, as a performance.

Have you performed 0'00"?
    Yes. It was always according to the directions. To be performed as an obligation. In Tokyo, it was the making of the manuscript in front of the audience. Another time I took my unanswered letters and typewrote the replies. Afterwards there was a big party, and someone asked me if I was a drug addict because they couldn't imagine my doing such a thing if I was not on drugs (laughs). Isn't that funny? Don't I say it should be under amplified circumstances? You see the typewriter was amplified so it made an horrendous noise which went on for a long time. And the bell-ringing of the carriage.

Isn't the term 'amplification' also ambiguous?
    I write directions that are mostly ambiguous. What makes you say it's ambiguous?

Amplification need not necessarily be electronic. Couldn't it be a matter of listening?
    Yes, that's true. However, generally, in the case of performance, some things won't be heard unless you do. One of the very early principles of live electronic music was that through the use of amplification changes take place in the quality of the sound — going through a sound system, coming through the loud speakers — changes which are interesting and introductory to present day living. We think (laughter). So that we like to use amplification even when it isn't necessary.

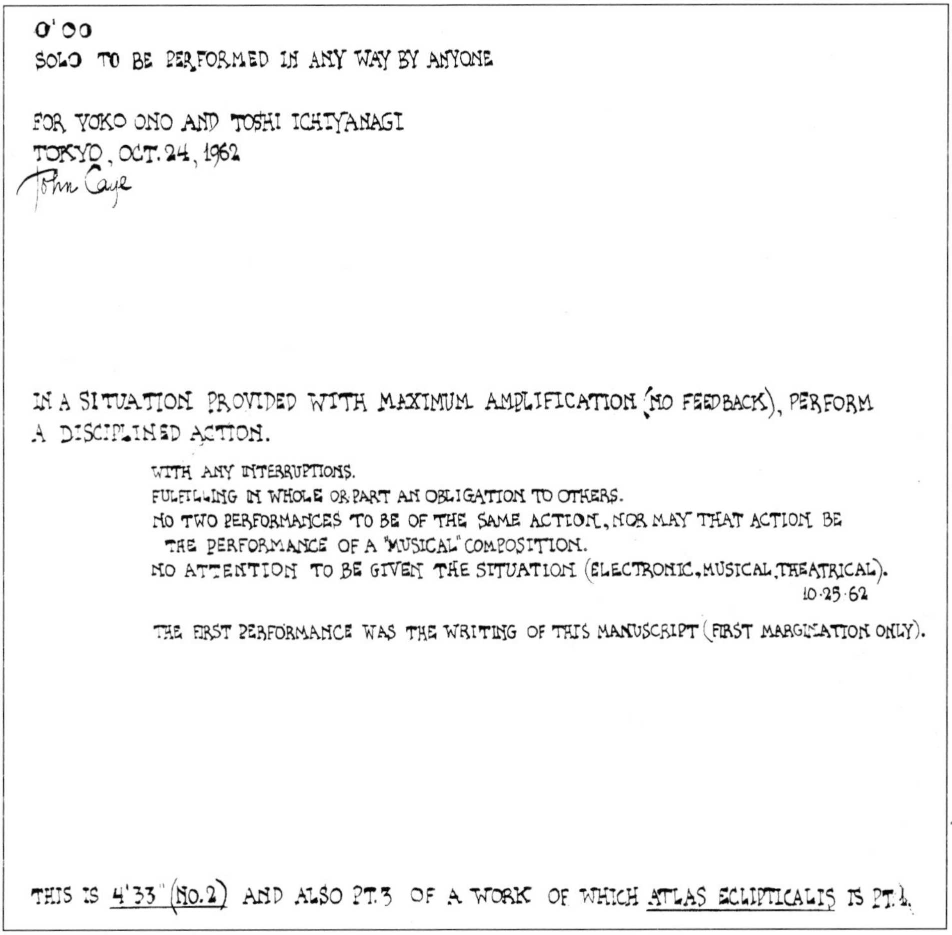
0'00

SOLO TO BE PERFORMED IN ANY WAY BY ANYONE

FOR YOKO ONO AND TOSHI ICHIYANAGI

TOKYO, OCT. 24, 1962

John Cage

IN A SITUATION PROVIDED WITH MAXIMUM AMPLIFICATION (NO FEEDBACK), PERFORM A DISCIPLINED ACTION.

WITH ANY INTERRUPTIONS.

FULFILLING IN WHOLE OR PART AN OBLIGATION TO OTHERS.

NO TWO PERFORMANCES TO BE OF THE SAME ACTION, NOR MAY THAT ACTION BE THE PERFORMANCE OF A "MUSICAL" COMPOSITION.

NO ATTENTION TO BE GIVEN THE SITUATION (ELECTRONIC, MUSICAL, THEATRICAL).

10·25·62

THE FIRST PERFORMANCE WAS THE WRITING OF THIS MANUSCRIPT (FIRST MARGINATION ONLY).

THIS IS 4'33" (NO.2) AND ALSO PT.3 OF A WORK OF WHICH ATLAS ECLIPTICALIS IS PT.1.

Figure 1 John Cage *0'00" (4'33" No. 2)* (c) 1962 by Henmar Press Inc. Reproduced on behalf of the Publishers by permission of Peters Edition Ltd., London.

Is there a third silent piece?

Oh, that's *0'00" No. 2*. Recently a very fine Hungarian musicologist, Andras Wilhelm, got a grant from Hungary to study my work. He made the most complete list of my works that I know of. You see, there's *4'33"*, then there's *4'33" No. 2*, there's *0'00"* which is *4'33" No. 2*. And then there's *0'00" No. 2*.

In other words, *0'00"* is the fulfilment of an obligation to others, whereas *0'00" No. 2* is the playing of a game involving several people.

It is some kind of thing that people do together that is not fulfilling an obligation, but which they don't normally think of as music, turned through amplification into music. Then, related to that, is another thing — *Instances of Silence*. This is simply a collection of — it could be a collection of any ambient or environmental sounds. Duchamp would have — in the case of found objects, which are his sort of acceptance of found environment — instead of a *thing* it's a found process. It could be any such process where intention doesn't take over. For instance, the sound of traffic is a plurality of intentions but intention is more or less wiped out by the plurality. I never wrote down the *Instances of Silence* or *Thirty Three and a Third*. That was done in the late sixties. *Thirty-Three and a Third* is a room with a plurality of sounds, preferably more rather than fewer — say eight at least — or twelve. And beside each record player — that's where the 'thirty three and a third' came from — beside each record player would be a stack of records. The room would be empty, and the audience would be let in. If they wanted any music they would have to put it on. (Laughs). A very nice situation arises because of it. Someone, for instance, will come up and take a record off, and then someone else will try and put it back on.

Do people try to listen to more than one record at once?
      There are a great variety of reactions. But it's also very — pleasant. So, the first pieces in that whole list, really, are the silent pieces, then the *Variations*, some of which I haven't written down, then the improvisations, the pieces for broadcast and television, then the Music Circuses, then things involving tape, taped music, then things involving the public.

To think of 4'33" as a performance which occurred in 1952, as you describe it in the notes accompanying the score, seems to suggest that the piece is tied to the formal circumstances of a concert-hall, even to the particular circumstances of that performance. Doesn't 0'00", as 4'33" No. 2, reject precisely this kind of limitation?
      It became *4'33"* by being composed in the same way that I composed the *Music of Changes*, with a deck of cards on which the individual durations were written. You see, *4'33"* was composed as though there were — it was music — as though there were lots of sounds, but none of the sounds had any definition other than their duration. They could have been low or high or anything, as they are. I think on the score I say it could be any length. As it was written by chance, it could have been any other length. Another thing that David Tudor used to say was that he didn't see why something that had a length of time as a title should last that length of time. You could call something *2'00"* and it might last two hours. Or an hour and a half.

And what strikes me about 0'00", as a revision of 4'33", is that…
> It doesn't measure the time.

…because that kind of 'movement' structure, and with it the concert-hall 'performance', isn't really necessary to the discipline you're setting out or to the discovery of the 'music' you would like to draw attention toward.
> But very few people have any discipline. (Laughs). It's really amazing how many disciplined people are undisciplined. It's quite amazing. Among musicians what happens is that all the three movements turn out to have the same length, because it would be the one they are just inclined toward if they don't measure it. However, if they're doing some actual work as in *0'00"*, or if they're playing a game, their mind is really taken off the question of duration and so they don't go toward the durations they like.

Read as a revision of 4'33", the performance of a 'disciplined action' 'accepting any interruptions' seems to qualify the situation that 4'33" describes, where one might listen to 'everything' that occurs. 0'00" seems to suggest that one might listen to something, only to accept interruptions or intrusions upon that focus. So the invitation is to interact with an environment, to acknowledge, in your listening, that you are within the flow of events. This seems to me much more akin to the kind of process and discipline that 4'33" is trying to get at.
> No, that's true. You know, the reason I said 'accepting interruptions' was that in the performance of the series called *Variations* people in the audience would come up to me while I was performing and ask questions or ask me to sign my autograph or something. I don't know whether I always refused or I was annoyed by that interruption, but I thought of it when I wrote 'accepting interruptions' (laughter). I think what I should say, right now, is that I write the directions the way I do in order that you can possibly discover something that I don't know. Hmm? For this reason I am in some ways opposed to punctuation, for instance, because it clarifies the writing. It points it, instead of leaving it ambiguous. And language — written language — began without punctuation. And was much more poetic, then. That is to say, much more ambiguous. Which is to say more useful. You can spend more time with it when you don't know what it means. (Laughs). I think that one of the things that occurs over and over again is a distinction between understanding and experience, and most of our education has been the attempt to start understanding. But the only things that we really enjoy experiencing are the ones we don't understand. I don't enjoy anything I understand.

You know *Variations IV* (1963), the one with the circles? That's very much like *0'00"*. I enjoy *Variations IV* best when it is done in a large space, in fact a space that can be defined by roughly how far one can hear.

Has it been realised outside?

Several times. On one occasion there were, say, twelve musicians, just speaking roughly. There's a cave in Ste Bohm, near Marseille, where I was asked to conduct a music workshop. What I did was to get all the people in the class to find out together how far away they could be, producing whatever sounds it was they were going to produce, and then used the transparencies of *Variations IV* to make a programme of activities for themselves to an established length of time.

And that activity would be simultaneous?

Yes. That was quite marvellous, both for them and for the audience. Because you see they developed a confusion between what was 'art' and what wasn't.

Have you visited the exhibition at the Saatchi Gallery? You see, many of those works in Minimal Art are, so to speak, 'silent', in that, if you don't pay attention to what isn't 'art' you don't have anything to look at. With the work, say, of Donald Judd or Richard Serra, it's really very beautiful. And you begin to see the effect of the changing light in the room. And also, the effect of your moving in the room. So that something that looks one way at ten feet changes as you get to five feet, and so on. And things that look well constructed turn out on close examination to be poorly constructed, and so on. It's quite amazing.

You have a long-standing collaboration with Merce Cunningham, yet such dance does not lend easily itself to the kind of confusion between what 'is' and 'is not' 'art' you see as so productive in music and visual art.

Well, they're different experiences. What's interesting about dance is different from what's interesting about music. What characterises dance is that there are human beings and that they're in a traffic situation, and its dangerous. It's a life and death question. Very often in a dance company people simply can't dance because of a muscle or knee or something. There was one performance in Ohio and one of the dancers had to be carried away at the end of the performance. She'd been able to carry on through the performance itself but she couldn't walk afterwards. Music doesn't have that kind of problem. But the fact that they're not sounds but human beings in this dangerous situation — makes it very moving. So that one's frequently made very exhilarated or brought to tears or all kinds of such things that

VARIATIONS IV

SECOND OF A GROUP OF THREE WORKS OF WHICH ATLAS
ECLIPTICALIS IS THE FIRST AND O'OO" IS THE THIRD

FOR ANY NUMBER OF PLAYERS, ANY SOUNDS OR COMBINATIONS
OF SOUNDS PRODUCED BY ANY MEANS, WITH OR WITHOUT
OTHER ACTIVITIES

FOR PETER PESIC

John Cage
MALIBU, JULY 10, 1963

MATERIAL NOT PROVIDED:
A PLAN OR MAP OF THE AREA USED FOR PERFORMANCE, AND
OPTIONALLY A COPY OF IT ON TRANSPARENT MATERIAL.

MATERIAL PROVIDED:
SEVEN POINTS AND TWO CIRCLES ON A TRANSPARENT SHEET.
(CUT SO THAT THERE ARE NINE PIECES, EACH WITH ONLY 1
NOTATION.)

PLACE ONE OF THE CIRCLES ANYWHERE ON THE PLAN.
LET THE OTHER CIRCLE AND THE POINTS FALL ON THE PLAN
OR OUTSIDE IT. TAKING THE PLACED CIRCLE AS CENTER, PRO-
DUCE LINES FROM IT TO EACH OF THE POINTS. (STRAIGHT
LINES.) THE SECOND CIRCLE IS ONLY OPERATIVE WHEN ONE OF
THE LINES SO PRODUCED (ONE OR MORE) INTERSECTS OR IS
TANGENT TO IT.
MAKE AS MANY READINGS OF THE MATERIAL AS DESIRED
(BEFORE OR DURING THE PERFORMANCE).

A. THEATRE SPACE (AUDITORIUM WITH DOORS)
  1. ONE FLOOR
  2. WITH BALCONY OR BALCONIES
SOUND(S) TO BE PRODUCED AT ANY POINT ON THE LINES OUTSIDE THE
THEATRE SPACE (EXTEND LINES WHERE NECESSARY). OPEN DOOR(S) PER-
TAINING TO A GIVEN POINT. (SOUND PRODUCTION MAY BE UNDERSTOOD
AS SIMPLY OPENING DOORS.) INTERSECTION OF SECOND CIRCLE =
SOUND IN TOTAL THEATRE SPACE (PUBLIC ADDRESS SYSTEM) OR
AT ANY SPECIFIC POINT ON THE PRODUCED LINE WITHIN THE
SPACE. TWO OR MORE POINTS MAY BE TAKEN AS A SOUND IN
MOVEMENT. (OPEN PERTINENT DOORS) MOVEMENT IS ALSO IN-
DICATED BY USING TRANSPARENT MAP IN ADDITION. A SINGLE NOT-
ATION WILL THEN GIVE TWO POINTS IN SPACE. SEVERAL OF
THESE MAY BE ASSOCIATED WITH ONE SOUND.

B. BUILDING WITH ONE OR MORE FLOORS.
WHEN NECESSARY OPEN WINDOWS INSTEAD OF DOORS.

C. APARTMENT OR SUITE.
THE PERFORMANCE CAN BE IN REFERENCE TO ONE OR ANY NUMBER
OF ROOMS. (THE MEANING OF "OUTSIDE" MAY CHANGE.)

D. CLOSED SPACE (CAVE).

E. OUTDOOR SPACE (ANY AMOUNT).

MEASUREMENTS OF TIME AND SPACE ARE NOT REQUIRED.
WHEN PERFORMED WITH ANOTHER ACTIVITY WHICH HAS
A GIVEN TIME-LENGTH (OR ON A PROGRAM WHERE A GIV-
EN AMOUNT OF TIME IS AVAILABLE) LET THE PERFORM-
ANCE OF THIS TAKE A SHORTER AMOUNT.

A PERFORMER NEED NOT CONFINE HIMSELF TO A PERFORM-
ANCE OF THIS PIECE. AT ANY TIME HE MAY DO SOME-
THING ELSE. AND OTHERS, PERFORMING SOMETHING
ELSE AT THE SAME TIME AND PLACE, MAY, WHEN FREE
TO DO SO, ENTER INTO THE PERFORMANCE OF THIS.

Figure 2 John Cage, from *Variations IV* (c) 1963 by Henmar Press Inc. Reproduced on behalf of the Publishers by permission of Peters Edition Ltd., London.

are less likely to happen in the presence of an experience of sound. The thing that is so marvellous about dancing — when it's good — is that it's a group of people that is not disgusting, mm? (Laughs). Whereas so much of human behaviour is disgusting. But in the case of beautiful choreography people are actually not disgusting (laughs). If you go down Tottenham Court Road, it's very hard to believe that you're in agreement with Mao Tse Tung that all human beings are fundamentally good. He said we *must* believe that every human being is essentially good.

Do you accept that?

I would like to. And I believe that good dancing makes us believe the practicality of that. But I think the effect of government and education on people in society, particularly the effects of economics — the division of society into rich and poor — makes it quite another situation. In which it's possible for all the things that are reported in the newspaper to take place. So that there's another practicality of the silent piece, it seems to me, in the realm of human behaviour.

4'33" and 0'00" also seem to reflect the wider importance to you of this notion of discipline, both in making and listening to work and in the relationship of art to life.

Well, you know, the central thing here I think is a drawing that Suzuki made when I was studying the philosophy of Zen Buddhism with him. He went to the board and drew an oval, and half way up the left-hand side he put two parallel lines. And he said, this is the structure of the Mind, and the two parallel lines are the ego, or mind with a little *m*, and the whole drawing is Mind with a big *M*. And the ego has the capacity to cut itself off from its experience, whether it comes to it from the world of relativity, through the sense perceptions, or whether it comes from the absolute, through the dreams, mm? But the whole thing is a complete circle. And what Zen wants is that the ego not cut itself off, but flow with Mind with a capital *M*. And thus subject it to divine influences. So, if one's involved just with Mind and not with the arts — one sits cross-legged in order to come to *no-mind*. But if you're already, as I was, involved with music, then you have to control your likes and dislikes with something as strict as sitting cross-legged. So I used chance operations. I explained this to you to show you that I try to use a discipline in everything I do. I don't think of art as separate from the rest. I try to do everything in such a way that I let that flow happen. Naturally, one isn't always successful.

So your music brought you to Zen?

Yes. Because I saw that following the precepts that I'd learnt at college, namely that an artist should have something to say and say it, wasn't working. When I said something perfectly serious people laughed. (Laughs). Or even something sad, they would laugh. I decided that saying whatever did not work, because I didn't know what anyone else was saying either. So I gave up that reason and decided not to write music anymore unless I found a better reason than communication. The reason I found came from India, and from England, curiously enough, from something like the sixteenth or seventeenth century. It was a reference Lou Harrison talked of where a composer, an English composer, said, 'to sober and quiet the mind thus making it susceptible to divine influences'. I thought that if it came from England at that time and from India at the present time, which is the same as saying from India at any time, mm? That it was the right answer and that my proper business was to find out the nature of Mind and the nature of divine influences. And I did that to my satisfaction through my studies through Suzuki.

In your paper Biology and History of the Future *(1972) you wrote that you were more and more interested in complexity.*

I'm always interested in complexity. It's just a recognition of the nature of reality. The nature of silence is extremely complex. It's not complexity with regard to my actions, but it's a complex situation that we're involved in. And it's getting more complex. (Laughs).

There's a sort of simplicity to the idea of accepting...

Yes, but what you're accepting is a very complex thing. Yesterday at the Institute of Contemporary Arts someone said, 'how could there be a coincidence?' And I said, how can there not be? Hmm? So, I would rather just foolishly experience things one way or another (laughs). In other words, through the way I place my intention I create the experience that I have. I will often — in the presence of something where chance operations have been used — listen as though it had been composed. Mmm? In other words, one of the things I enjoy doing really is noticing how things begin and how they end. In, say, the *Etudes Australes* (1974–75) or the *Freeman Etudes* (1977) which were written in a detailed way with the use of chance operations, the cadences are all perfectly beautiful. There isn't a single one that isn't beautiful. Whereas Debussy was unable to finish his *Trio for Harp, Flute and Cello* except in a conventional and very foolish way. Mmm? But through the use of chance operations I was able to make the most elegant cadences. Simply because I didn't mean them. However, if the word 'elegant' arises when I say I did mean them. Mmm? Then they become elegant. So I can listen one way or the other. From the point of view of chance operations there's actually no reason for them to have occurred that way. But the fact that they did is very beautiful. It's a bit like having your cake —

— And eating it.
        Yes. (Laughs).

What you don't do, though, is — when you listened to things like the Music of Changes...
        I think you're moving toward something you needn't. You needn't be too purist about it. That is the effect of Germanic thinking, wanting everything to be —

Logical.
        And unified. I received a letter today. I can't quite understand it, but it makes me think along these lines. It goes on and on about the coincidence of association I have made in my writing and that the writer of the letter had made in his thinking, and then he imagines that if someone were interested in Thoreau that he might be interested in Zen. So far so good. And then he ends — I can't quite understand why — he says — don't you think you've carried the use of chance operations too far? And I don't quite know how to reply — I can't think what's going on in his mind. And — I'm on the point of sending him a note saying 'no' (laughs). You see, the common denominator is not 'chance' operations, really. What it is freeing the work from my intention, freeing work from the fact of my ego.

You've said before that people sometimes don't understand that chance is a discipline.
        No, I would agree with that. You see, David Tudor was suggesting yesterday, in his remark that I was a chance operation, that I could drop chance operations, being one. (Laughs). But that's not true, because I'm an ego — with just as good a set of likes and dislikes as anybody else.

CAROLEE SCHNEEMANN

Since the early 1960s Carolee Schneemann's work has pre-figured and influenced a wide range of departures in performance art, as well as dance and film. Alongside her performance, Schneemann's work has consistently engaged with painting, collage, and environments, and, latterly, video art and installation. Her early performances included *Eye Body* (1963), a response to the treatment of the body 'as object' in Happening performances, and *Meat Joy* (1964), an ecstatic group performance drawing on dream sensation and imagery. During the 1960s, Schneemann presented several of her early performances, including *Lateral Splay* (1963), as a member of the Judson Dance Theatre in New York, as well as participating in early Fluxus concerts. At this time, alongside the development of her own work, Schneemann performed in Happenings by Claes Oldenburg (1962, 1965, 1969) and Wolf Vostell (1964), with Robert Morris in *Site* (1964) and in 1965 directed Allan Kaprow's *Push and Pull*. Her performances in the 1970s included *Up To And Including Her Limits*, developed as a performance and installation from 1973 to 1978, and *Interior Scroll* of 1975. Schneemann's uncompromising explorations of the body, identity, the gaze, and her concerns for myth, dream and the recovery of suppressed histories and imagery, have consistently challenged and set the ground for new work in performance. This interview was first recorded in September 1988, following a performance of *Cat Scan* at the *Edge 88* festival in London. The text was substantially developed and revised in collaboration with the artist in 1993 and 1994.

*　　　　　*　　　　　*

Were you performing in the early eighties?

My first New York City exhibit, in 1983, was a retrospective of twenty years work. Gallery Dealer Max Hutchinson said it would require four years to really position the context of my work, that it wasn't going to take hold if I continued to perform in New York City. The culture can't absorb it. If a painter also does performance art, the art world is extremely skeptical — it's considered a trivialisation of one form by another. A painter has to fulfil a prescriptive authority connected to both investment economics and traditions of the heroic — the masculine.

I would associate New York in the sixties and seventies with artists working in a variety of media.

'Performance art' really starts with a painter's or a painterly vision extending tactility and movement into lived time and space. The young men who became the main forces in Happenings were originally painters. They later individually made decisions to go back to making objects, sculpture, paintings, and that's where their enduring success has been; Oldenburg, Dine, Whitman, the Austrians — with some exceptions. Most performance art in the States now has moved away from vision and intimacy towards spectacle, theatre, TV. In 1983 I had to agree with Hutchinson that I would only perform outside of New York City for the next few years. New York City had become saturated for me as an exploratory performance site. But it was wonderful to be able to show the objects and installations — which I consider to be my primary work — for them to be given independence, identity apart from performance works, where I'm always central, both subject and object. In the 1980s I wanted to locate spaces that were not already culturally surfeit, that had no association with performance art or theatrical traditions and forms. Performances where I felt an ecstatic connection to my materials and to my audience took place in Winnipeg, Canada; Iowa City, Iowa; Hamilton College in Northern New York state; San Diego, California; Florida; New Haven, Connecticut.

Why do you consider the objects and installations to be your primary work?

I'm a painter, a painter who does not necessarily work with paint and brushes. My thinking is visual, tactile, imagistic, dimensional. My use of the body in conjunction with my early painting-constructions, and the development of my Kinetic Theatre in the later 1960s both visually and physically vitalised a conceptual and 'painterly' space. Landscape and the animal in its relationship to both the suppressed feminine in my culture and archaic archetypes has been an underlying iconography in my work. There is a wide range of works in which landscape formed my central metaphor. *Eye Body* (1963) is the earliest documented work using my body as central to *36 Transformative Actions*; in one sequence, two garden snakes appear on my naked torso. Performance works between 1965 and 1968 use film, slide projections and sound scores to introduce or insist on the displacement of landscape. *Illinois Central* (1968) is built on the imagery of the tree as a vertical key linking the human destruction of the Vietnamese landscape with the open plains of Illinois. *Up To And Including Her Limits* (1973) takes the delineation of horizon as rope into a solo vertical activation: suspended first in a tree-surgeon's harness the anti-gravitational trance-like state of suspension produces a continuous web of strokes and was later developed into a film and video installation with performance (1973–78). My film *Fuses* (1965), now an 'erotic classic', was self-shot as film-maker and participant in love making. Here the erotic bodies are in continuous dissolution within landscape as site and texture, and within the hand painting, stretching, cutting of the film. *Homage to Ana Mendieta*, a 1985 tryptich, is composed of eleven series of paintings and photographs. I created a sequence of paintings in the snow using blood, syrup and ashes. In the photographic series which encapsulates this outdoor work my hands are active in an image relay of reaching and falling. These paintings are combined with the photographs to form a twelve-foot high tryptich.

What is it that brings the work to performance as opposed to an object or installation?

Usually I don't *choose* to perform. When there's an accumulation of images that are very insistent I'm forced to make those images 'actual'. For example, I was sitting in someone's office, having an interview with an editor, and suddenly images appeared — they're very fleeting. So I had to stop the discussion and start drawing. Once there's a drawing, a process opens.

Do you enjoy performing?

Yes and no — it's an ordeal finding funds for materials, the space, editing, sound, film, slides... It's a nightmare. But it's also ecstatic when I'm lost in the action and my material is enveloping — a wave carries me between unconscious content and the pressure, the risk of exposed moments. That can be ecstatic. There's also the flow and intercut of text. I've been engrossed by text in its conjunction with images for a long time. *Meat Joy* in 1964 starts with self-referential layers of collaged text. By the 1970s, for example, text became increasingly less abstract, less musical, if you will, and more concerned with strands of information that are implied by the imagery. And a didactic motive to introduce sexual taboos with deepened cultural references and contradictions.

Is an awareness of cultural context particularly important to your work?

'Context' for me has to do with what's missing, suppressed, diverted. Culturally, we're missing woman's history, we're missing our unconscious archetypal connections, we're missing the generative femaleness of the universe, we're missing being able to read the variousness of our experience. We're missing our keys.

I'm interested in the way Cat Scan *weaves very personal images, such as the cat, that appears in a lot of your work, through a presentation of images and texts drawn from ancient cultures and civilisations. What are you seeking in this?*

I took the smallest personal archetype, following it as a thread. The cat, in some of its many attributes, has an association with the femaleness of the universe that has been tamed and trivialised, sentimentalised. There are several keys to the piece. One is the mouth; the kiss. And the taboo of inappropriate intimacy. So the inter-species kiss was one thread out of which the performance work started. When Cluny was a kitten this was something he did that was remarkable. Every morning, whether I was in bed with my lover or not, the cat would slowly walk up to my body, lean his face toward Mike, then he would be kissing me, his tongue probing my mouth, purring, his eyes closed. A unique expressivity. So Cluny had made a step across the threshold between species, toward the human with whom he was bonded. There is also a photographic series that was made over the course of his life, *Infinity Kisses*. I recorded these kisses — because they were so wonderful — with a hand-held Olympus. There's a wall of kisses printed and permutated, nine feet by six feet, which is now in the permanent collection of the San Francisco Museum of Modern Art — the first work purchased by an institution.

Part of my curiosity is to examine the ordinary erotic. The motive for my 1965 erotic film *Fuses* was similar to this 1980s photographic sequence. What does this interchange look like to my camera eye? When Cluny died — he died of a rat bite, a rat that he had brought to me. Bringing the rat to me was a demonstration of his power to guard me. But he 'bit off more than he could chew'. It was at a time when suddenly we were living alone. My partner of eleven years had left. Within a six month period my best friend died. My mother died. Devotions were being stripped away. And I began to associate that with ecological denuding and abuses of the universe, as well as the de-sexualising and draining of my own persona. So the culture was denying my integrity and identity, and I experienced that as parallel to the denigration of ecological systems. Just as the femaleness of the universe was always denied, projected upon, trashed, glorified and vilified. The Western splits, dualities…

Is the reference to ancient culture specific to this piece?

I think it starts with *Meat Joy*, I think it starts in 1964. A realisation that I am dealing with the sacred-erotic, deflected from Judeo-Christian culture. The only precedents I find are from earlier, archaic cultures. It might be native American, it might be Aboriginal, it might be Cretan, where I can begin to imagine integrations…

Figure 3   Carolee Schneemann *Cat Scan* (1988) (photo: Plautus) (courtesy of the artist).

A powerful aspect of the performance seems to come from this attempt to place a missing key before an audience.

     Yes, because what I inhabit physically also communicates energy fields. It's the mind penetrated by the body's immediacy. The voyeuristic space of audience to performer, that hierarchical distance, has to be assaulted, aggressed upon.

I'm interested in the connection between this challenge and your address to the 'sacred-erotic'. Do you think your address to the erotic serves to undermine or attack this 'hierarchical distance'?

     Yes.

Is there a danger that by engaging with the erotic the performance plays into the voyeuristic space the audience constructs?

     Always.

I would associate the work, as you describe it, with some European ritualistic performance in which aspects of ancient culture are re-presented to a contemporary audience. I'm very struck, though, by the way in which you directly link archaic imagery with the personal.

One of the ways in which that happens is through dreams or synergistic events. For instance, to me the most startling key to the performance — as it was developing — was finding this Egyptian frieze reproduced in a book on Egyptian astrological hieroglyphs that someone had accidentally left in my house. I'd never seen anything like this frieze fragment. It's called *The Breath of Life*. The translated hieroglyphs describe this frieze as a kiss exchanged between a priestess and a lion. And the priestess and the lion cub are raised together from infancy. A measure of the empathy or para-normal power of the priestess, is that they've chosen the right child to grow with the appropriate lion cub if the ritual kiss, the 'breath of life', is exchanged.

Figure 4   Carolee Schneemann *Cat Scan* (1988) (photo: Lona Foote) (courtesy of the artist).

In the section of the text 'New Nightmares, Ancient History' the male voice has very laconic explications. I've written a relay of re-attributions of gender and symbolic significance, a whole set of imperative gender iconographies which are simply and intentionally incorrect. As a painter and a performance artist, I can project a slide of an androgynous or male figure —

and insist it is a female priestess or Queen that's been mis-attributed. So the male voice in *Cat Scan* has this intertext: 'The smaller figure is not the king... but the queen... the queen who was granted accession'. And then, while doing my research, I discovered things that unravelled my personal key underlying the piece. A hieroglyph is shown on a slide, and the performer's taped voice states: 'Here you can see a potent amulet for the opening of the mouth ceremony... This hieroglyph shows the mouth... It has the sign of 'R' as Rat'. This one I didn't invent. This is a literal transposition from the Egyptian.

CAT SCAN 'NEW NIGHTMARES/ANCIENT HISTORY'
(MALE, LACONIC, VERY SLOW, 'H' — HISTORY; FEMALE, INTENSE, 'D' — DREAM)

D. there was a strange a strange dream a huge vicious dog was biting her cat's head and she couldn't save him... one night he slept apart from her...! she didn't know what it meant in the middle of winter the dogs became mysteriously fat... she followed them to the frozen stream bed... there lay the body of the fawn — wounded by hunters — captured and eaten by her dogs...

H. the smaller figure is not his 'wife'... but the Queen through whom she was granted accession...

D. once she dreamt the womens psychic group came to take away her blue metal trunk she protested you can't have it! it's full of love letters... and the corpse of my cat

H. this Goddess is believed to suckle the dead... to sustain them on their journey to the next world

D. and then she dreamt... Andy Warhol died suddenly after a gall bladder operation... and she dreamt that artists became the most reactionary of people and only wore black clothes for three years while discussing money and media deals...

H. the Goddess Hathor is seen holding the sun in one hand and 'man' in the other...

D. dreamt she had a magical cat who travelled everywhere she went

H. the cat Goddess was an ancient deity... worshipped as long ago as 3500 B.C.

D. in that dream square blocks of the ancient biblical cities of Tyre and Sidon were bombed away... there was not a single intact structure nor any person to be seen there, nor in Damour...

H. the Lotus flowered... and when its petals opened a child was disclosed

D.   in order to take the bus from the Port Authority... in order to get to
     the country she dreamt... they had to walk between rows of homeless
     people stretched out in puddles of urine vomit blood
H.   cats were held in great honor
D.   in that nightmare... the rat he triumphantly laid at her feet had bitten
     him under the tongue... he continued to wake her with morning
     kisses
H.   the wrapping with its deep religious significance took time...
     seventy days passed between the death and the completion of the
     wrapping... on the final day the mummy was taken back to the house
     of mourning...
D.   dreamt that one year a friend died of AIDS every six months... then a
     friend died every month... then...
H.   she was sent forth as a lioness to maintain human honor for the
     Gods...
D.   dreamt B. left... married a German lover and had a baby... or two...
H.   the Queen's mummy was not in the tomb... the sarcophagus was
     empty... except for two silver bracelets set with butterflies of small
     bright stones

Carolee Schneemann, from *Cat Scan* 'New Nightmares / Ancient History'
(1988) (courtesy of the artist).

*The artists Marina Abramovic and Ulay, in their work together, have made an
analogous address to archaic symbol, but they don't link what they call the male and
female 'principles' to the personal in the same way.*

I may work in the reverse. I'll have something happen in my own
life that seems to be something I have to pursue. I begin to pay attention, and
then the symbols appear. I never start with the symbols. I'll just describe how
it happened. Recently, I was in Austin, Texas, applying for a job, staying with
Deborah Hay, the dancer and friend from Judson Dance Theater days. I was
to sleep in her studio — it's all white, and she said, this is also where the
Austin Buddhists meditate once a month. I told her I slept in a room like this
once before in Ohio also with a dancer friend named Deborah! and I had an
incredible vision that time. So I went to sleep on the little mat in this all-white
room with these Buddha faces around and I woke up and I said to my friend,
aha, nothing happened, nothing special. We were preparing breakfast and I
looked out of the window and there's a cat crossing the road. So I went out to
meet this cat and as soon as I touched it, this amazing dream recall hit me.

And what it was, was that I had dreamed that I had opened my red notebook — in the dream it was an oversized looseleaf. And there inside was Cluny's arm and extended paw... He said, this is as much as I can offer back to you now, I can't bring anything more through. I stroked his paw, weeping — it was definitely his. It was his colouration. And I said, thank you for this, what should I do with it? He said, you're to use this. I asked, how? And then in the dream he showed me that I was to take this paw, like a rod or small staff, and rest it on my knees and raise it up to my heart, and take it down and raise it up. I started to do that and I was in tears, my whole body axis opened, suffused with a strange comfort. It induces deep, deep breaths. When I was doing *Cat Scan*, I took this gesture to the performers — just this gesture, I told them nothing about it. I said, try it with your arm and tell me what it makes you feel like. They said amazing things: it's like a physical gift; it feels very ancient; it feels very sacred; it makes me breathe. We did it for a long time and each of us went into a trance-like state. So I decided to follow this motion. I told the original performers to go home and bring in any kind of simple book on Egyptian symbolism, Egyptian history.

So you're pursuing a coincidence between dream, intuition, the logic of another ancient culture and ancient symbols.
    Yes!

Where did the furniture imagery in Cat Scan — *the wheel and chair — come from?*
    It comes from different places. It's one way of following the performers through space. In order not to say to the performers, I want you to collide and embrace, I offered them objects as an extension of their bodies, creating very particular extensions in the space. When you meet another object you have to make an exchange with this object, that's become a part of your body, this cumbersome and impossible shape. And it's in the combination of cherishing and exchanging objects that the intimacy results. Another image had to do with the way a cat watches human life. You see all this obsessive effort that repeats itself over and over again — we're always carting and carrying and sweeping and putting things in little boxes and taking little things out. These are the compelling directives that seem to reveal and obscure the essential structures of our lives' organisation. But really they don't make any sense at all. And then the disruption of the function of the object — it was very important that the object never be in a position that resembled its function. This also comes from an early Jim McBride film about the end of the world, called *Glen and Randa*, where a little boy is, presumably, the only survivor. He tries to invent and imagine culture by finding things in garbage refuse and he's trying to re-ascertain

what was, what existed. At one point he finds a live horse! He never climbs on the horse. He never rides the horse. He never puts anything on the horse. The horse is his companion. He finds ropes and he guides the horse, but he carries things on his own back. The horse is like an — equitable companion, not for use. That's an influence in there somewhere.

Also because that detritus was — filling this space — and we began emptying it, filling it and emptying it, and making it almost impossible to come in blind and penetrate that space with solitary trust and concentration. So I filled it in then emptied it for other actions to develop.

Which just makes me think about the way the piece has been organised. It's like a visual, sculptural texture.

In this case the text precedes the action. And I'm looking for an equivalence to all the loss and dissolution, some of which is from daily news, some of it seems to be from someone's personal life — mine, but it may not be. So that was intercut in the 'Ancient History and New Nightmare' section. Our movements become correlatives. It's all real, although it's all proposed as dream.

Your work as a whole seems to have been freer than a lot of the work that, particularly in the sixties, surrounded it. I'm thinking more of the, actually, male-dominated Happenings which seemed to have more formal concerns.

They really didn't have more formal concerns. Kaprow, of course, was more linear than, say, early Oldenburg. He was always interested in a 'passage', a journey, in which everyone had an equal amount of information, an equal degree of action. My pieces were always more rooted in a physicality that's heightened and that's coming through me and that's engaging a degree of sexual energy, of eroticised space. It was distinctively different from the others, although their work was very messy and spontaneous and visceral. The conceptual work comes later, like the more theoretical, pared-down work. Then, of course, parallel to this is Fluxus, with the purity of the object, the denial of the body as a force-field. The notion that everything, *everything*, has its particularity to *demonstrate*. But for Fluxus the 'thing' was never physicality, as such.

I think what was influencing me was a resistance to a conceptual deadening, the disappearance of the body and a concern for the vitality of material being taken through the self and back into space. There was always a cultural separation, where the self was positioned as 'outside', as superior, controlling. So my sense of being drenched, that's the Aphrodite metaphor, is that you are subsumed, you disappear, you are drenched, and it's a sensory submersion in the materiality of the process of work. A submersion into the group, into the interchange.

Despite the fact that much of your work has been collaborative, your performance has been associated with Body Art, which has been largely a male activity.

One of the real differences has been with the female use of the body as something ecstatic and integral to a lived life whereas most of the male performance artists approach their own body in terms of challenges, violence, and degradation, abuse. It's not ecstatic, it's tormented. And so it usually involves a mythic or heroic ordeal.

Reading More Than Meat Joy *there's a sense of an alienation from male artists that you worked with in the sixties and the seventies. And there are obvious differences in the work…*

Performance works entered into a male contextualisation of space as gender specific to the male imagination. So that women internalise themselves as being a part of something that's dreamed by the men. Trying to tear these veils is central to my work. The classic male nude stands for a mythification, an idealisation; just as the female nude traditionally in our painting and sculpture has always been mythicised as an idealised object of male desire which does not correspond to what women actually experience or feel about their bodies. We incur that separation as well as a deeper fracture — if you are a desired image you lose authority as an artist. A woman is immediately an expectation of male sexual projection: 'Do I want to fuck this or not?'

One of the attractive aspects of your work to me is the way you have readily drawn on very different kinds of practices. You adopted Contact Improvisation and you seem open to various theatre practices. The early work employs some of the methods the Judson Dancers were using, including rulegame, one example of which would be Lateral Splay. *Is this eclecticism something you would have any comments on?*

My Contact Improvisation begins with *Newspaper Event* of 1963, which was a piece conditioned and motivated by the fact that dancers never touched each other spontaneously or intimately. They would pass bricks between one another, they would touch a hand or a foot. But real loss of individuation wasn't part of their movement vocabulary. For me that seemed to be an essential investigation.

Figures 5 and 6   Carolee Schneemann, preparatory drawings for *Lateral Splay* (1963) (courtesy of the artist).

Which is very much to do with finding something beneath the surface of behaviour.

To let that kind of spontaneous joy and risk come in. To get rid of the calculation. To dig towards the suppressed latent content.

And you had to work for this?

You have to work very hard for it, yes. But that's how I began to perform. I would bring in a drawing of a figure jumping off a ladder and landing while they had two cans of paint in their hands that would fling out and splatter the space as they leapt. So I'd bring in these drawings and ask the group — which was to become The Judson Dancers — who would go up the ladder and leap off? And to a person they all refused because of their ankles, their knees! I always have this conviction that if I can draw the image it can be done.

MOVEMENTS

1. backward run
2. forward run
3. low crawl-run
4. turnings and falls with run

VARIATIONS

1. climbing
2. swinging
3. and other*… extreme change of locus

SPEED: fast as possible

DURATION: long as possible or: encounters with objects, walls, people

*Objects: try for 'Variations'
Walls: mean automatic change of movement or rest
People: collision, embrace, grabbing allow you to rest; the person caught
            must rest with you
Objects: if variations actions are not to be explored at full momentum
            you may rest beneath or by object
People: if touched or kicked into you may change motion immediately

DIRECTION: random

Carolee Schneemann, instructions for *Lateral Splay* (1963) (courtesy of the artist).

So I would start with little stools, little tables, little ladders. And we'd practice jumping off until finally someone would say, I'd really like to go to the top and just leap off! And I'd say, how about carrying a couple of cans of paint in your hand? So the training always has to do with never going directly for what I want. The drawing is there, and that's the key. And then you have to go through many circuitous changes. There is a journey to approach the essential image. *Water Light/Water Needle* (1966) was very complicated. I had to learn rigging. I mean the drawing was simply of these bodies and pulleys guiding each other through space on layers of 3/4" manilla rope — of anti-gravitational fluidity. So I had to learn rigging, metal tension. And then when I found St Mark's Church where I could rig the ropes onto steel pillars we discovered that it would take us three weeks to build enough calluses just to hang hand over hand, to move and develop muscle memory. As a painter, I didn't understand this until we went out on those layers of horizontal ropes —which I had drawn so swiftly!.

Because of the focus on the present moment and the actual circumstance of the performance, performance art frequently takes on quite different qualities from conventional theatre productions.

My work is much more ritualistic. It becomes ritualised so that the individual elements are all addressing something that's within it but also centred beyond it — reaching *towards* that rather than being given a form that you have to fulfil, in which you're trained to excel.

Do you feel that your current work has an affinity with other work going on in New York or other American performance?

It's very hard to be a progenitor and not find affinities with many things. And I have been economically punished despite the scope of my influence. It's as if performance process recapitulates an ontology. Everybody has to explore certain sorts of things, and a lot of potent ideas are familiar. There's wonderful work happening in New York in a myriad of forms. Theatre has gotten much looser, more adventurous and more political. At the same time there's a commodification in some independent spaces. A lot of new people go into performance art as a launch to get to MTV or Hollywood.

There does seem to be a point at which the way that performance art was entered into changed.

Oh yes. It's changed drastically. It used to be about ritual and intimacy and, of course, feminist performance can and still does address transformative gender politics. Gay, Lesbian, Black, Asian, and Feminist work insists on revelatory intimacy. Some artists leave performance because it marginalizes their issues, others embrace it. And these political aspects are often motivating the most interesting formal developments, because they have to do with breaking time, expectations, with extending space. It's interesting and odd for me to be back in the context of *Edge 88* where I make something that begins at a certain hour and ends at a certain hour, which is frontally focused with fixed boundaries. Because that was what I wanted to get away from. It's mysterious. I don't know if my work is going to create historical energy or not. I just do these things — so, it's always kind of a surprise that people are paying attention and seeing a whole cultural shape evolve.

BARRY LE VA

In his work of the late 1960s and early 1970s, Barry Le Va's concern for process, and the *event* of the work's production and reception, gave rise to object-based art which could be read in terms of theatre or performance. In his scatterpieces, first presented in 1966, and his introduction of progressively less controllable materials in his three-dimensional work from 1968, Le Va came to present the viewer with arrangements of unconventional materials, such as flour, chalk, glass or oil, which invited readings through their tracing out of an earlier action or event. Following studies in mathematics and architecture, Le Va had studied fine art of the Otis Art Institute of Los Angeles County, graduating in 1967. In 1968 his work was featured prominently in *Artforum* and in 1969 his first solo exhibition was shown at the Minneapolis Institute of Art. In the same year, Le Va showed the *Velocity Piece*, a stereo installation tracing out his earlier occupation of the gallery space. In 1970, he moved to New York, where he continues to develop work through a variety of media. In 1988, the Rijksmuseum Kroller-Muller, the Netherlands, presented a twenty- year retrospective of Barry Le Va's work. This interview was recorded in New York in March 1993, and the text was edited by the author and subsequently revised and developed by Barry Le Va during the summer of 1994.

*　　　*　　　*

In the criticism surrounding your work, the terms 'theatre' and 'performance' have appeared despite the fact that you don't present performances to an audience. Do you think these terms are useful to a consideration of your work?

If you're talking about an audience that has to look at the work, and the work is only a clue to the actions that have taken place — if that qualifies for the 'theatrical' — then yes, but that was more so in the past than now. There were drawings that functioned like scripts which I followed to complete certain specific works — the drawings were like dance notations or architectural floor plans. Let's say that the script in itself may or may not be how the work is actually going to end up. Liberties could or would be taken depending upon certain architectural features within or of the space or place. For example, if the space was larger — the work is possibly going to be larger or possibly smaller — those kinds of things. Also the work allowed for spontaneous improvisations, but within the logic of the processes involved. But I did not think of it purely as theatre.

As they are met in the gallery, the elements of the work seem to refer to something other than that which is present, as if they refer to a past activity.

Absolutely, and that still has continued. In the case of the early work what you had was the result of a physical activity — and that traces itself back. A lot of the work was about cause and effect. For example, if a sheet of glass is dropped and a sheet of glass is thrown they will have two different kinds of dispersal patterns or effects which you can trace back to their cause. Much of the work had to do with making distinctions like that. That this lies the way it lies is because of doing this activity from this position. That would be the only aesthetic.

So the work was, in a way, concerned with 'events' rather than objects — or, at least, with traces of an 'event'.

Are we speaking specifically of sculpture or of performance in real time, real space?

Could it not be either?

Yeah, it could. I'm saying that a lot of the things that I was interested in when I was first involved with the sculpture — I didn't know what to call it. At school nobody knew what to call it. That was before the term 'process art'. I was going under the notion that I considered everything I was doing was sculpture — but I called it 'event-structure'. It wasn't about composition. It wasn't about setting it up in the space, except by activity. It was a result of an event that took place in the space. A very structured event. So somehow the only structuring principle of the sculpture was *exactly* what you're talking about — those traces, the residue of the *event* or many events.

It grew out of a lot of things. At the moment, I'm just trying to put it in perspective.

I went into art school with the notion of being a painter. Somewhere along the line — I realised — either I didn't understand the issues in painting, or it seemed too easy, too contained or confining. I was just working toward an end. Since I knew nothing about three-dimensional work, I just started pursuing that. I was making three-dimensional situations that I considered were — not objects, because there were five or six elements placed around the space to set up some kind of a dialogue, this thing to be placed here, this thing to be placed there — but, in a sense, it was still working toward an end.

One day, I turned around and everything that was on the floor — the residue of the making of this sculpture — was more interesting than what had been made. I could literally piece together the day's events or my activity by how things just accumulated or lay on the floor or the table. The arrangement was unconscious, but it was a result of a conscious activity which included a variety of processes. I didn't know what to call it. I started to read about time and space. At that period of time Something Else Press was printing a lot of Fluxus, and that was very important. Reading them enabled me to articulate some of my own thoughts.

The one that really interested me — was the Daniel Spoerri book, *An Anecdoted Topography of Chance* (1966). I did not find the events that led up to how the various objects ended up being on the table very interesting, but the situations that he presented, the notions of residue accumulating through chance or through an activity interested me. I think that somewhere along the line those books led me to think more in terms of an 'event'. At that point in time, though, my justification was sculpture. Not that this in itself was a piece of sculpture, but that the binding core to make this what it is, was the event that led up to it. I felt 'event-structure' was as much an important aspect of sculpture as making a square box and not showing anybody you made it.

At the same time, the concern with 'event' is a point from which many artists have stepped into performance.
Yeah.

In the case of the Velocity Piece *(1969), the reference to a performance becomes explicit, doesn't it?*
The *Velocity Piece* was interesting. Friends of mine at that period thought about it in terms of Body Art. I didn't. I looked at it as a sculpture in time — where all the aspects of an extended sculpture — non-objects — would come out through an activity — the durations, stereo and acoustics of a particular space/place. I thought of myself as an object — but it was not about me, it was about the space — its architecture — distances — materials of the walls and floors. It was me running from one end of the space into the wall and back again. That's what I needed to do to make and complete the work. I could not trust someone else to do it. I could only end the work when I couldn't run anymore. I could not think of any other reason to end the piece. It was about an energy drain of a moving object.

So there's an emphasis here upon a 'real' action having taken place in 'real' time.
Yes, and real space to me means that it was installed (played back) in the space/place where it was recorded. The first one that was done lasted for an hour and forty-three minutes — and there was one sound engineer working out the stereo, so that when you played it back you could hear —

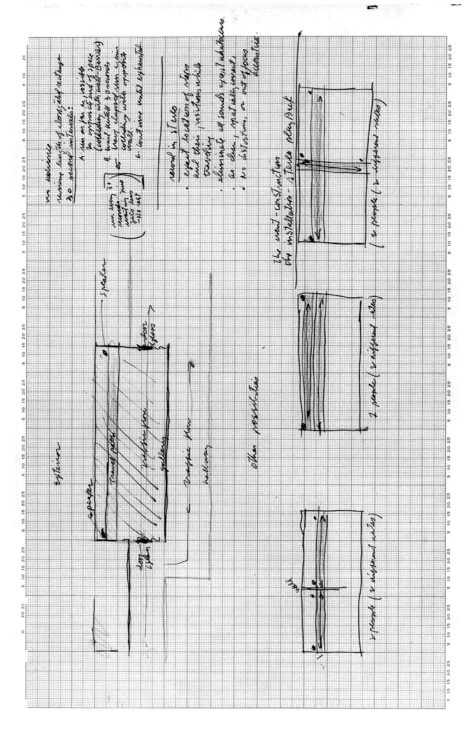

Figure 7 Barry Le Va Notes for *'Velocity Piece — Ohio State University'* (1969). Ink on paper in 2 parts, each part 11″ × 16″ (courtesy of the artist).

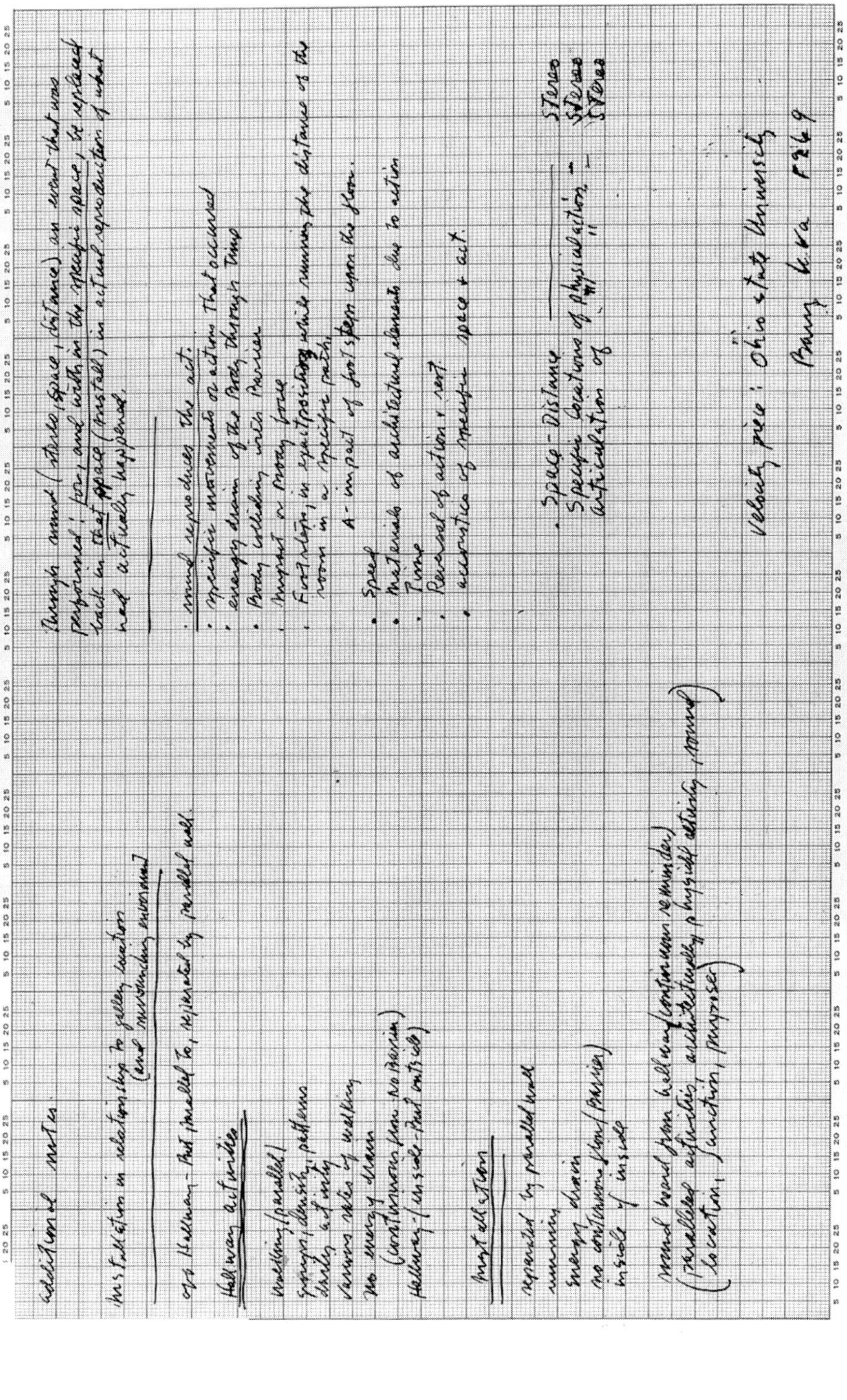

Figure 8 Barry Le Va *Notes for 'Velocity Piece — Ohio State University'* (1969). Ink on paper in 2 parts, each part 11" × 16" (courtesy of the artist).

and *feel* and *visualise* — all the activity going on. But what's interesting is that at the actual exhibition there was just a tape and two speakers. People came in and sat down and — instead of just hearing it — they *watched* it. That's what interested me. So I guess there's a sense of performance and theatre — that probably is the closest — meaning that people literally did watch something but there was nothing to see.

In making the piece, did you consider the audience's response?

Not directly, only as a receiver of information. I was thinking of the sense of the sound, the location, of making convincingly a piece of sculpture. A lot of the work had to do with the notion of locations in time — that patterns or appearances are a result of a certain kind of cause, that if the wall is wood or sheetrock or plaster the sound is going to be different. To me it was all very sculptural.

A lot of the work that was being done at that period of time was a result of specific activities, such as *Cleaved Wall* (1969–1970) or the broken glass pieces — [for example, *Shots from the End of a Glass Line* (1970), *On Center Shatter — or — Shatterscatter (within the Series of Layered Pattern Acts)* (1968–1971)] — or even some of the early felt pieces — [for example, *1-2-3 (eliminating strips)* (1968), *Disentangle* (1968)] — or some of the ones that had to do with throwing and dropping or an activity in a place or space. It grew out of that. I was dealing with certain physical materials and I just tried to switch over — to have a piece of sculpture only through stereo. Since everything was a cause and effect at a certain point — since the pieces were, one might say, points in space where this or that occurred. I asked myself — could I give something that much flesh and that much physicality while not having any physical thing there?

I assumed the audience would come in and be standing around and listen to it for a few minutes. Maybe just walk around. What I found was that they didn't want to walk around the space because they didn't want to get in the way of my running path. That's what I found interesting. And since it ran the distance like this — it went (footsteps) BOOM! that way, then (footsteps) BOOM! that way — every thirty seconds I would run. Eventually it got to where it was taking twenty-eight seconds to get from one end to the other. So I got two seconds of rest. After a while, that comes through in listening to the piece. So a lot of people were willing just to sit down and go through the whole duration, which I was very surprised at. I had never even thought of that. And when they were doing it, I realised it worked on an entirely different level than the one I had considered. The whole idea that their heads moved as if they were watching a ping-pong game. That somehow there was a sense of reality.

Figure 9 Barry Le Va *Cleaved Wall* (1969–1970). 22 meat cleavers embedded in wall, Whitney Museum of Art, 'Contemporary American Sculpture' exhibition, 1970 (courtesy of the artist).

It strikes me that by not appearing you stepped back from a direct confrontation with the audience.

I didn't think about that. I thought of it as research. I have thought about a lot of the work as research. I still think of it that way. I don't know how the work is going to end up. At that period I was not thinking of it in terms of confrontation. I was thinking of it just in terms of sound and acoustics. It was done at another time and space/place and I just had to do it all over again, because you can't take this tape and put it into another space — the distances are different, the acoustics are different, the walls are different. I was trying to make where I was at each moment in time and space, in that particular space and that particular time and location, as clear, as physical, as possible without being there. And the confrontational aspect — if I was a performer, if I was there, it would seem like a step backward. I would feel self-conscious, the audience would focus on me and the activity, not the sculptural aspects I was interested in. I did not want it to be an actual performance.

It was done first of all at the University of Ohio and the second one was done at the La Jolla Museum of Art. The second one had many more problems. At the University it was much more object-like, meaning that the positions of the feet going by were very distinct and located. At the Museum, the sound engineers had a very hard time trying to get that object-quality to it. That's very much what I was after — really pinpointing the sound into the sense of it being a physical object — having weight, distance, place, and force, all as a result of this physical activity.

One of the notable things about the Body Art performances that were occurring at the same time as you were making these explorations is a catching of particular pieces between the presence and absence of the artist or the performers. Pieces such as Vito Acconci's Seedbed *(1972) or Chris Burden's* White Light/White Heat *(1975) seem to pose analogous questions about the activity of the audience — the spectator's role — by leaving traces or hinting at presence, but refusing to appear.*

But Vito actually was in appearance. You couldn't see him, but he was just underneath the ramps. You knew he was there. He set up an interesting kind of tension. I mean, maybe he wasn't there, maybe it was a speaker. But there was something about just knowing or believing that he was under there, at least if we can assume he was under there. That was a very interesting piece for me. It's like something very private and also something very vulnerable. It made me feel very vulnerable because I was forced into being a participant of somebody's very personal, private situation.

But there's something else, here, isn't there? Burden's White Light/White Heat *presents what appears to be a piece of minimal sculpture high up in one corner of the room, which, we're told, he may be lying on top of — but you can't see him. There's a statement to the effect that he's present, even though he's not in appearance. This possibility changes the whole perception of what might be or might have been a piece of sculpture. Either it's a Minimalist object or a platform or both. And the possibility of Burden's presence charges the space up. So one of the questions is — is it my belief that Burden might be there that charges the space up or is the fact he's there, the sense of his actual presence that does it. Without this question of presence, it would be a completely different situation.*

Assuming or even implying that there is something there or not there — one really doesn't know — sets up a form of confrontational situation of some sort. The situation has to be believable, even if there is doubt.

And it changes it completely for the person who is looking, doesn't it? The piece becomes durational, for a start.

Yes. I would also say it becomes — again I would use the word confrontational. I would say very few people like being placed into those

A conventional gallery room twenty-five feet by forty feet; halfway across the room, the floor turns into a ramp that rises to a height of two feet at the far wall. The piece is one of three pieces of mine in the gallery, one in each room, each performed live; the performances of the pieces alternate, while the setting for each piece remains in place. This piece, then, is activated three times a week; each day, the piece lasts from opening time to closing time, from 10 AM to 6 PM: I'm under the ramp, I'm moving around under the floor where viewer's walk, I'm maintaining a constant masturbation — in order to do this, I use the viewers as an aid, I build up sexual fantasies on viewers' footsteps, my fantasies keep my masturbation going.

(The viewer, entering the gallery, walks across the floor and, almost without thinking about it, up the ramp. The viewer hears my voice come up from below: '... the person to my left... I'm doing this with you now... I'm touching your hair... I'm running my hand down your back... I'm touching your ass...' Whenever I reach climax, the viewer might want to pick himself or herself out of the crowd; the viewer might want to think; he's done this for me, he's done this with me, he's done this because of me.)

Figure 10   Vito Acconci *Seedbed* Performance/Installation, Sonnabend Gallery, New York, January 1972 (courtesy of the artist).

situations. They like to have the choice of just looking at something. A lot of videotape to me is about that. That, actually, you might not want to be a witness to somebody doing these actions right in front of you. And the medium seems to kind of make it more comfortable. I guess pieces like Chris's or Vito's certainly made you feel much more uncomfortable, just by assuming their presence.

It is confrontational, but, like the Velocity Piece, *in this work there's an element of absence which triggers something for the viewer or creates a situation of involvement. Is it not also, in pieces such as* Seedbed *and* White Light/White Heat, *this sense of involvement, coupled, perhaps, with the emphasis upon real actions in real time, that makes them so uncomfortable or objectionable. That by being there and watching you're somehow responsible —*

You become a participant. And once you become a participant you have to be responsible. But it's not only real actions in real time, it's also real space. It's like we're within the boundaries of the performance. A play or opera can use real time and real space, but there is still the distancing factor of watching something. In the late sixties and early seventies there were a lot of performances in lofts. Everybody would sit around and watch — and people had their video tapes going so they could document it — and then it might become a video. But if it's just you in that space and one other person then if you're in a gallery situation and it's Vito's piece and he's under the ramp and you're the only one in the space — or there are just two people in the space — then you become aware of no distancing factor. And there's so much space to wander around in. It also sets up an odd relationship with the other person who's in the space and to what Vito's doing. You all become participants.

Do you think of your work as activating a space?
          Does the space seem important?

Could they be described as site-specific?
          Some of the work definitely was. With certain specific pieces — the felt pieces — I would say they were almost site-specific in the sense that they were done just there, they weren't in the studio then brought to the space. The boundaries are set up by the space. There are certain kind of logical or illogical decisions I have to make for the space. But in terms of activating or existing in a space — they probably do both. I've actually never been clear precisely what people mean when they say 'activating a space'. What do you mean?

Well, what I mean, in my sense of watching it, is that a piece points out something or reveals something in some way integral to that space. And my entry into the space is not simply an entry before an object.
          Yeah. I can say in some cases there definitely was a symbiotic relationship between the space and the work. That that work could not exist unless the space was like this or that.

One of the things that interests me about the notion of an 'event' is not simply, in this work, the event of which the work is a trace, but the event this reference back provokes between the one who views and the thing itself. This strikes me as being part of what you're talking about with 'event-structures'. As I view, I become aware of the effort and engagement of retracing your steps, and so of an event in the here and now rather than simply in the past.

And hopefully you're correct in your perceptions. Which gets to be a big thing. One of the problems in a lot of the work — like where I'm walking a stick and I cut off the ends of the stick — [*Unequal Lengths Cut Circular (walked end-over-end in their own paths, ends touch ends cut)*, 1972–1973] — also started to interest me. Can you really tell the difference between something that's been dropped and something that's been thrown? Maybe something that has been thrown doesn't break, maybe the one that has been dropped doesn't break either. All of a sudden you're in a confusion over which one really is dropped and which one is placed. Or which one is thrown. I started finding those kinds of things interesting — about false perceptions. In retracing you can run into a lot of false premises and incorrect information based on your own perceptions. All of a sudden this changes the whole notion of locations, activities, relationships.

Do you mean, in a way, that there's a correct answer?

Not a correct answer, but what I'm saying is that — for example — there's a thrown glass piece which is in someone's collection, and one of the glass sheets that's intact was the one that was thrown with the most force from the farthest distance. The result fits into the definition of the activity, but it doesn't fit into the definition of what you think it should be.

It's just that people say, Barry, you have so many things there — like the *Accumulated Vision Series* (1976–1977) — do you really expect us to trace back through everything? I kind of had two answers. I said — it took me a long time to set those up, maybe I expect you to spend that much time with them. And if you don't then you aren't giving it enough time or concentration. I think it's possible. It may seem impossible because it takes so much time and effort — and unless something is moving in time, spending time with something static can be an ordeal. And more so if one has to retrace back. Within the duration of thought, I think frustration and anxiety enters in, and that in itself starts clouding your perceptions. You have limited visual information, but then to keep it all tracked in your head, to go through it logistically in terms of a sequence of events, either linear or non-linear, gives you so much information that it all gets befuddled. In a sense, I expected people to do it, but also deep down I liked the anxiety and the frustration. I think that when people find themselves with something very simply presented, yet the information it produces is so much of an overload, it's bound to cause misperceptions.

In these respects your work seems caught between the kind of 'systems' work that a viewer could unravel quite specifically and the Fluxus multiples and 'events' where the puzzle is insoluble.

I never really used clear-cut systems. There's more or less a loose programme. They're logical, but the system or the activity allows for certain changes to occur dependent upon the here and now of the space. The resulting appearance of things might have changed, but the logic of the activity won't be changed. The logic is just subject to certain realities of the space. As a viewer, these kinds of considerations should be taken into account because it is both about that activity and that space.

You have also suggested that you are interested in unrelated things becoming related by proximity.

Yeah.

This seems important here, because it suggests that the elements you present are in some way resisting being related. They may be related by proximity, but they're not simply being absorbed into a single system.

Right. A lot of that can even come out of making these false perceptions. It could be, say, two different sets of actions, two different sets of materials, two different causes and effects. Yet by proximity they become related. Maybe that's the intention. The underlying thing, though, is in real time or real space or it's the real intention, and that has nothing to do with their relationship to each other.

For the last three days I've been watching a lot of Godard films. And I can look at these films and see those kinds of things. I've always been interested in fragmentation, and fragmentation can come from a variety of sources. The thing I've always liked about Godard films is that there's one action taking place and then off to the side there's another action taking place. They only seem to relate to each other because they're in the frame.

If you create a situation where there's a tension between the unrelatedness of two things and their possible relationship, it invites you into a reading but it also tends to resist your particular reading, doesn't it?

Yes. I like to subvert one intention with another intention.

Isn't that another strategy that can give rise to an awareness of the 'event' of reading the work?

The subverting of one intention with another also gives rise to different kinds of readings. What it does, for me, is that it destroys, at a certain point, what I was interested in — any sense of correct judgment, any sense of stableness. It doesn't produce confusion, but it does set up a situation where one has to question one's own thought processes. The situation becomes active, organic, it grows and seems to be in a state of flux due to the constant re-adjustment and re-evaluation of your perceptions. If that makes sense. All of a sudden things are being subverted and you realise the work wasn't about what you first thought at all.

So in that way it becomes more about the engagement than the solution.

Yes. Well, you may just have resolved my problems. When people ask me about these, I can say — it's not the end, it's the engagement.

Is this not the way you've thought about it?

Yes. What I always found interesting about a lot of work that I was doing at that period of time is that people would almost talk about it in terms of Abstract Expressionism. I thought of my work as much colder and more calculating, much less expressionistic, more detached and more theory-oriented. I think what's interesting is that all the things that you're talking about are aspects of that, it's more of a theory-orientation — a focused and silent investigation towards a very physical and intellectual situation.

Yet doesn't the whole notion of focusing on the 'engagement' rather than the object makes it tempting to set the work against some of the implications of Abstract Expressionism? For example, you talk about the process of collage as building, rather than collage as painting —

Oh, that's something that I do talk about a lot. Some of the drawings I always thought of as collages, more of a sculpture process. People will look at collages and talk about paintings — and I just say — no, it's not that.

Doesn't this relate to some of the routes away from Abstract Expressionism and into performance? Allan Kaprow suggests that his own move from Abstract Expressionism to the early Happenings was through a reconceiving of collage as a process of building instead of a fixed form.

Right.

In the really early work, like with 18 Happenings in 6 Parts *(1959), he tries to establish a field in which the viewer is forced to engage in the same process of building through their looking.*

Yes. Form layers of meaning and content, just by the physicality of layers, one over another.

And the interest is in the process of engagement.

Which is possibly a process of confusion.

But in your work there's a much stronger focus upon structure and system.

Yes. It's like somehow the sparseness of materials — in some cases, real time, real space, real durations. Yet it seems to be out of the realm of physical reality, but it's — do you know what I'm saying? A lot of the Happenings — even Kaprow's early work, or a lot of it, no matter how disorienting, seemed to draw on daily life events or imagery — like car crashes, these kinds of things. A lot of the Happenings, even some of the early performance pieces, seemed to be about bringing life into art because they wanted to get rid of the aesthetics of art. And my work was almost in the reverse. It's not that I'm trying to bring back the aesthetics of art, but I don't really want to ground it in daily life, in those expressions. It's more grounded in some kind of mental situation. It's the complex of thought processes as opposed to perceptions of, let's say, related imagery that exists in real life.

So then it becomes really important to drain the materials of references beyond the structure or system.

Yes. Definitely. That's why I considered it cold, detached.

This goes back, in a way, to this idea of 'absence' that we were talking about, doesn't it? Certain things being eliminated in order that other things can become traces, rather than complete in themselves.

Right.

So it creates a space for the viewer.

In a sense, yes. It presents information or lack of information in a more direct way. It's not a mental space that serves as a framing device, but the space acts more as part of a process of destroying viewer distance. The space becomes a space for the viewer, because the space itself is taken into account as part of the decision-making processes that occur when creating the work that it will eventually house. There is something of a fundamental relationship that exists between the work and the space, a relationship that places the work in the here and now of the duration of its existence in that place. The activities involved, and the work resulting, exist in the present, which includes the audience as part of it when placed in that situation.

I wonder if the questions that this work has been dealing with are coming up again, now.

I think they are. I know there are times when I give lectures in universities, and I see some of the work and a lot of very young people at school are reinvestigating these kinds of things. I get a sense that they want to investigate something again, as opposed to just putting their arms around a market or gallery sensibility.

DENNIS OPPENHEIM

Dennis Oppenheim's work has embraced sculpture, Land Art, Body Art and performance, as well as photography, installation, film and video, alongside other less easily named events and presentations. Rooted firmly in the conceptual turn in art occurring in the late 1960s, Oppenheim's first performance work was executed while he was living on the West Coast of the United States in 1967, a year which also saw his first engagement with Earth Art. From 1968, Oppenheim worked between California and New York, participating in that year with Robert Morris, Michael Heizer and Robert Smithson in the influential *Earthworks* exhibition at the Dwan Gallery in New York. From 1969, Oppenheim's work was exhibited widely in Europe and the United States. In that same year, Oppenheim became friends with the artist Vito Acconci, and began a six year engagement with performance and Body Art, among his other forms of activity. In 1974, he produced his first 'surrogate' piece, *Theme for a Major Hit*, in which he substituted a mannequin for his own presence as performer. Since then, Oppenheim has continued to work across a wide variety of media and through innovative forms. In 1990 the Institute for Contemporary Art, New York, and P.S.1 Museum, New York, presented a major retrospective of Oppenheim's work since 1967, a show which was seen in Europe in 1994. This interview was recorded in New York in March 1993, and the text corrected and qualified in April and May 1994.

*   *   *

In coming to performance were you influenced by work outside of an art context?
    I came into Performance, or Body Art, through doing large scale land projects in the late sixties. Land Art levied a heavy blow against discrete objects as well as the traditional system that supported their belief system. All of a sudden, what constituted a conventional art object was threatened — it was now dematerialized. Sculpture could be a hole in the ground, for instance, un-movable, un-sealable and in some cases, un-seeable. Of importance was the fact that the artist was now outside of the studio, in real time, activating works within an ongoing system. I began to travel. It wasn't as if I had influences outside the art context — art had actually invaded these contexts. Body Art invaded one's home. It took in your family.

It seems important to make a distinction between considering a live action in terms of these processes and the kinds of terms that surround representational theatre.

Yeah, it is. It's quite important. I think one of the most catalytic aspects of Body Art, as it was extrapolated by some of the younger people who carried it into other areas, was this connection it had with the real world. The fact that it did not engage or mediate in a kind of a 'method'. When I did a piece where rocks were thrown into a circle — [*Rocked Circle — Fear* (1971)] — in which I was standing and I was trying to get a configuration that represented fear, it was very important that it was not seen as 'drama' in the traditional sense of acting. It wanted to be *real* in the simple sense of the word. And, I think, within the realm of the real, it wanted to find perversions.

Quite often when one's young and under the impression that you're breaking new ground, which is always overstated, the tendency is not to reach historically into things which might connect with it. The temptation is to engage in a belief-system where you've actually invented something, and there are no corollaries. Body Art seemed to be capable of fracturing into many radical areas — some of them would buttress closer to theatre. I was always afraid of 'method', the idea of method acting as something to be compared with, because most, if not all this work, was *real*. The artist would execute or engage in a process which, over a period of time, would release a psychological state — it would be about exhaustion or about some kind of slow eroding of a certain stable position. So when one was coming to Body Art from sculpture — one didn't want to be seen as coming from theatre. At the same time, though, there was a kind of naivete on the part of the Body Artists, because theatre was actually far more complex than one was feeling. It was quite advanced even then. In the late sixties, it was a rather simple version of theatre that Body Art wanted not to associate itself with. It was the simple suppositions of 'theatricality'. A lot of the Body Art performance

---

ROCKED CIRCLE–FEAR

"I was concerned with turning the face into raw material, like plastic, then creating an external situation that was going to change the face, the way it looked ... I wanted to alter it by forcing it to express the sensation of fear.'
DAO with Willoughby Sharp, 1971.

A situation was created which allowed registration of an exterior stimulus directly through facial expression. As I stood in a 5' diameter circle, rocks were thrown at me. The circle demarcated the line of fire. A video camera was focused on my face. The face was captive, its expression a direct result of the apprehension of hazard. Here, stimulus is not abstracted from its source. Fear is the emotion which produced a final series of expressions. *DAO.*

One half hour video tape, with super 8 film loop.

Figures 11 and 12 Dennis Oppenheim *ROCKED CIRCLE — FEAR* 1971 (courtesy of the artist).

works — it's like Conceptual Art's relationship to philosophy, like Kosuth's flirtation with philosophy as an artist — when it came too close to the real thing it showed its relative shallowness.

Much of the Body Art performance, and even the actions that were documented on video and film, were, on my behalf, so concentrated on the possibility of uprooting information that could be used within the sculptural domain that the idea of form became unimportant. It became unimportant that I was rolling two hours of video on an activity that nobody would ever watch. There was, throughout — I'm speaking for myself — this highly enriched interrogational procedure at the cost of very uninspired form. The documentations that were often the residue of these enquiries, this engagement, lacked formal energy and interest. Often they were haphazardly displayed. So there was this sort of imbalance. It is very much this imbalance that was corrected by the picture-theory art — the artists of the eighties — like Sherry Levine. These people looked at the documentations that were done by the so-called first-generation Conceptual Artists and they began to take away the rough edges, to redirect the content towards more available subject-matter.

As you use it the phrase, 'Conceptual Art' seems to suggest an address to the viewer principally on a discursive level — perhaps an awareness of the uprooting of the languages of sculpture. The emphasis you place on the 'real', though, seems to suggest that Body Art's centre lies elsewhere.

Well, I can see why it would be a bit confusing. It is true that while the impulse to do this work resides in more of a conceptual orientation, the actual execution, as it becomes physical and perhaps given to certain ranges of improbable or difficult to calculate outcomes, might dovetail back into something that doesn't seem to be cerebrally housed. The impulse, though, germinates from a desire to uncover, to advance, to, oddly enough, make clear some sort of rather deep and difficult region with which form is asked to engage. In some of the performances or activities I did with my children, using them as so-called 'surrogates' or 'agents', I would initiate an action, and they, being biologically connected with me, would be asked to carry on an activity — [*Two Stage Transfer Drawing (Advancing to a Future State)* (1971), *Two Stage Transfer Drawing (Returning to a Past State)* (1971), *Colour Application for Chandra* (1971)]. Clearly, because of their relationship to me, I was asking the viewer to consider the fact that I was able to operate in a different time frame because these agents were younger. There were a lot of conceptual acrobatics going on in some of these things. In that early period of the seventies one replaced certain ways of talking about sculpture with words like 'energy-fields', 'transference', 'energy-zones'. It got into a vocabulary of de-materialisation. I think the attempt to radicalise the making of sculpture lies in this world of de-materialisation, which was very much a corollary with the performance area. It was a fundamental in the thinking of other sculptors as well — in the distributional sculpture and in a number of more visual, dormant counterparts to that. I know that in 1970, 1971 and 1972, I was pretty much immersed in this vocabulary. I would call pieces *Energy Transference, Feedback* — [*A Feedback Situation* (1971) *Feed-back: Kristin*, (1971)].

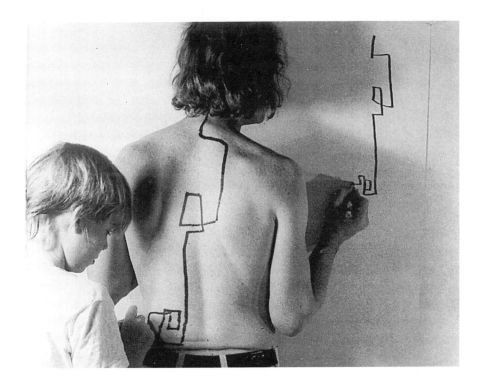

TWO-STAGE TRANSFER DRAWING. (ADVANCING TO A FUTURE STATE).
1971
Boise, Idaho
Erik to Dennis Oppenheim
'As Erik runs a marker along my back, I attempt to duplicate the movement on the wall. His activity stimulates a kinetic response from my sensory system. He is, therefore, drawing through me. Sensory retardation or disorientation makes up the discrepancy between the two drawings, and could be seen as elements that are activated during this procedure. Because Erik is my offspring, and we share similar biological ingredients, my back (as surface) can be seen as a mature version of his own... in a sense, he contacts a future state.' *DAO*

Figure 13 Dennis Oppenheim *TWO-STAGE TRANSFER DRAWING. (ADVANCING TO A FUTURE STATE)* 1971, stills from videotape (courtesy of the artist).

TWO-STAGE TRANSFER DRAWING. (RETURNING TO A PAST STATE).
1971
Boise, Idaho
Dennis to Erik Oppenheim
'As I run a marker along Erik's back, he attempts to duplicate the movement on the wall.
My activity stimulates a kinetic response from his memory system. I am, therefore, drawing
through him. Sensory retardation or disorientation makes up the discrepancy between the
two drawings, and could be seen as elements that are activated during this procedure.
Because Erik is my offspring, and we share similar biological ingredients, his back (as
surface) can be seen as an immature version of my own... in a sense, I make contact with a
past state.' DAO

Figure 14   Dennis Oppenheim *TWO-STAGE TRANSFER DRAWING. (RETURNING TO A
PAST STATE)* 1971, stills from videotape (courtesy of the artist).

*This idea of constructing a mental configuration which is, in a way, the point of the
work, seems linked with the impulse towards performance. A 'mental configuration'
does not reside within an object, but the traces or elements offered in place of the
object — the text, photographs, whatever — might provoke an engagement with the
set of ideas which 'are' the work. It strikes me that if that's what 'conceptualism' is
it intersects with what 'performance' might be. It's 'something that happens', an*

occasion or event provoked under certain circumstances by the traces or elements the artist offers.

Well, yeah. I would say that that is very much a description that I feel comfortable with as one of the conditions in which some of these early programmes were founded. I mean in spirit, *in spirit*, there was the feeling that these activities were charges to activate the periphery of the things. There was a tendency to see even discrete performances and works as being charges that opened up doors that were not going to be found on the paper that you were presenting the work to. It was a characteristic of that work which was quite unlike Minimalism — Minimalism was supposed to be succinct, completely understood, grasped, totally comprehended by viewing it. Here was something that was quite the antithesis.

The language in which the pieces are couched also seems relevant to this, and to be a means by which sculpture and performance are brought into some kind of collision. Your account of Arm and Wire *(1969) uses terms derived from conventional sculpture — you talk about 'artist as material', 'artist as instigator'. Yet these terms no longer seem able to adequately contain the implications of this kind of circle of actions. The presentation of an act upon one's own body as in* Arm and Wire, *or the marking of one's own body, as in Vito Acconci's* Rubbing Piece *(1970), seems to go beyond this kind of formal description. It's as if one of the tensions in the work lies in the way in which its implications exceed the language through which it is offered or documented. Elsewhere you've talked about* Arm and Wire *in terms of artist as 'victim' and 'victimiser'…*

Well, you know, this aspect is very interesting. Acconci and I used quite often to give lectures to students, and we would be showing slides over long periods of time. And it always occurred to me that I detected in myself, and very much in Acconci, an attempt to leave a tremendous amount out of the information. It was almost as if — like in describing the *Rubbing Piece* Acconci would simply describe the activity, knowing full-well there is this whole range, but leaving it out. Of course we were all taught — I mean, it came through some sort of unprescribed course — that, as an artist, if you discover something, and you don't fully engage it, if you don't over use it, it leaves a lot of remaining energy. It's kind of a peculiar thing to say, it seems too calculated, and one wonders, well, if you discover a thing how can you control the use of it, aren't you inclined to do it again and again? But if there is a pulling back — not making a career out of doing one variation after the other, but leaving it very early — it somehow adds energy to the initial work. I noticed that very much in Acconci's lectures, where he just skimmed over these things that had considerable depth. I think he's inclined to do that. It's an inclination not to unnecessarily uncover those regions and a desire to

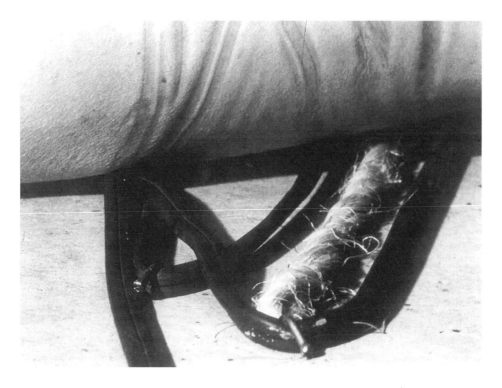

'ARM AND WIRE incorporates a very close shot of my arm rolling across electrical cording, receiving the impression on the skin. Basically I make no distinction between the material and the tool. The impressions produced by the expenditure of downward pressure are returned to their source and registered on the material that expends the energy. It was this economy I found interesting. ARM AND WIRE was an attempt to make what you are making and how you are making it one and the same thing. It consolidated output and compressed it into a single act.'
DAO with Willoughby Sharp, 1971.
fed back to the source.

Figure 15   Dennis Oppenheim *ARM AND WIRE* 1969, stills from 16 mm film, with Bob Fiore (courtesy of the artist).

keep them open. And probably on some levels an inability on his part, with the correct energy, to invade them.

Isn't this concern with language, or with the taking of terms from one system and putting them into another, present in other aspects of your work — in particular, the Earth Art?

It was one of the ploys that I engaged in in executing the Land Art pieces. The temptation early in Land Art was not to scribe onto land

RUBBING PIECE
Max's Kansas City Restuarant, New York; Saturday, May 2, 1970; 2-3 PM

Project:

Sitting alone at a booth, during the ordinary activity at the restaurant.
Rubbing my left forearm for one hour, gradually producing a sore.

Notes:

My performance has been announced: my performance keeps being announced (my performance consists in marking myself as the performer: marking time).

•

Performance as spread: breakdown of specific channels of adaptation, so that the reaction is forced to spread over different areas (expansion of the sore, exposure of a secret).

•

Performer as producer (of the sore); performer as consumer (receiver of the sore).

•

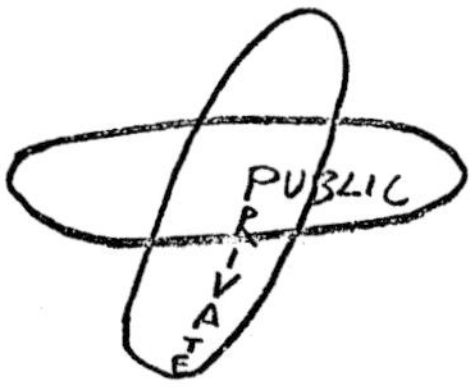

Performance as overlapping situations: one place in two different social occasions at one time.

PUBLIC PRIVATE

•

Performance as slip: a presented piece of biography that ordinarily would not have become part of one's active biography at all: performance as handicap.

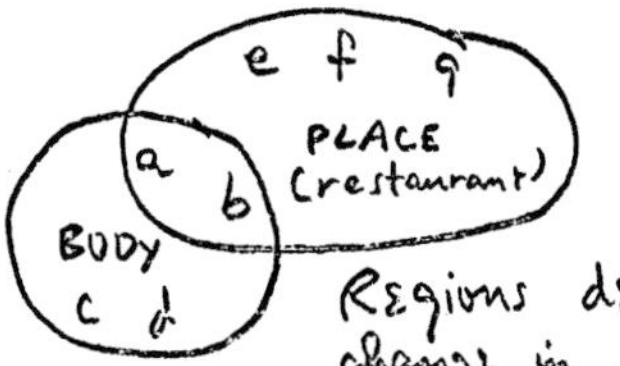

PLACE (restaurant) e f g
BODY a b c d

Regions determined by change of state: change in state of a does not influence c or d but b, e, f, g.

Progression of the sore after the activity: development of the sore on its own.
(Performance as after-effect: performance as place -- stepping-off place for the sore that is the result of the performance: since I do not happen to be there, after the performance is over, the rest of the performance occurs wherever I happen to be.)

Figure 16 Vito Acconci, notes and diagrams for *Rubbing Piece* 1970 (courtesy of the artist).

gestures that would easily echo from traditional art — abstract gestures or subjectively derived images. One didn't want to treat the land just as a canvas to reinterpret Abstract Expressionism, for instance. Nor did they want to be formal. They didn't want to be a continuation of geometric or even minimal, after a while, forms on land. So the tendency was to take information from other areas, what I would call 'information lines', lines that *meant* something. At that point it began to operate on a conceptual level. For instance, I would use lines that would indicate rainfall or topological lines from one mountain to another, just in an attempt to come to grips with a dialogue, a conversation that wouldn't, again, echo some of the more traditional, sculptural interests. I always felt that Body Art, in my hands, had far more substantial vein in which to engage, and was much more mysterious and radical — if I could use that term. Earth Art was radical in the fact that in one gesture it countered major canons of traditional art, such as sellability, accessibility, mobility. I mean, you can't see the art, you can't buy the art, you can't have the art. Of course, we took photographs, but even so it had that radical aspect in relationship to the methods in which art was available to an audience. Body Art had a far more substantial vein in which one could slowly build a case for art, for sculpture being able to survive and live within this dematerialised zone of psychological topology. And the kinds of persuasions and currents that an artist would succumb to and would be affected by within that dematerialised, sensory core, were really unknown. One was really throwing oneself to the wind. There was no 'programme', so to speak, and I'm sure this is true of Acconci. One had a sense of a hierarchy, of what areas seemed more deserving. Acconci is not a psychologist, yet his programme seemed to be very much — as he was swept into these orbits of self-referential interrogation — a dialogue with certain psychological states and mysteries and the after-effect of certain transactions. I think mine was equally as mysteriously undirected. I would always use the term 'up the ante'. Quite often 'upping the ante' during the early seventies meant more risk. Risk, and in some cases danger, seemed to be a kind of admixture within the process that would make one work better than the other. If one work had it, it just seemed to be elevated. So it became a kind of a ploy that one would use as an agent to thicken the cake.

I find it interesting that you use the word 'ploy'.
    Well, because I think there is a feeling in some of these works that the artist is a little bit out of control and driven by honest impulses that are not necessarily his own. Seventies artists were not near, *not near* as convoluted, as cunning, as schizophrenic in their pursuit of careerism as those eighties

artists who had a cold, calculated procedure of elevating their personae. There was a term in the eighties that was coined to describe a certain kind of art going on then, it was called 'smart art'. Well, I think the roots of smart art may have been discovered somewhere in the seventies, but there was the inability to actually make it work by the practitioners.

You've suggested that at the time the Body Art pieces were being executed, some without audiences present, you weren't especially concerned with their documentation. Didn't this pose certain risks for the work and for those who would be an audience to it?

I think I made a statement that was picked up by Jean Cristoph-Arman, who's a curator in Basel, that, even though I'm making something, it's not necessarily what I really want to make. There is this kind of feeling in much of that work that the ambitions are often so overwhelming — particularly when the artist got into this dematerialised mechanism — that there was probably a richer kind of theoretical, conceptual vein than one had the ability to objectify in form. One would pull back and give excuses for the photography as the evidence, because there was all this sensory stuff and all of these states which were, certainly, seated within the orchestration of the event, but were thrown out when the documentation had to cut through it and save what little there was left. Again, the overwhelming feeling that, often, the installations and the activities themselves were shadows of the real desires. It was so prominent then. It was a constant feeling of getting just percentages of the work.

I wonder if the danger is so important because it's something you can't finally commodify or reduce to a 'documentation'. It has to be at that moment.

Yeah, I would agree that the reason why it was so much of an inducement was that without it the results often had certain problems of authenticity, certain problems of the calibre of the pursuit. It seems that with that element of danger, one's work, in every way, became more substantial. It seemed to satisfy the urges inherent within this whole programme to raise the work and to raid the real. It dissuaded sentimentality. It was an instrument by which one could hone in on a more rigorous outcome. Even though, as anything which is used over and over as a method, it can become weakened.

But was it not also what brought you to the end of that mode of work?

Well, yeah. I would always say that I started to do the surrogate puppets because my work was getting too dangerous.

Yet you have expressed some doubts about the puppet pieces.

    Well, a number of things bothered me about them. The fact that these would be looked at within a historical field of figurative work bothered me. I used to make these as a child. I used to perform a little bit with marionettes, so I had some experience with them that I drew from. I didn't feel, though, that they could be expected to contain the type of rigour I wanted to put them through. *Attempt to Raise Hell* (1974), which crashes into a bell, may be the one that was the most successful in making legitimate the claim that if Body Art were to continue in my hands — Acconci and I both said to ourselves when we were thirty or so that we didn't expect to be around when we were thirty-five. There did seem to be this desperation about the work and, of course, one was always dissuaded by the Viennese Aktionnist work — which was kind of myth about dying — and it didn't interest any of us. But there was this feeling that the work was getting more and more

Figure 17 Dennis Oppenheim *ATTEMPT TO RAISE HELL* 1974. Cast aluminium figure, bell, felt suit. Timing mechanism forces figure to lunge forward and strike every sixty seconds. Wooden base. 6′ × 4′ × 3′ (courtesy of the artist).

rigorous. I just couldn't really fantasise how one could k
certain stage. So there was always a feeling that at som
change. But one didn't want it to be weakened by its e
surrogate, the marionettes, were not an adequate, I think,
carry the energy attributed to Body Art. I think it's at that
energies attributed to Body Art remained — they didn't g ---. .ot to any
great degree.

*Thomas McEvilley describes your work as 'anti-Modernist'. Is this a position that
you recognise?*

    Well, McEvilley is a spokesman for the new kind of 'postmodern'
position — of multiple cultural positions. In diagnosing a career he
is going to be very perceptive about areas where he thinks this shift
may have occurred. I admitted to him that if I have evolved to the nineties
attaching myself to certain signs that could be construed as postmodernist,
it's not with a great deal of consciousness.

*Interestingly, he doesn't say you're 'postmodern'. He talks about later work, post-
1980 work, perhaps, as 'becoming' postmodern, but he hyphenates 'post-modern',
suggesting it's a kind of historical category. He suggests the work is
programmatically anti-Modernist and at the same time Modernist. It's anti-
Modernist in the sense of being anti-Greenbergian, but also Modernist in the
sense of paring things down, of 'going on to the next step'. You might say it's 'anti-
Formalist', perhaps, it's against non-objective, self-contained, autonomous art, but
it's Modernist in its thrust forward.*

    I think that's true. I would say that one of the impulses that spirited
a lot of the seventies work, definitely the zone of the mid- seventies where
much of the performance and installation work was self-referential,
autobiographical, self-interrogational, was a sense of art as a tool to uncover
itself. That's when a lot of relatively uninspired form, on my behalf, was
initiated, because the enquiry into the art-making process was so intense
that one's guard was dropped in the final requirement to minister in the
form. A good deal of the impulse at the time was directed towards faults
within the Formalist practice, particularly the 'signature' art — works that
would carry a theme on endlessly. There was a supposition that a certain
amount of dishonesty was being practised there. Many works were given, on
my behalf, to the question of motive. In *Theme for a Major Hit* (1974), with the
puppet, the song is 'It Ain't What You Make It's What Made You Do It'. Even
though I didn't know what made me do it, I at least acknowledged that it
was interesting. There was a great deal of challenging of one's position and
trying to be honest.

You keep on returning to this notion of form and the fact that in Body Art the emphasis lay elsewhere than with 'good' form or 'pleasing' form. Yet, in resisting 'good form' while calling into play or referring to these 'energies', the work might be read as refusing to fudge it, particularly with respect to danger or pain, to these uncomfortable contents which can be referred to or provoked but not embodied by the object. In other words, might 'good form' not detract from what the work is aiming at?

Well, you know, even Greenberg said that quite often new or radical art appears to be ugly in the beginning. I know Acconci and I both said that content is relatively easy, form seems to be the problem. I think these are kind of misleading statements, but it's circling around what one means by 'elevated' form. I know it's true that strictly formal pursuits are quite often unrewarding. I've always targeted them as shallow pursuits, certainly not rich enough to justify being an artist, even though there are many who are highly evolved in this area of formal art, working on some meta-level of esoteria, beyond the sublime. But, with all that in mind, there still is this characteristic that one might detect in extremely good work, work that has this elevated content and has somehow been able, in describing that content, or giving way to it, to become imbued with an enlightened formal counterpart to it. I mean, it just seems to be a magical uniting of powerful content and the perfect armature for its containment. So as I approach a work I feel that I have to at least wish for this other part, which is supposed to open up the avenues to inspired form, to engage in this middle pursuit, the pursuit in which all this stuff is supposed to be figured out before you lay it on the floor. But when I begin to steer the form to what I hope is enlightenment, I find that I don't have the adequate vocabulary. The mental procedures which one can trust to carve the content into deeper rings do not work on the form. The form is some kind of haphazard, hit it or miss hope, some kind of accident. It seems that the form is the thing that does not pay attention to the methods of coming to bear, the methods of genesis. In generating content I seem to be able to use cerebral methodology. Form is non-verbal, it doesn't respond well to intellectual dictation. Some artists are able to manoeuvre themselves in peculiar ways which trap some of these awesome formal outcomes. I think Bruce Nauman occasionally. It's just a gift. It's some kind of gift they have of knowing the temperatures by which to de-control the intellect, to unplug it at certain disjunctures and plug it in at others, thereby handling this delicate thing so that when it's finally administered it doesn't look over-intellectualised, it doesn't look under-intellectualised, it doesn't look contrived — it looks as if it was born in heaven. And all I have to come in proximity to this is desire. I don't know how to do it. I know that intellect bears a heavy crease on it, though.

I realise that when I'm using too much intellectual stimulus in trying to answer questions along this falling or pursuit, it under-nourishes the outcome, it taints it too early and it doesn't allow it to be in this elevated formal state. I mean it sounds like I'm talking as a formalist, but I'm talking in the best way I can about a very straightforward sort of — about a certain differential between the two. Just by years and years of working, the kind of fear, the degree of difficulty and the degree of chance there is in matching the formal constituents of an idea, of a work that generates from an idea and then needs a form. Most of my works seem to be that disjointed, you know. They all come from notebooks — from sketches and words. So in this early point of showing itself to me, the words quite often stimulate images, and images spiel off words in this tangled onward mechanism towards some sort of stream which is going to start to increase its velocity. And the thing I distrust the most is when formal determinations are made by cold intellectual decisions. You want to feel like ideas happen — like when they discovered DNA. Oh, yes! You know, that's it!

You talk about form as if it is something beyond language.
　　Well, I mean, this a very kind of Modernist — you know, I'm talking like a heroic Jackson Pollock, virtually.

Well, we have been talking about ways in which the Body Art work resists explanation or, at least, tensions that arise out of a refusal to explain. Is that not consistent with what you're saying now?
　　I think it's true that a tendency to keep a lot of the stuff floating in some ways translates into almost a formal portion. It just enriches the whole thing. When I look at works that I think are successful, where the form and content are somehow both allowed to live in a state of suspension, there are few examples. You always want it to happen again, but they are always works that I can't explain. It's as if it is a non-verbal region. And I know this is true of Nauman. He doesn't seem able to talk about this stuff, but he is able to do it, which is an interesting thing for one of our better artists.

This point at which it's difficult to talk about the work interests me, because it seems to be a point, again, that challenges or disrupts the terms by which one finds access to the work. It also makes it difficult to write about.
　　Well, just because these things are difficult for the artists to talk about doesn't mean that they are difficult to talk about. I think it's simply a question of the practitioners' hierarchy of use of energy. We used to say, well, it's OK for an artist to be inarticulate because they're so exhausted! After trying to make this stuff they just have no energy to talk about it. But — I

don't know. I went to school in California in the late fifties and there was a general kind of position where artists didn't want to talk too much about their work. So I grew up in a climate of Bay Area sensibility, which is very inarticulate. And this became really a problem, because I knew this stuff could be talked about and these people were pretending that it was too difficult. So I was glad to come back here where you could have a conversation. But I do know that there is this region that seems to defy language. And it's in the area of form. And rightly so. And one would say, and why not?

STUART BRISLEY

Developing out of his formal concerns with kinetic and audio-visual environments, Stuart Brisley's entry into performance in the late 1960s drew Body Art practices toward explicitly political contents and purposes. Following a period of work in the United States between 1960 and 1964, and, subsequently, exhibitions of object-related work in Europe and America, Brisley's performance emerged not only in relation to earlier American performance and contemporary Body Art practices, but as a means of addressing specific cultural and political contexts. In this respect, Brisley's work looked toward Eastern European performance, with which he engaged directly in the film *Being and Doing* of 1984, made in collaboration with Ken McMullen. From 1981, following a major retrospective of his work at the Institute of Contemporary Arts, London, Brisley gave emphasis in his work to installation, photography, sculpture and sound, as part of the developing the project, *The Georgiana Collection* (1981–1986). Stuart Brisley currently teaches at the Slade School of Fine Art in London, where this interview was recorded in May 1994.

*　　　　*　　　　*

Are you still doing live work?

Yes. Very occasionally. If I'm invited I may or may not do it, depending on whether I think it's interesting or not. The only thing I've tried to generate was an anniversary of something called *10 Days*, which I did in Berlin in 1972 and again in London in 1978. It was agreed that I would do it in a place in Frankfurt last year. Then they got cold feet for some reason. It would have been a good situation because it's very similar to how the Acme was in the late seventies.

What was important about the space?

In 1978, it was a development in the sense that the Acme had three or four floors, so I was able to separate two aspects of the work which were complimentary to each other on different floors — they had their own discretion. I'd better describe it. It was based on the idea of making some sort of collision, as it were, with Christmas and the New Year. I decided, I suppose, to do the inverse of what is normally done at Christmas when there's a lot to eat. At the same time, I decided to give everything that I might have eaten to anyone who wanted to eat it. I set out a structure so that there were two tables that would accommodate thirty-one placings — thirty-one because we started on the 21st December at 8 pm and ended at 8 pm on the 31st December. Each of the tables had to be long enough to take into account breakfast, lunch, dinner — breakfast, lunch, dinner — and so on. Downstairs, the table was laid for a banquet, or a celebration, a New Year's celebration. For every meal that I was presented with in the upstairs space, the waiter would lay a place — and the places were actually underneath each other — at the banquet. So slowly over ten days the placings for the banquet were completed. Upstairs, all the food that wasn't eaten was left on the table, but it was ordered day by day so that you could see the remains of each day. We opened at 8 o'clock and closed at midnight. I slept there, so did the chef and the waiter. I don't think anybody ate any of the breakfasts, because it was too early — nine o'clock in the morning — but all lunches and dinners were eaten. At midnight we would take all the bits of food –- like bits of potato, potato peelings, whatever — and put them onto the table with a sort of strip of tape put across — and, I don't know whether I dated them — and then put a dusting of flour over it, just to give it a separation. The food would get old and rot and give that sense of passing time, in contrast to downstairs where you have this anticipation of a celebration. And that just slowly accreted, of course, during the ten days.

Did you have a fairly free interaction with the visitors?

Yes, but not when they were eating. I just sat at whatever point at the table the next meal was going to come from. What was interesting about that was the way in which people were sort of inveigled into performing. People came in and went out — and there would be a lot of conversations. It was very open in that sense. What was also interesting was that — well, it got into the press, I suppose, and after Christmas day people began to phone up wanting to book tables (laughs). And some of them were quite genuine, they were assuming it was a restaurant. So we had to say — look, you know, there's only one meal. It doesn't cost anything, but if you come and somebody else is eating it, it's too bad. So various other sorts of connections began to be made. For example — it's just my perception — we seem to get a lot of Italian people coming — I don't know if they were specifically in London for Christmas. And waiters from various London hotels and restaurants. It sort of determined its own audience, which has happened before with works. The other thing was that it was in an area in London — around Covent Garden, as it was then — where there was quite a lot of homelessness. On Christmas night, for example, we got two tramps. It was

Figure 18 Stuart Brisley *10 Days*, for Fifth Year Anniversary, Acme Gallery, London, December 1978 (photo: Janet Andeurn) (courtesy of the artist).

difficult to explain to them that there was only one meal — so we split the meal in half. Then they wanted to know, you know, where the beds were, where the whisky was. So it did connect with a number of other dimensions, that came to it without, you know, any kind of will on my or the gallery's part. The nature of the thing opened into this social sense which I thought was rather interesting.

At the end, I wanted to have a really open celebration, for anybody — but the gallery were opposed to that. They wanted to make it a celebration of the gallery. They won this argument — I mean, it didn't really matter to me — so thirty-one people were invited and there were speeches and so on. I had my first meal. What I did — there was also one live action between these two events which was that I took my clothes off and I crawled through all that old food — once up and once back — and then I got up and went into the banquet situation.

The invited audience changes the situation completely, doesn't it?

Yes, it does. But I recognised it was part of an institution, so I felt I was prepared to make certain agreements.

In describing the work you seem to stress its permeability, as if the performance might become indistinct from the various events it gives rise to or provokes.

Yes, that's right.

I wonder if this aspect of the form is one reason why you haven't pursued documentation to any great extent?

I have, actually. But I always regarded the primary act as being that of the performance. If I were to change that — there's no reason why one shouldn't — the work would have to change. It would be an entirely different work and a completely different relationship to the camera. I'm very conscious of the camera, but when I'm making performances the act is the primary issue. It's a problem, because I don't actually believe in documentation — I mean, how does one do it? There is another challenge — which I don't think that I've resolved. Because of this predeliction for the act, as it were, I haven't been able to properly constitute the residue in a set of terms which make it another work. I suppose the closest was with a photographer called Leslie Haslam, because of circumstances in relation to the act when we collaborated in *Moments of Decision/Indecision* (1975) in Warsaw. I was blind, so I needed the photographer to work with me way beyond what the camera required. We made an agreement that he would use the camera from certain positions, but also that he would collaborate with me to let me know where I was in relation to everything else, because I didn't have a clue. That gave him the opportunity to enter into it.

How did the piece come about?

I was invited on DAAD to go to Berlin. And I really wanted to go to Poland, for all kinds of reasons — that goes back to when I was a child. So I went to Warsaw and the first thing I did was to look up a guy called Joseph Shiner who'd worked at the Edinburgh Festival in 1971. I had read a review of his work which I found very interesting. He happened to be the director of the Theatre Studio in the big palace that is in the centre of Warsaw — which was built as a gift from Stalin to the Polish people. He invited me to work in the Theatre Studio. What I was going to do there was kind of open.

What was the space itself?

It was a big theatrical space, although it didn't have rows of seats or anything. There was really nothing there. To get a nail took two or three days. On the other hand there was lots of paint. So I used what was there and within that given space I worked out how I would start the work.

Figure 19 Stuart Brisley *Moments of Decision/Indecision*, 6 days, Teatr Galery, Palac Kultury i Nauki, Warsaw, Poland, 1975 (photo: Leslie D. Haslam).

Did you conceive of what you were going to do before you went?

        No. I never did that. I just went, probably, with some idea of the last thing that I'd done. Then in that situation, I structured something that could be enacted, but without knowing what the parameters were. Working there was just extraordinarily peculiar. It was early on, given the situation between East and West and cultural exchanges, so this business of not seeing was, in a way, connected to being in a condition of not seeing anything, of being suspended somewhere else. I had no idea about the language, I didn't understand what the institution was up to that was working with me. The whole thing did have a tendency of feeling Kafka-esque. There was another agenda — of course, there always is — but it was an agenda of which I literally had no idea. It was like being on another planet. That was really rather shocking. I think that's expressed in the way the work reveals itself, although I can't say that I was actually thinking like that when I did it. I was very much responding and reacting to the situation. I had this idea about making work, that it should be possible to be placed in the next room, or wherever, somewhere, and you do something. You do it. What is it? What are you doing? Although it isn't quite as obvious as that, because I'd set up a whole process whereby I was able to make that work.

Was your step into performance from an idea about the social and political role of art?

        Yes. Sure. And another essential factor to that would be that you had to put yourself into a position. You have to declare yourself. One had to be, in a sense, open, naked, if you like, so that if one was saying something that necessarily implicated the way other people might think about their behaviour, one had to actually demonstrate that one was not doing this from any elevated position. That one was doing it from *being* it. That was an essential characteristic. Right at the very beginning, though, I came to a stop with making objects — although I'd been a painter as well. I came to a stop because there was no purpose to making anything else. I'd reached a point where I was using mathematical equations to exemplify something fundamental to how we are, such as gravity. I was making works which related to the x-y-z co-ordinate. Neon works which dealt with it in time and perspex works which were structures. And I realised that once you'd made an object, the object wasn't an expression, somehow, which gave volume to the idea of the x-y-z co-ordinate in the terms that I wanted, that it was in some sort of ideal world that these things worked. And therefore, what was the *real* world? Well, the real world is where you walk about and do things. So the very first work I did was between two people eating, *White Meal* (1966). That's how I came to it — well, let's do something that's fundamental — we have to eat. After that, I did bits and pieces of making objects.

Presumably, the fact that you were making work which was time-based, even though it took the form of objects, established a frame within which something could occur.

Yes, that's right. At some point I did make one of those things that I walked into the middle of. So there was a kind of messy area around there. And also — anyone who starts doing performance having not done it before — it's actually quite cathartic — for all kinds of reasons, I'm sure. After that, then, there were suddenly lots of things to do, whereas before there'd been this awful crunching point of it not being possible to do anything. Of course, there was a context of things taking place — the *Destruction In Art Symposium* (1966) — all those people. It was in that ethos that this was taking place.

Formally, your work seems to have had a strong relationship with North American Body Art, despite often very different kinds of concerns. I'm thinking of such things as the use of risk, endurance, events in real time and space, the use of documentation, as well as in the intersection between the performance and its immediate contexts.

That's probably because I spent five years in America. I came back from the States two years before I did *White Meal*. I was in New York when all of those things were taking place, like the Judson Church work, and Jim Dine's *Car Crash* (1960), all of that. So I've been heavily influenced by American art.

But did you not have a strong reaction against it in certain ways?

No, I accept that. What happened was that I — I actually got thrown out of America, let's put it that way. I had to leave, because of my visa. I was there for five years and then it was over. I'd left to go to America to emigrate — I think this is relevant to this question — I really wanted to leave Britain. So when I found myself back again, I had to do something. Five years at that point was a large part of the time that I had spent as an artist, and I had spent it somewhere else. So it was a matter of actually getting engaged, and my engagement took on much stronger political colouring — as a sort of self-education, I suppose. By the time I'd got to 1968 and I was invited back to America, I wouldn't go.

Why?

Because I had become so engaged with what I was doing here that there was absolutely no point in going to the States. And the issue of art-language, as it were, would only be a part of this. Certainly, art-languages as they existed in New York were important to me when I was there and have been important to me in various ways since. But to come back was to become much more politicised. One of the things that did happen to me was that I found it more and more difficult to think of the idea of becoming American. There was that as well. I mean, I knew, in going to a place like that, one would meet all kinds of people. I met a lot of Hungarian refugees, from the '56 uprising. They were, mostly, terribly upset and sad about being refugees. And I realised that I wasn't. That I had a choice. So I had this developing sense of being alien from wanting to be American, but finding that New York — that kind of urban-scape — was a very comfortable place to be in. Coming back was like a deep shock — having to shrink to fit, to find a path. I think all of that was part of how I became much more politically conscious.

So the sensitivity to context draws you away from the North American practice and politicises the work. It's also why, presumably, the performance becomes, in a way, permeable. You go along to a set of circumstances and engage in an act which in some way activates or is in dialogue with the contexts in which you find yourself.

Absolutely. And that was one of the main premises of the whole thing. I mean, to the extent that in 1970 — I tried all kinds of things — I tried to extend the nature of performance and by doing so stepped outside the art-world.

What were you have responding to?

Well, I can give you two examples. I did something in a park in Sydney called *Lying, Standing, Walking and Talking* (1976). I was given some strips of wood, laths, a hammer, some plastic. I had no food, no water. I just walked into the park and selected this part of a road to live on. I decided that whatever it was, was going to take place in this park for two weeks. One of the ideas was — is it possible to live and at the same time make an art-work, as it were, where the living is almost inside the art-work and the art-work is an essential part of the living? It's pretty well impossible, but that's what I was trying to do. I can't exactly remember how I started this, but I remember somebody came past and said, what are you doing? It was a guy, on his way to work. And I said, well, this is what I'm doing. Then two hours later this girl appears from the other side of the park with a cup of tea that had come from him. Slowly more people came to this thing. They started to tell me things. I'd built this structure to live in — it was raining like hell in Sydney at that time — at spring going towards summer. I mean, people would come and bring so many things — clothes, food — and people would take things, so it was like an exchange centre as well. All out of control, of course. So I became like a silent centre. A lot of the intention in my work was to get to a point where I didn't have to do anything, where the work was doing it and I just had to be, where the whole thing was actually articulating itself. That was one of the things that I had experienced and then found that I could reach, not by having a kind of presumption about how to do it, but I did it time and again.

Figure 20 Stuart Brisley *Lying, Standing, Walking and Talking*, Sydney, November 1976 (courtesy of the artist).

And in this work it quickly became rather important, because people came and wanted to give me things, to tell me things. Then the press and television got involved and the question was — well, what sort of work is this? So we had a kind of open discussion about how we should end this. How should we end this work? And the overwhelming desire on the part of these people was that I should put myself into the position that they were in, which was that they were all in prison in various ways. They had to go to work. You know — it was very simple. They were all doing things they didn't want to do — and I was doing something I really wanted to do, and yet the circumstance was such that I could — not as an individual, but as a figure — become an image which presented their own kind of sense of their constriction. So I had a lot of debate about this, because I didn't want to do this particularly, quite frankly (laughs). But I thought, well, if I don't do this then I'm actually working against my own argument. I can no longer be discrete about the way I choose — I've got to take all this into account. I did that, and almost immediately there was a lot of aggression, which was really very interesting — not from the same people. So it was a work that moved way beyond the point where I had an individual control, but it still existed within the terms of there being some kind of symbolic representation for those people. It still had some reference to something which is not entirely pragmatic. It had an art-content of some kind.

So that's one where the question of art actually still exists. At the same time that I did that in 1976, I started to work in Peterlee in County Durham. I worked there for eighteen months. I'd been invited to go to Peterlee by Artist's Placement Group. They had made some arrangements up there — I was probably the last artist for them to contact — I signed a contract and agreed to work as the town artist for, I don't know, nine months or something. The town had been set up in 1948 as a New Town, but obviously there was a history prior to that. So I set up a project called *History Within Living Memory*. Rather than to make art, the intention was to engage with a public or publics in relation to their own history. They were to be the subjects of my attention, and that collectively we could create circumstances where someone might want to make art. And it wouldn't necessarily be me.

History Within Living Memory was significant in the sense that people were still alive who had, as children, been brought to that area from Ireland and Cornwall, from all parts of Scotland, because their fathers were manning the new mines that were being sunk between 1900 and 1915. So *History Within Living Memory* had at that point an actual, significant context to it all. The project had three parts. The first part incorporated talking to people, taping people. The second part was to do with the history of the Development Corporation, which I did in relation to the Sociology Department at the University of Durham. The third part was workshops about current issues — why is nobody allowed to paint their doors the colour they want? Why doesn't the town allow there to be allotments, etc, etc.? All kinds of specific things like that which are critical to daily life. The only thing that I held to — so far as I could — was that all the visual and textual material had to be treated as though it were art. It didn't matter what it was, one had to pay attention to it. I got lots of posters, lots of snapshots, stuff from the twenties, thirties, and I had them blown up and given status as photographs. They were then associated with text, which were people's own memories, of their choice, edited with them. I wanted it as far as possible to be objective. In the process I employed six local people to do all this. We started a workshop and archives. We had daily public openings, we had reports to various arts centres, etc, etc. The whole idea was that the place itself was its own university. But what happened at Peterlee was that I was overtaken by the Labour party (laughs).

Really?

Well — I say the Labour party — I suppose it was the Labour party. The Development Corporation had completed its work in Peterlee — thirteen years of making half-size, first-generation new towns. They were all going to be 60,000 people except Peterlee, which was a late addition, because the miners had petitioned the government wanting to have a centre for the villages around — and Peterlee became it. They were given a half-size — and the Development Corporation was given responsibility to realise it. This was just coming to its end at the point that I was there, so I wanted the project to get out from under the Development Corporation and into the local District Council. And there'd been a lot of attention on this project towards the end of it — national newspapers and so forth. So the Corporation were very aware of it. They were also aware that within it there was a lot of critical material. Part of that critical material — some of that critical material was not made public but was around in relation to scandals.

Right.

Right. So the minute you actually look into the history of the Development Corporation in Peterlee you run into political scandals that run throughout the region. You know, T. Dan Smith and all that. So they became very edgy because they had a lot to hide. People had committed suicide over this. It had actually hit some hard areas. That was one aspect. The second aspect, which was my third part of the project, was local people setting up their own workshop in relation to what the hell was going on — why is only a Japanese company being invited in and nobody over the age of 35 being allowed to work when there's 25% unemployment. Why? So these were the things that were causing lots of anxiety and I was trying to avoid being snaffled, as it were, in relation to this, realising that I had reached a point of no return, really. So the transition from Development Corporation to the local council was done between them — excluding me. Parts two and three of the project were removed and burned and part one, *History Within Living Memory*, was kept.

Literally burned?

Yes. All the documents were got rid of.

The way you describe it, the project soon departs from any terms one would associate with making art or with an art-product.

Yes, that's right. But I regard that as a kind of model, really.

Which brings me to another aspect of the performance that I wanted to talk to you about. I found Being *and* Doing *(1984) a fascinating film, because of the way it weaved a notion of social and political efficacy through a reading of ritual — ritual as a communal doing. What was it that brought you to an interest in ritual?*

I think it came out of the way the work developed. I found that I was having to think about things I hadn't thought about before. But I have difficulty with the idea of ritual — maybe because I have a limited view of what it is. What I was interested in in *Being and Doing* was contextualising contemporary activity in a way unrelated to high art.

And you chose to look at work which was deeply political because of the context in which it was occurring.

That's right, yes. I was making a claim which Milan Knizak had made in 1968, that in the West this work was easier to do, that in Eastern Europe it brought severe dangers. I was pretty mindful of that. I suppose I was very self-conscious about it. Again, because of this desire to go to Poland, I bumped into mainly Polish artists. So the film is coloured by that, by an awareness of what certain people are doing in certain circumstances and my limited view of the history of Polish art since the Second World War. As far as the stuff that still goes on — the Haxey Hood and so forth — what I really wanted to do was to suggest that there was nothing new in performance. In performance, ritual, of course, is an issue that immediately arises — but if we think in those historical terms, that folk activity is a kind of mad necessity. It's something which is irrational in the sense that it, I presume, allows one to make comments of some sort about things that one can't come to terms with. Like, why do the seasons change — about fertility — about things which don't have rational answers to them — or didn't have rational answers to them. So you get this engagement with elements that are extraordinarily persuasive in the way they deal with one's life — that one can't control in any way. One relates to them in these strange human ways which have a collective sense to them. It's a kind of collective creativity. If you take industrialisation — those classic arguments — that contemporary performance starts from this alienated, isolating position, the claim would be that there is a possibility that this can be overturned. It's a matter of how you strategize the process — and whether the imagination can be transferred from the individual to the collective — and then, how it actually operates. I mean, within that ritual plays a part.

Looking at your practice, I'm not suggesting that it is ritual, but that the idea of ritual as you set it out in Being *and* Doing *provides a set of terms which, in your own description of your work, you're elaborating.*

Yes, that's right.

It's not to say that the art practice which relates to that aspect of ritual is necessarily mystical — that it has to be overtly shamanistic — but there's a certain social engagement, social doing, within that — that ritual presents an enactment enmeshed within specific social relations — and that art might tap into this kind of social doing. It also, again, provides ways of talking about performance that are not to do with theatre.

Yes, exactly.

More recently, you've entered into a period in which you haven't made live work —

Well, the Peterlee experience changed my views about what I should be doing, in a way. So I made another project called *The Georgiana Collection* (1981–86), in which I sort of invented my own institution — so the model was more controllable.

But there's a kind of continuity there with the earlier performances.

Yes. In a sense. I went forward, but I went back and I opened up to it in a different way. I decided that wherever I lived next, that would be the subject of the work. It happened to be Georgiana Street. So I made a number of events, a number of different kinds of categories of work.

What was the nature of the events?

Events in the sense of sound works and so on. I decided that — this is what I thought at the time. I don't think it's the real reason that I did what I did, but I don't know what the answer is. I felt that these performances weren't specific enough. That within these institutional terms — *not* the Peterlee things, but the other ones I was doing — that I wasn't getting what I really wanted to say across properly. I guess you could say, well — if you do performance all kinds of things happen sub-consciously, and one can never really determine what the readings are going to be. I was feeling that this was too loose for me. I wanted something more critical. And I decided that the only way to deal with that was to get into more text. So I moved into what I called 'radio space' and the whole idea of radio space as performance, using the voice and so on. Of course, what happened was that they eluded this critical intention just like all the other things had (laughs). So I ended up in this abstract 'radio space' — and I was having exactly the same problems.

Were they broadcast or distributed on tape?

They were distributed as tapes. I made that for eight years, on and off — I did quite a number of those. And I incorporated them into site-specific situations — for example, I did something in Interim Art [*Conversation Piece (The Red Army)*, London, 1985] where you would go along the street, knock on the door, go in, and be invited to sit down on a chair in a very small space and there was a six-minute everlasting tape. The tape was about the Red Army, as it happened. But it incorporated into it the idea of walking along the street, knocking on the door, walking into the space. So it brought into the nature of the work what one would have just experienced although one might not exactly have paid attention to it. It was site-specific in those kinds of ways. I did one or two things like that, but I found what was happening was that these were all, in a way, too peripheral. They were very marginalised. There is a real — and this has continued to be a problem — there's a real problem about how one relates works that don't fit particular canons, and yet could intervene in that sort of central area in some way. And the continuous experience of marginalisation actually reduces the capacity to work, because you repeat the syndrome — that marginalisation repeats itself time and time again. And I find that that's just as bad as the other — of being invited by institutions to do these things. So there's a problem right the way through it. So, I've been struggling around with that.

Well, you end up having to act within the contradiction rather than resolving it.
          Yes.

And to have the work disseminated by other means would really put it back into one canon or another.
          That's right. So I have that position in that unhappy area, really. I don't think there's an answer to it, as you point out. So, living with it, I've made different kinds of interventions, as it were, in one way or another, which has included performance — or live activity — but within that scenario. Another reason why I moved away from live performance was a kind of re-institutionalisation that was taking place, where I felt that what I would be doing was all being too pre-determined. I didn't want to do that at all. I felt really resistant to that. I don't know what the solution to that is.

And these things become part of the subject matter of the work, presumably?
          Yes. Sure. And also, you know, because the things I've done in the past, most people have forgotten them — but some people haven't. Therefore, if I poke my head over the parapet it usually gets shot by people who want to settle old scores. Because the climate of opinion now, the climate for art activity, is so much more to the right than it ever was. If anyone from the past, from the left, pokes their head up, it's going to be cut off regardless of what you're doing. That also has its effect.
          I think that — perhaps paradoxically — the political implications of what I've been doing with live work very recently is, possibly, less clear, I suspect. Which is also interesting. It's not true of other work, but

Stuart Brisley

from CONVERSATION PIECE (THE RED ARMY)

Sitting on the chair, remember? The door painted grey, an elusive mid-toned grey. Carefully selected and expertly painted. Inside, a dark, soft carpeting, almost matching the stairs painted dark grey. I couldn't quite tell what colour it was — brown, or blue-black. Then down a few steps, two or three. I sat on a chair, placed in the alcove on the left, facing a mirror on the opposite wall, so close I could almost touch it. Remember that? I was sitting in this position exactly, bathing in red light. We swam toward the ice. I walked towards the barracks which faced the mainland, crossed a small bridge and went through an arch in the wall. On the other side, I walked to the corner of the building and turned left. The buildings were painted a warm yellow ochre, but were harsh and vaguely forbidding. I was afraid to go on, as though every step took me further out of my depth. I turned and left quickly, not wishing to be seen. Across the bridge [looking into the mirror] and walked among the trees [I was thinking as though you were there, when I was informed that the prisoners from the Red Army had been held in captivity on the island] sitting on the chair and looking into the mirror, I was thinking, as though you were there. Remember the street? Sitting in the chair [perfect pavements] I was thinking [and the door] that you were here [an elegant grey door]. Inside, [sitting in the chair] dark carpeting [looking in the mirror] almost matching the dark grey stairs, in a narrow corridor passing the doorway by the stairs on the right, down two or three steps. There's a chair placed in the alcove immediately on the left, facing a mirror. Remember that? Locked in the ice. I was sitting in this position exactly, looking at myself in the mirror [I'm sitting exactly in this position] watching myself [looking into the mirror, watching myself] you return the gaze [and I can see you] you return the gaze [looking at yourself in the mirror] and we recognise each other [we recognise each other]. We saw from the boat that the army had left its mark on the island. On our return to the mainland, they were prodding the ice with long, thin poles. A large apartment building, just behind the square to the right of the quay was pointed out. And I was informed that it had been the headquarters of the Red Army. A red flag [locked under the ice] flag. Locked under the ice. We looked down into the water, absolutely still, mirrored against the sky. The air was clear and cold. The cries of birds careening over the frozen lake mingled occasionally with the distant sound of traffic. I climbed into the lake, and breaking the surface swam towards the ice, turned and came up thrashing wildly. I lurched out on to the jetty in 30 seconds flat. There is a dipping in the light when the sun sinks below the horizon. Sitting on the chair, I was thinking about you [I was looking into the mirror and thought] I thought you were [you were looking at me] at me. We were bathed in [I saw myself] red light [I saw myself in the reflection of your eyes] I saw myself in your eyes [which would be to all intents the reflection of yourself].

Stuart Brisley, *Conversation piece (The Red Army)* WINDOW, WALL, CEILING, FLOORSHOW Interim Art, London June 1985; sound installation. Extract from 6-minute everlasting tape (courtesy of the artist).

it's certainly true of live work. I suppose, in a sense, it's more personal. It doesn't necessarily have another agenda attached to it, but you find that within it there are a number of other things that are taking place which might be perfectly viable, but don't actually connect with the socio-political intention. So it's — you know — it's slightly complicated.

Yes.

Yes. But you'd probably have to see something I did in order to see whether that was right or not.

Thanks.

JOAN JONAS

Joan Jonas' performance has roots not only in her training as a sculptor in the early 1960s, but in her work with 'post-modern' choreographers, including Trisha Brown and Yvonne Rainer from 1967–1969. Influenced by the concerns of Process Art of the late 1960s, but rejecting the Minimalist aesthetic out of which these concerns arose, Jonas' performance from 1968, and her use of video from 1971, engaged with mythological sources while making use of acutely personal objects and imagery. From 1974, Jonas turned explicitly toward fairy-tale and myth, using narrative structures alongside her own complex iconographies. Jonas' work has been influential not only through its complexity in the wake of the Minimalist aesthetic and her shaping of early video art, but also through her concerns for issues of identity and personal history, as well as the meeting her work presents between vocabularies drawn from fine art and theatre. While continuing to produce her own work across a variety of media, Jonas has also collaborated with the Wooster Group, performing in *Nyatt School* (1978) and *Brace Up!* (1990). This text is derived from conversations recorded in New York in April 1990, at the time of her work on *Brace Up!* with the Wooster Group.

*   *   *

I'd like to begin by asking you about the changes in your work. What was it that took you from the early work, the dance and outdoor pieces dealing with space and discontinuity, to the more theatrical presentations dealing with mask and role?
      In the first place, even before I started doing those outdoor pieces and the mirror pieces — and while some of my inspiration came from art, because my background is in visual art — it also came from literature, myth and ritual. Although there weren't so many images or references in the earlier pieces, these influences were underlying. Then, when I went to Japan in 1970 — where I bought a portapack — I saw the Noh Theatre. I went with Richard Serra. That had a really deep effect on me. It was the first theatre I'd seen that I felt really related to my work, because it was ritualistic and formal. When I came back, the way I started working with the portapack was to sit in front of the TV screen or the camera in a closed circuit situation and work with myself and try on different disguises. I wanted to

get away from Minimalism, to really step away from Minimalism. The Noh was a kind of doorway.

Do you feel that the sensibility of Minimalism underlay the performances you were doing before that?

I think so. I was very close to the whole group of the Minimalist movement. My early work was very simple. I kept it very abstract. I was very interested in the materials, the movement and the space.

How did your interest in myth and ritual inform those performances?

Well, the early mirror pieces were actually inspired by Borges. I mean, information came from various sources and there was always reference to things I had seen or read. The early work came out of poetry, too — American poets, like William Carlos Williams and Ezra Pound — very consciously. Just the idea of how to structure an image and the sequence of images — I structured it like poetry. The outdoor pieces were composed as a series of images, even though they were based on issues of space.

So at the time did you feel close in your work to other performers?

At the time I was. When I first started performing it was at the end of the Judson period, although I was not a part of the Judson Dance Theatre.

You'd had contact with some of them.

I knew them all. Coming out of art history, I felt that I had to know the history of performances. I saw Oldenburg, Robert Morris, Yvonne Rainer, Trisha Brown, Simone Forti, Deborah Hay, Lucinda Childs. So I could say, in particular, Yvonne and Simone. Then I took a workshop with Trisha. I knew the whole group and I did that purposely because I wanted to learn what they had done so I could go on.

It's interesting, because although Simone Forti was concerned with game and task in the early sixties, she soon seems to depart from a focus on found movement. She begins doing these animal pieces, doesn't she? I can't remember exactly when it was, but it was a departure from the address to performance as object.

She did, yes. She went more into dance. The early pieces were related to sculpture, then she became more involved in this kind of poetic movement. And inner spirit. I found the work she was doing around the early seventies, when I got to know her, very poetic. She made up these Italian songs that were really beautiful. She worked with Charlemagne Palestine and they did very simple collaborations. I thought they were absolutely beautiful. Of all the dancers, I can feel some relation to her.

Was there a particular way in which this concern with ritual and myth came out in the early performances?

This is the way I can put it. I had no background of performance, so when I started performing, even before I started working with the idea of persona and making video pieces, I had to see myself as some kind of persona. Now, in between the time I got the idea I wanted to do performance and when I actually started making performances, I went to Greece because I was very interested in Minoan art. I spent a year there. And they have these little seal stones in which there's an engraving of the mother goddess. That was something that attracted me — the idea of this goddess. Not that I was involved with feminist art in that sense, although I was involved in the idea of searching for my identity as a female and if there is something female in imagery. Then I was very affected by *Portrait of the Artist as a Young Man,* and the idea of Icarus and Deadalus, and the way that myth is incorporated into literature and so relates to contemporary experience. All I can do is say that I had these things in my mind. In my very first performance I made a mirror costume. Later Peter Campus and I went into the snow and made a film [*Wind,* 1968]. I thought they were kind of shamanistic characters, these two figures, the man and woman in the mirror costumes. And it did turn out that way. I mean, you can have these things in your mind and you wouldn't purposely think of it being that, but then somehow it would come out that way. That's all I can say. So I entered into this idea of shamanism without really saying, I am going to be this or that. It was just that it was there and it happened naturally.

One of the things that interests me about this is a certain coming together of interests in ritual and identity and a sensibility from the visual arts, from Minimalism or a formalism. It seems to me that throughout the work the theatrical languages that you use are always self-conscious. When you take fairy tales, in Upside Down and Backwards *(1980), for example, you collage them in such a way that the viewer doesn't easily become absorbed into a single narrative.*

Yes. When I started working with fairy tales, I wanted to make these ancient myths relevant for my audience. I more or less took them apart and analysed them visually and in a sculptural sense, they became familiar territory.

It seems to me that to set up a fairy tale or a mythological framework is to do something very powerful, but to treat it in the way you do is to get a distance on it, to refuse to allow it to completely unify the piece.

Yes. It's about different forces and how these forces affect individuals. Well — I use the word archetype, the archetypal elements in fairy tales. *The*

Juniper Tree (1976) had all kinds of references. Red is blood and white is snow is a kind of fairy tale cliché — but I would relate that to blood and female and so on and so forth. I tried to free associate with all the elements. I'm not a *structuralist*, but I made my own structure around the fairy tales.

This kind of association seems important in the earlier mask pieces, too, even though they would appear to be concerned with identity and role. In Organic Honey's Visual Telepathy *(1972), in particular, there seem to be oppositions coming into play around your use of the mask and the idea of a role, but as the piece develops the relationship between images becomes more and more complex and any straightforward oppositions become displaced.*

    I was playing — first collecting props, objects, ideas. I would play with making a series of moving pictures for the monitor — my ongoing mirror — and play with the elements of theatre, illusion, developing my own visual language, pretending I was a sorceress. I did think I could be one — an electronic sorceress. And in dealing with this electronic imagery I'd try to create a magical atmosphere. And these masks and disguises enabled me to enter this non-verbal world. I couldn't tell you, but I could show you what that identity was. I experimented with the idea of female imagery, for instance, and I imagined an erotic landscape that a woman might inhabit. Few critics talked about it seriously. Hardly any critics were writing about performance, and those that did were mostly formalists.

    Some people also called my pieces autobiographical. They weren't explicitly autobiographical, but one reveals things. When I started doing these imagistic pieces, the *Organic Honey* pieces (1972), I'd let anything out within the parameters of the structure. I accepted whatever worked. It made some people uncomfortable. They thought I was exposing myself. And I was, but it didn't bother me because I was protected by a formal distance from the audience.

By the fact of the mask?

    The mask, yeah. I masked myself, but I showed myself through gesture, props, activities of drawing, howling, for instance. I think the mistake some people make when they look at performance art is to think it's you. Of course, it is, in a certain sense, but I always try to go beyond representing myself. The last piece I did, *Volcano Saga* (1985–9), is based on an Icelandic myth which begins with a young woman's four dreams. Some people assume I wrote the dreams — but the point is, they're not my dreams but our dreams. It's complicated because you choose the material you identify with, but there is also a distance.

You said a sense of playfulness was important.

There were lots of things I was dealing with. After all this use of the mirror and all those group pieces dealing with space I felt this tremendous freedom to make images. Then, when I got into using the video in a closed circuit situation, all of a sudden I'm by myself. So I wear the mask, I hide myself from the audience, because it wasn't about my individual personality. I was only interested in these characters, these disguises, all of which had to do with — all I can say is — a kind of magic, different magical characters. Organic Honey was my opposite. Then I was dealing with the idea of using video. I was always thinking about film as opposed to video, that was my reference for certain moves and elements in front of the camera. So *Vertical Roll* (video, 1972) is like frames in a film. I was playing with the idea of making a film. Then very simple alchemy, like light and dark — opposites. I would deal with the light situation of video, how to manipulate the iris, for instance. I was playing with things like that. The way I started those performances was working on that little tape in my loft and then realising that it was interesting for an audience to watch this process, the actual making of the tape. Then the idea of the female — is there a female imagery? Also, of course, all the objects that I used, and still do, are objects given to me or objects I had from my family, like the fans and the little dolls and the silver spoon. That created a certain kind of aura or atmosphere — a language, a visual language. I guess the only way you could describe it would be to list the different activities. Then, as a child I liked the circus and magic shows and the musical — those are the three theatre-forms that I saw and that I loved. All these things were behind my motivations for making this non-narrative, poetic structure.

At the same time, I was involved with mysticism, especially in the middle and late seventies, although I've never expressed it directly in my pieces. I was involved in a very practical way. I was very attracted, for instance, to the imagery of, say, Tibetan Buddhist rituals. When I first saw those I was immediately drawn into them because I felt my work had something to do with it. The use of sound, colour, movement. All those things were part of my work. I suppose Artaud, for example, would be somebody whose ideas I could relate to.

My concern was with a complex layering of elements. My body was only a vehicle for these. I never thought about myself as involved with Body Art, for instance, even though I did that *Mirror-Check* piece (1970). I don't think we even called it performance, then, you know. I called them pieces or concerts. I did think about theatre, music, layers of meaning, and complexity. I was involved with art history and the experience of looking at paintings and always seeing an iconography.

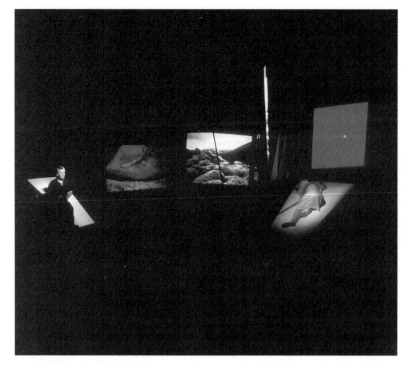

Figure 21   Joan Jonas *Volcano Saga* (1985) (courtesy of the artist).

---

1. VOLCANO SAGA

VIDEO BACKDROP

Pan of river running through black volcanic landscape, intercut with bubbling hotsprings and slides of vari-coloured mountains and plains — interior view of Iceland.

Intercut with *slide-stills* pictures of bare desert-like rocky mountain ranges, sun streaked golden, under grey skies.

ACTION

Scene: a studio-like setting with a table and a microphone. A map of Iceland is on the table.

A woman dressed in a raincoat measures with a yardstick the video backdrop, and then the map, the slides (stills), comparing scale, distance. On this map is indicated the locations of where the action will take place.

Close-up on map, measuring devices.

WOMAN

The wind was blowing. The day was sunny. I drove out toward the glacier. It started to rain. So I stopped for lunch in a big pink restaurant. I drove on, and just after I had reached the peninsula — there were mountains and shallow ponds on my right — the sea was on my left — big flat green slopes, and large areas of sharp black lava. I lost control and went into a skid. In those few seconds I couldn't see the end. The car bounced a bit, went off the road, and turned over, leaving me hanging upside down. The wind whistled and blew. Everything was moving.

Joan Jonas, from the performance *Volcano Saga* (1985), (courtesy of the artist).

Wasn't it this consideration of meaning that made your work different from that of most other artists involved in performance at that time?
    Yeah.

Doesn't it also open the work up to all kinds of usually distinct languages?
    Well, that's why I wanted to do performance art instead of being a sculptor. I could use all these different things at the same time — music, movement, imagery. That's still what interests me and keeps me in

---

VOLCANO SAGA

SCENE FOUR: THE FIRST DREAM

SLOW PAN DOWN A NARROW WATERFALL TO A WOMAN SITTING BESIDE A STREAM WITH HER BACK TO THE CAMERA. SHE TRIES ON A HEADDRESS BUT QUICKLY THROWS IT INTO THE STREAM. PICTURE BREAKS APART TO SHOW BLACK AND WHITE SCENE IN SLOW MOTION OF A WOMAN SITTING IN FRONT OF A MIRROR IN WHICH THERE APPEARS TO BE A STREAM. SHE QUICKLY TRIES ON A SERIES OF HATS AND THROWS THEM, ONE BY ONE, AT THE MIRROR. THEY SEEM TO BE SUCKED INTO THE MIRROR AND THEN INTO THE STREAM.

GUDRUN: I dreamed that I was outside standing near a stream. I was wearing a headdress on my head, but I felt that it didn't become me, so I was anxious to change it. A lot of people warned me not to, but I paid no attention to them and tore the headdress from my head and threw it into the stream. That was the end of the dream.

SCENE FIVE: THE SECOND DREAM

CAMERA PANS BLACK ROCKS LINED WITH WHITE CLAY IN THE STEAMING BLUE LAKE. FADE TO C.U. OF HAND SINKING IN WATER WITH A SILVER RING ON THE THIRD FINGER. FADE TO PAN OF BLACK ROCKS EMERGING FROM THE WATER. FADE TO A SHOT OF THE LAKE WITH A WOODEN RAMP IN THE FOREGROUND WHICH SLOPES INTO THE WATER. FADE INTO BLACK AND WHITE OVERHEAD VIEW OF THE SLOPING RAMP WITH TWO FIGURES LYING ON THE RAMP. THEY ARE HALF IN THE WATER AND STEAM OBSCURES THEIR IDENTITY. ONE OF THEM SLIPS OUT OF THE ARMS OF THE OTHER AS THE SCENE BECOMES STORMY.

GUDRUN: At the beginning of this dream I was standing by a lake and it seemed to me that a silver ring appeared on my hand. I was sure that the ring was mine. It seemed to become me extremely well and I thought it was a wonderful treasure and I was determined to keep it forever. But when I least expected it the ring slipped off my hand and into the lake and I never saw it again. I felt this loss much more keenly than I would have expected from losing a mere ring. With that I woke up.

GEST: That was no less of a dream.

SCENE SIX: THE THIRD DREAM

A WOMAN IN A YELLOW DRESS IS SITTING ON A MOSS COVERED LAVA FONDLING A LARGE GOLD RING. SHE STANDS AND WALKS. C.U. OF A BLACK SHOE STEPPING ON THE MOSS. SHE STUMBLES, CATCHING HERSELF ON A ROCK. THE RING STRIKES A STONE. C.U. GOLD RING WITH BLOOD. THROUGHOUT THE ABOVE SCENE THE IMAGE PERIODICALLY BREAKS APART TO REVEAL A BLACK AND WHITE SCENE OF A WOMAN DANCING, FIRST WITH ONE MAN AND THEN ANOTHER IN A WALTZ AMONG SHARP ROCKS.

GUDRUN: I dreamed that I had a gold ring and it seemed to me that the ring was mine and that it made up for the previous losses. I had the feeling that I would enjoy this ring for longer than the other one, but it didn't seem to me all that much better even though gold is supposedly more precious than silver. Then I seemed to stumble but in trying to steady myself the gold ring struck a stone and broke in two. The two pieces seemed to bleed. What I felt now was more like grief than mere regret over a loss. Then it occurred to me that there might have been a flaw in the ring and when I looked at the pieces I thought I could see

> many other flaws. Yet, I felt sure that the ring would have stayed whole if I had looked after it better. And with this, my dream came to an end.
>
> **GEST:** The dreams are not drying up.

Joan Jonas, from the videotape *Volcano Saga* (1989) with Tilda Swinton and Ron Vawter (courtesy of the artist).

performance. I think a lot of theatre has been influenced by performance of that kind.

To what extent were you concerned to make an address to the audience?

In all my pieces I spend a certain amount of time drawing the audience into the work, into the atmosphere. I was always concerned with the way the audience saw the work — what they saw and how the picture was perceived.

In the earlier pieces, things like Delay Delay *(1972), there's always an aspect of the piece which lies with the audience, isn't there?*

Well, the audience was in the space of the piece. In the mirror pieces they would be reflected in the mirrors, then in the outdoor pieces they would be in a particular viewing position. Even if it didn't take place all around them they would be part of it, because I would be sending signals to them. The audience was a part of the piece.

Also, the mirrors had a lot of connotations of narcissism — and I was interested in narcissism because it was such a taboo and I knew it made the audience uncomfortable. When I did the *Mirror Check* piece it was like the culmination of the abstraction of all the mirror pieces. It was about voyeurism and — it's hard to express. My relationship with the audience was partly in making them uncomfortable. I also tried to entrance, to attract attention.

Does that then become different when you start to deal with mask and this more overt layering of elements?

Maybe lately — maybe I've gotten too far from that original vision. When I started doing the video pieces I still passed a mirror in front of the audience at the very beginning. I kept that signature. Then the way I would draw the audience in became a little bit more theatrical — through the atmosphere. I would draw the audience in by addressing it. Not directly, but through the video, through the story.

Figures 22 and 23   Joan Jonas *Volcano Saga* (1985) (courtesy of the artist).

It becomes different, I suppose, when you start performing inside. The space becomes much more demarcated.

Well, many people have said to me that they feel like the pieces are very private. That when they look at them they feel like they're looking into a private space. It makes some people very uncomfortable. Other people really like it. Or they like it and they feel uncomfortable. I'm definitely in my own space and I'm doing something private to which they are witness.

It's quite a complex space, isn't it?

It's a very complex space with complex relationships with the objects and then the close-circuit television. That was just because I was honestly wanting to communicate to them something about my perceptions about things. Just showing it in a certain sense.

Claes Oldenburg describes his happenings as a 'pressing of his vision closer to the audience'. They're not objects, they're not finished, they're not perfect in that sense, they're about a process, a way of looking.

I'm sure I was influenced by process. To me the most important show that I saw in the late sixties was the Process Art show with Bruce Nauman, Eva Hess and Richard Serra. I found that work the most interesting. And I had friends like Robert Smithson, who was a Minimalist of course.

I'd like to talk about Upside Down and Backwards *(1980). There's the use of the various narratives, there's the two descriptions of landscapes, there's the music, which is collaged from various sources, then, the most difficult thing to get hold of from reading the script, your place within this. It seems to me that there are many kinds of narratives within the piece, each one being broken down by another. As a spectator, you're not drawn into a narrative, but become aware of the promises made by the various narrative elements precisely because of the way they're played against each other.*

I'm not really interested in just telling a story. I'm interested in the different ramifications of it.

But so many performance artists haven't used narrative.

Oh — you mean, why do I use narrative? Because I love stories.

The reason I started using narratives was that I was commissioned to do a piece for children [*The Juniper Tree*, 1976]. I chose a fairy tale, as I thought that would be the best thing to do. Then, when I started working with fairy tales, I realised that it wasn't so different from what I'd been doing before.

It was like the same poetic or mythological imagery, but with a narrative structure. It drew me into characters and a richer kind of imagery that was given to me from the outside, that I could then deal with. I got interested in this double-track, the sound-track and the image-track. That's why I stopped doing video for a while in my performances, I wanted to concentrate on another kind of double-track. In *The Juniper Tree* I had the story going all the way through the performance on a sound-track, while I represented the story visually. Then, in *Upside Down and Backwards*, I felt it would be interesting to try it another way so that the audience wouldn't have to make a connection between the words and the imagery — so I separated the story from the visual track and told it at the beginning and again at the end, so that they could experience the work instead of trying to figure out what it meant. I also got interested in shifting away from a kind of esoteric concern for the tradition of poetic language. I wanted to use the same kind of poetry but tell stories so that maybe I could reach a different kind of an audience. Through storytelling, even though I deconstructed it or pulled it apart, I felt that I became linked with a different kind of tradition.

I've been thinking a lot, especially since *Volcano Saga*, that I want to go back and reincorporate some of my early concerns. You know, I jumped into narrative. I could have brought those other things further along. For instance, now, working with the Wooster Group — they're using TV. In a way, what they're doing now is an extension of the things that I started — but I would take something, then drop it, and go on to something else. Matisse said something which I've always remembered from the very beginning, which is that if you feel stuck you just go back and look at your work and look at the threads that run through it. So — I've been commissioned to do a performance this Summer, outdoors in Riverdale. I'm going to have some of the piece take place indoors and some outdoors. I'm going to do it with the light changing at dusk, and the sound and the landscape and so on. I'm going to go through my book and find old images and try and develop them, put them together. It's sort of an experiment. I'm going to try and make a piece that's very free-form, open, with people doing lots of different things in the space, using some of my old images. I don't think it's necessary for me to constantly look for new ideas. I did think so.

Have you found working with the Wooster Group on Brace Up! *very different from making or performing your own work?*

Actually, it's so close to my work. Right now they just happen to be doing a piece with a lot of video, so it's really strange. The main thing that I like about it is that I get to perform in a different way and somebody directs me. It's a slightly different style of performing.

Brace Up! *uses Chekhov's* Three Sisters. *Is this the first time you've worked on a dramatic text?*

I worked with them on a piece called *Nyatt School* (1978), that used Eliot's *The Cocktail Party*. It was just a section of that piece, though. This is much more, because play Masha, one of the sisters.

With Richard Foreman or Robert Wilson, and to a certain extent in the Wooster Group, isn't there a way in which individuals enter into a piece for the qualities that they have rather than the qualities that they can portray? Isn't it at this point that the languages of performance art tend to differ from theatre, through a certain concentration on presence and what is there?

Oh, definitely, that's true. That's true. We had some open rehearsals and Peter Sellars introduced the group. He said that technically, the Wooster Group is really good, and it's true. It's like being part of a machine, almost. It's really about this movement and energy. After a while, you don't think about the character. It's more important that you think about the breath and words and energy. So that's why they ask someone like me to be in it, because I'm not traditional actress. I can't play emotion.

Yet it's still different from what you're doing when you take on a mask in the Organic Honey *pieces.*

Well, the thing that's different — and that's making it very defined for me working with the group — is that my pieces, although they are rehearsed and planned, have a kind of looseness about them that allows me to move in them. In this work, though, there is an extreme attention to detail. I'm really interested in a different kind of construction, although my pieces are musical, too. I was influenced from the very beginning by the idea of musical form, but with softer detail.

Karen Finley has talked about the differences between the pieces that she does which she says are performance art and pieces which she says are theatre. The difference seems to be that the theatre pieces are rehearsed monologues, with perhaps some interaction with the audience. The 'performance art' is something that she prepares herself for mentally.

Oh, and then she just does it.

She just does it.

Right. For me, the main thing I don't like about theatre is the endless mechanisations, the props, the setting up and getting everything perfect. All the things that you have to do to orchestrate. And I do love different things. I want to keep performing, but I also want to make visual pieces and video tapes. I can't spend so much time on a performance. The difference between my rehearsals and, say, theatre rehearsals, is that my rehearsals are just about working the piece out. I don't really rehearse. I work it out and I try and get the moments as I want them to be. I try and work the piece out and then I perform it. It's like a preparation, but the piece is not improvised.

Despite these differences, there is a great deal of continuity, isn't there, between your work with the Wooster Group and the concern with role in your own performance?

Yes, it's very close in that sense. I like it because it's more like the way theatre-people deal with roles. There's a separation. When I do my performances I enter very much into the world of the material, and in this I'm not doing that. I'm keeping a distance, because I don't want to get that involved in their work. So I'm finding myself getting more and more separated from the character, which is good. It enables me to represent the character in a more objective way and not be submerged within it. I think that's what Liz LeCompte wants. In a way, working with them is giving my performance and my performance style — the one thing I can think of is *muscle*. I don't know if that explains what I mean, but it's like exercising, in a way. I feel that I'm getting stronger. It's giving me a kind of strength. I enjoy very much working with other people, and those people in particular. It's giving me a dimension of performance that I really like, and that, if I'm going to go on making performance art, I feel I need.

RICHARD FOREMAN

In its origins, Richard Foreman's *Ontological-Hysteric Theatre* calls on the eclectic mix of influences acting on art and performance in the late 1960s. Under the influences of film-makers such as Jonas Mekas and Jack Smith, the aesthetics and practices of Minimal and Systemic Art, and notions of performance elaborated by the choreographer Yvonne Rainer, Foreman sought in his early writing to systematically invert the 'good practice' he had acquired through his training as a playwright at Yale during the 1950s. In doing so, especially through the development of work throughout the 1970s, Foreman rigorously tested the conventional languages of theatre, frequently working with familiar dramatic conventions and signs within a framework and according to strategies which denied them their conventional efficacy. In his writing, Foreman has always drawn explicitly on a wide range of philosophical and critical sources, including aspects of psychoanalysis and contemporary literary theory. His practice includes the *Ontological-Hysteric Theatre*, musical theatre through his long-time collaboration with the composer Stanley Silverman, as well as the production of plays such as Kathy Acker's *Birth of the Poet* (1985) and collaborations with the Wooster Group, including *Symphony of Rats* (1988). This interview was recorded in New York in April 1990.

*   *   *

I'd like to begin by asking you about some of the influences on the work. You've talked about film — Jack Smith, I think. Kate Davy talks about the influence of Gertrude Stein.

Yeah. That's all so far in the past. Sure, Gertrude Stein was a major influence. Brecht was a major influence. Neither of those people mean that much to me today.

There also seems to be a coincidence with Cage. Not in terms of what you do — though I know that in some of the manifestoes you talk about chance work — but in terms of a sensibility, an idea about presence or ways of looking. I wonder if that was important?

Well, I would say — even though I know John slightly and find him a wonderful person and obviously a very interesting and important figure — I think he was so important that probably I was more influenced by people who were influenced by him. And I never spent much time actually paying attention to the source. But certainly when I started in New York all the people were dominated by the kind of thought that Cage was a fulcrum for. If not exactly he himself.

How about visual art? At that time?

Well, I was never that enthusiastic about contemporary trends until Minimalism happened. And when Minimalism happened I thought, for the first time I didn't seem to be alone in the world. Even though I later realised that in my heart I wasn't that Minimal, there was something — a clearing of the decks — that Minimalism forced that was akin to what I was trying to do when I started making theatre, which was really to begin from the basic building block elements, to reground my theatre and learn a new language. And then as the years go by, eventually, that language is used for more and more romantically oriented projects. And projects whose interests are other than pure Minimalist interests. But there's no question that — two things — Minimalism and a very superficial encounter with some of the ideas of alchemy, the kind of work that one did in alchemy, were really at the centre of the way that I began in '68 or so.

Could you expand on this concern for alchemy?

I had read a few secondary texts just talking about the way material was processed and reprocessed, you know, how the stuff was mixed and remixed or boiled and reboiled. And the repetition of that activity again and again and again, in the hope that at a certain moment, grace, or if you're going to read Jung, the unconscious, or something else, would take over and cause a transformation that you had not purposefully aimed at. You were just creating a space in which this grace might descend. Also, at the beginning, the whole notion of working only with the materials, not letting ideas and theories and so forth interfere with the work. Sort of, attempting to be totally honest about reworking physical materials. So in the early plays all the talk was about the physical manifestations, about the physical feelings in the body and things like that. The language was pared down so that it was just a kind of notation of those feelings without allowing any interpretation to enter through the characters.

Doesn't Minimalist sculpture also open itself up to a kind of theatre in the way that it confronts the viewer? Was that important?

Yes, well I felt all that very strongly. And I felt especially that the demand it made upon the spectator to recognise how he was dealing with the confrontation with this bare, brute fact was important. But, as I say, that has softened over the years. Except, I don't know, I'm always trying to change, I'm always trying to do something different, but in a sense I'm experiencing at this moment a kind of need to retouch some of those sources. So I don't know what will come of that.

I think you've suggested that Eygptology *(1983) may have been a point at which things changed.*

    People are always asking me to locate specific change points and so forth. This is really very hard to say. I do know that there's been a drift from this Minimalist beginning to a kind of Post-Structuralist stance, which was an attempt to deal with the fact that the objects and the presence no longer seemed to be anything except the interaction of all the codes and all the languages and so on. So the style got much faster, in the obvious sense, but also objects were shuffled in a way that to me implied that the object itself didn't really count for much, it was just garbage to be discarded. These days, I think there is a shift, frankly, to a quieter mode, perhaps where some people were able to start but I wasn't. And that is to say just let it flow, really, and totally destroy any intellectual effort to control any of this stuff and just not to think. I've been working for twenty years to read everything so that I could throw it out (laughs). And I do want to throw it out and I do want to get rid of that mind that has been straining to find out which are the keys that will allow one to make contact with whatever energies are desirable and so forth. I always claimed that I was trying to get rid of that and I feel that in the work, now, I'm starting to get close to being able to do that. And to start really doing I know not what.

It sounds like you're talking about something that is more intuitive than intellectual.

    Well, I've always worked intuitively. But the intellectual concerns and the reading that has accompanied the making of all of this stuff must have informed me and must have informed the angle at which I came at all of these things. Even though working was intuitive.

Isn't one of the changes to do with genre? Penguin Touquet *(1981), for example, seems to refer to a murder-mystery. At the same time what interests me is that there's no taking apart of the genre in any simple or systematic way. One of the things that seems to happen is — this is a genre in which objects and their meanings are very important, yet here objects seem unable to acquire the kind of significances that they should be able to. And so there's a kind of breaking of the genre which leads to something which is much more open, chaotic and slippery.*

    I think that's because I certainly was not thinking in terms of playing with genre. The impact that that has, partially, is to do with a different modus operandus in the way that the plays were staged, in the way they were cast and the pull of the theatre. Those analogies with things like a detective story were simply a much more conscious effort on the part of me as a director to try and make the material cohere. I've always been unhappy, in a sense, with myself as a director because as I get to working with people in the social situation of the theatre I feel that I tend to make the texts cohere and become organised in certain ways that the writing does not necessarily imply. But in a sense I haven't had the courage to let the mis-en-scene be as fragmented and non-coherent as the writing. I think at various times I've told myself, well, that's a strength, there's a struggle between the writer who dares just to put down all kinds of disassociated material and the director who's more concerned with finding thematic lines in this material. This tension, perhaps, is productive.

It must also require a certain kind of performer to enter into that kind of fragmentation and maintain it.

Well, that's why at the beginning I used non-professional actors. Then I worked with Kate Manheim for many years — until she stopped acting — and she developed a particular kind of technique of her own and urged me to do things because she wanted to do them, things in which she needed to be playing off of people with more technical virtuosity. So that changed the texture of things also. Now its interesting. In the piece I've done this last year, *Lava* (1989), I went back to using non-actors. One of the reasons being that most of the material was me talking on tape and the performers interacting with that. I'd like to continue in that direction, but in a practical sense it's difficult. Space is becoming so difficult in New York. I have to do my play next year in a theatre that has a contract to use equity actors. So that has an influence that's not totally desirable.

Watching the work there seems to be this constant disruption that puts familiar material into question.

Well I always want to try and notice material that has less than official status within the scene. Like, if you have a scene of conflict between husband and wife, what are you supposed to notice, what is supposed to be important? Well, yes, but what is the rejected part? The part that psychoanalysis, for instance, would obviously say is the crucial part, the little details that don't seem to count.

And also points where there might have been a clear focus when a distraction enters.

Oh, absolutely, absolutely. But I think sort of for the same reason. I mean mostly I spend my life being bored, seeing everything, yeah, I know that. I go to the movies, think, oh this is a great movie, but, OK, now we have this, the scene between the husband and wife, that's going to take about five minutes and we've got to wait until that's over. That's what has driven me up the wall occasionally when I've had to — not had to, you know, I have also directed quite a few 'normal' plays, and every time I find myself sitting there, and some of them have been quite successful, and I'm sitting there in the middle of rehearsal and going out of my skull with boredom. I mean, we *know* that this emotion is going to be worked through in this scene. Once you see it starting to happen, it's time to move on. But, of course, normal plays work through it, fulfill the expectation.

One of Cage's central problems was always that of the consequences of giving up his compositions to trained performers who then, inevitably, introduce their own decisions and intentions.

It is a big problem. It's a big problem. On the other hand, I remember a couple of years ago when I did this Kathy Acker piece, *Birth of the Poet*. And at one point, when we were in Rotterdam, Kathy came to see what was happening and she said, 'Yes, but the actors are being so expressive'. And at first I said, well, Kathy, that's actors. And she said, but, you know, I want them to be cool. And I said, well, my take on it is this, that your text is very concerned with recycling the junk of our culture and, in the same way, with the performers. I would like to try and recycle all of that schtick, all of that gunk, all of that expressiveness that is what we all hate about actors and see if that can't be used in the mix. And I guess that I would say that that was my justification for being able to continue using actors. But it also explains, I think, why a lot of people say, oh, well, there's a lot of silent movie technique in your performances and other quotations of kinds of more obvious theatrical styles.

In one of the reviews of Symphony of Rats *(1988), you were reported as saying that the piece was political. I wonder if you could talk about that aspect of your work.*

Oh, that's two separate things. I've always thought that the work was political in the sense that, especially in the American context, the conservative, reactionary forces in America are the product of a character structure that cannot function in ambiguity — which needs to know if things are good, bad, black, white. And progressive character structure has always been people who know you're never going to make those distinctions. So an art that teaches people to exist in an evolving mesh of those various qualities that we perceive in our lives is essentially going to promote a progressive character structure which does not panic when finding itself in a sea of ambiguity. To me that's progressive. Now, something like *Symphony of Rats*, when I say that that was political, the subject matter that I chose to play with had political references and that, huh, was just publicity hokum. One is always looking for ways to make people interested in what you're doing. It happened to be ostensibly about the President of the United States dealing with the fact that he thought he was getting messages from outer space, but it was no more or less political than the other things, really. To get the *New York Times* to write an article you have to think up some new angle, there has to be some gimmick.

At times I have wanted to make directly political theatre. And to raise people's political consciousness. However, I've always felt that in order to talk to people you have to be 'understandable'. Yet if you are speaking most honestly, using the language that is closest to you personally, to be 'understandable' means using a language that no longer reflects the woop and warf of your own sensibility. And you are therefore choosing a language which is not yours and so, in a sense, speaking down to people so that they will understand. I mean, that corrupts your work.

It's very hard for me. I can do a pretty good job of telling people what the subject matter is, but when I look at my work, and I'm honest, it's very hard. And I've spent twenty years trying to frame for myself exactly what it is I'm getting at, and I know it's something very specific. The greatest compliment that was ever paid to me in my life was along those lines. Once somebody brought Foucault to see one of my plays and he said, you know, I'm very interested in this because I can see that there is a rigorous system at work but I can't figure out what it is (laughs). And I thought that was a gigantic compliment, especially coming from Foucault.

One of the things that struck me watching the documentation, particularly Pandering to the Masses: A Misrepresentation *(1975), was the feeling that it wasn't the structure or the system that was important, but the way in which these structures somehow got in the way of the thing that was being presented, the material that was somehow at the centre of the work. There seems to be a tension between the text and its structures and the presence of the performers themselves. It's as if a constant referral is being made to the ways in which these structures can't encapsulate something that is there, as if the structures are being presented in order to show what they cannot do. This seemed to become explicit at the end, with this sequence of, kind of, ironic questions and answers: Where's the meaning? The meaning is in the book, the meaning is in the text. On reading the text my focus had been very much on the idea of being disarmed, of arriving at a point at which you focus on the present because you're constantly being tripped up — you're promised something and then it's taken away. But watching the tape it seemed also to be about something that was there on the stage yet which the structure couldn't capture, but tended to destroy as it structured it.*

Right, because in those days I was trying to wipe out the text and whatever intelligence and whatever interest was in the text I wanted to wipe out with the brute fact of — of presence. As if to say whatever intellectual

construct you make of it and whatever intellectual construct you make in
your life, it's so contingent.

*Because that is partly what it's about, isn't it? It's concerned with a kind of failure of
these structures. It's rather like the impossibility of naming or something.*

Yes, and that's even true today. Of course, that was a long time ago.
It's hard for me even to remember. You might not like as much what I'm
doing these days, I don't know. It is true that the last play I did, *Lava*, for
instance, was still me talking about how language didn't work. I mean
hopefully I was making fun of its associations with Derrida and so on —
with that kind of approach. But it was certainly about the total self-blocking
quality of any kind of language that one would attempt to use. The language
problem, to me, is the most interesting problem. And I'm interested in
problems and I'm interested in solutions and to me the most interesting
solution is the *no-mind* solution. So it is a war between those two tendencies,
I think, that takes place in my language.

*This brings me to one of the things that has come out of being here for me, which is
the recognition of a sort of fundamental current that seems to underlie a whole
range of performance — a kind of denial — denials that are made in order to produce
something that could not be there except by way of that denial. Cage is obviously
involved in this, but so are a number of other artists that might at first appear not to
be. It's to do with language as a contingent construction, but it's also to do with an
admittance of things into the frame of the work which can't be there simply by
making them or taking control of them, but which require a crossing out of the
artist's intention or structure in order to be admitted. And part of that in your work
seems to me to be an attempt to capture a kind of elusive but fundamental moment of
experience.*

Again, though, I've always found that easier to do in the privacy of
writing than in the social situation of staging the plays. Even though some of
that, I hope, is still present, and you're implying that it is present.

*I'm saying that it is. For me this is what the documentation brings out; the way in
which the whole edifice of the text is in tension with the sense of presence it seems to
reveal. And this tension is established in a whole series of ways, one of which is the
performance style, where some quality or emotion that is alluded to in the text, for
example, is drained from the performance itself. Or the way in which the performance
comes to show you what should be there and yet offers you only an empty
signification. It all seems to point toward something about what these constructions
do to experience.*

You see I'm not sure if I'm still doing that. I think I may be doing
something slightly different and which may be less interesting or it may be
more interesting.

I think that the thing that's happened in my work recently, you know, my work has always been terribly personal, of course, but I'm older and I blush to admit, because I know that in the circles in which I travel it's a horrible thing to admit to, but I'm becoming more Jungian (laughs). And the plays are partaking more in an attempt to, in the course of letting material float through me as a writer, to — God, I'm blank, I don't know how to say it because it's not going to sound any different from what I've been saying for the past twenty years. So maybe it isn't. I know it is curious that the last two years I've started doing plays in which the dominant things in the plays is hearing my voice, all the time, just telling stories and speaking and working against that. And I know that in the last couple of years — you talked about this crossing out of material — well, I've gotten so sick of people saying that they mostly relate to my theatre because of its visual impact that I'm desperately trying to think to make a theatre in which people aren't basically looking but they're listening. I'm finding that hard. *Lava* was an attempt, specifically, to do that. I think I succeeded in a certain way, but it was still too visual for me. I may get bored with that effort, but everybody says, but Richard, you're trying to eliminate all the best things. But, of course, that's the point.

Presumably, if one of the things you're dealing with is the attempt to overcome languages that replay familiar experiences then you don't want to get caught in your own trap.

Oh, but I do. And of course I'm aware of the fact that I, just as any artist, am caught in my own trap. But it's very tough to get out of your own trap.

Isn't that one of the subject matters of the work?

Yes, it is exactly part of the subject matter. I am under no illusions about the extent to which I am caught in my own trap. But every time you try to escape the trap you feel that you're doing things arbitrarily and they have just as little connection with the necessity that is you as all the bad things you see. So it's a tricky situation.

It interests me what you say about this change, this difference. It reminds me of the idea of trying to find a centre — you were talking about no-mind *— a centre which is a sort of clear point that is free of things in some way. And you say the work is very personal. But at the same time it seems to me that within those terms it's absolutely necessarily personal. If you're going to deal with the moment, with this idea of arriving at a centre, it's necessary to do it from a personal point of view. But in pursuing that it becomes public.*

Of course, in trying to arrive at this centre, the work is mostly the documentation of all the things that are not the centre, things that get in the way of it.

What's interesting to me is that it seems to be precisely all this clutter that enables you, in some way, to get to that point.

Well, I don't think I've got to that point.

I mean that through the way these things are treated, it might become apparent that it's not these things, the structures, the objects, that you're really interested in.

Yes. That is the effort, that is the effort. The subject is not anything you can see. And that's very difficult for people to understand. Very difficult.

I think it's just, like — one is continually attacked by form, you know — you start to make a move and immediately form, inherited form, says, hey, that belongs to me! So you find yourself pushing through this morass of form that just clings on to you as if you were a magnet. Indeed, I feel often that, I've never thought of it this way, but making all of this stuff it's almost as if, you know, you want to get to the *no-mind*, you want to be still, you want to get to that point, but you are a magnet, unfortunately. So you're spending all your time dealing with these things; forms, objects, ideas; and everybody sees all of that and they say, oh, that's very complex, how's he put that together? But really, no, that's all the garbage. And you're trying to say: help, help, there's something else underneath!

This is the problem with reading the text, because reading the text makes it seem as if the work might be a play of autonomous form. It's difficult to see beyond that to the effect of the work. This may be compounded by the idea of Richard Foreman the playwright, because it seems to me that while the plays aren't unimportant, and they are the means, the work is pre-eminently performative rather than in any way literary. The work is performative because it's only under the circumstances of the performance that an audience can discover this questioning of the text itself.

I think it is becoming, in my opinion, a little more literary. This may be good, it may be bad. And that's a conscious choice also, again for practical reasons. It's not particularly important or interesting, but it's getting more frustrating to do these things, certainly in New York.

This acknowledgement that just to move or to speak is to replay inherited form interests me very much. And this is very different from, say, Cage. It seems to me that Cage is enormously influential and yet in a way quite different from most of the people whose work in one sense or another may have a relationship with his. On a fundamental level with Cage, there's an assumption, which is acquired from Zen, that meaning can be overcome in the simplest of ways. Yet part of the subject matter in your work seems to be the impossibility of getting rid of all this baggage of which language is a part.

Well, it's just that John is purer.

Yet its seems to me that your work suggests that it is impossible to escape, that if you're enmeshed within language, within these systems, then there's no stilling of the mind to a point of nothing. I mean that in a way you have to go through all this.

That's right, I find it impossible to escape. Now I always thought, in a way, that that was a character failure on my part, because I would like to get rid of all this baggage. I mean, I'm not particularly happy about that for myself, speaking personally. So that's the struggle. The work is about that struggle. At the same time, it may be a convenient struggle — that I have chosen to sit in a particular hall of mirrors telling myself this is my struggle, because it gives me material for my work. Who knows if there's anything genuine past the hall of mirrors? I don't know.

Basically, I've always said that I feel like I'm living in a world that does not satisfy me. That does not seem to be built in such a way that the world refracts the energies that I experience when I'm awake. So I'm trying to build in my work a new world in which I can exist in which everything that happens — being it having a cup of tea, being it shooting somebody, being it worshipping somebody, whatever it is — is built in such a way that it refracts that generating energy that I feel is the source of my being awake and perceiving in the world.

Because normally gestures and actions that one performs, I feel, get lost and absorbed by intention. And intention is controlled by the particular intentional patterns that a particular society you're living in has set up. And I don't want the impulse of gesture and thought and action to get sucked in to those intentional patterns. I want to put up those mirrors strategically that bounce back the impulse. And that's what the phrase does, that's what the bit of staging does, that's what the bit of music does, ideally. They say, no, don't get swamped by the tidal wave of intention that everybody gets lost in.

Part of this seems to me to do with the fact that as soon as you start with theatre you're dealing with a complex of action, interaction and physical presences that, music, for example, simply doesn't encounter.

Now this is very interesting because for many years I've said I'm in the theatre because I have all these fancy ideas about how one should attack life. And it seems relatively easy to make this point of view happen in words or in visual imagery or in the sounds of music. But theatre, being concrete, three dimensional, in time, with real bodies — if you can make your vision happen there that proves that it is true or it's real because it's the closest to real life. Over the last couple of years I've started thinking, well, that's absurd. That maybe, in a very Gnostic sense, this is a fallen world. So the idea of taking these intuitions of how being might engage itself, manifest itself, *be* differently, should not be dragged down to the concrete reality of three dimensional concrete life. And the plays have actually been addressing that issue of trying to be 'not there', and they're full of images of not making art, of retiring, as a reflection of that and dealing with this whole notion of why on earth make things that are mental, spiritual, what you will, be fleshy things? Maybe that's a perverse thing to do, in a sense.

MICHAEL KIRBY

Michael Kirby's work as writer and director for the Structuralist Workshop was shaped by his work as a visual artist. Following an engagement with 'Happenings' in the early 1960s, Kirby produced Minimal and Systemic painting and sculpture. With his founding of the Structuralist Workshop in 1975, he brought his procedures for the production of Minimal Art directly to bear upon the generation of plays for performance, in pieces such as *Photoanalysis* (1976), *Double Gothic* (1978) and *First Signs of Decadence* (1985). Yet Kirby's work through the Structuralist Workshop is just one aspect of a wide and influential engagement with avant-garde performance. In 1965, Kirby edited the first full-length volume documenting the new performance by artists, *Happenings* (E. P. Dutton, New York: 1965). Other volumes include *The Art of Time* (E. P. Dutton, New York: 1969), *Futurist Performance* (E. P. Dutton, New York: 1971) and mostly recent the collection of essays, *A Formalist Theatre* (University of Pennsylvania Press, Pennsylvania: 1987). From 1971 to 1985, Kirby was the editor of *The Drama Review*, based at New York University, where he was appointed Professor in 1971. Since 1983, Kirby has been an associate member of the Wooster Group, performing in *L.S.D (...Just the High Points...)* from 1984 as well as scripting the film *White Homeland Commando* (1992). This interview was recorded in New York in April 1990 and revised by Michael Kirby in March 1994.

*   *   *

I'm not entirely clear on the history of the Structuralist Workshop.

Well, it began with the performance *Eight People* (1975). At the time of the first rehearsal, I had very little of it written. I was Chairman of the Department in addition to teaching and editing *The Drama Review*, and I didn't have much free time, so the idea was to work with other directors. I got these eight people together, which is where the title came from, and started writing the play, and as they rehearsed I wrote. But by the time things had finished, I was directing it all. At the same time, we started having workshops. We would meet once a week. Anyone who wanted to could come. Each week I would have a project, and if they wanted to work on it they could. The next week, we would see what they'd done, and I would give them another problem. It was pretty interesting. Then during the summer, we got the use of the *Artists' Space Gallery* which was at that time at the corner of Wooster and Houston. We — several Structuralist playwright-directors — did a series of plays, and one of the evenings was short pieces that had been developed in the workshops. The next year we didn't continue with the workshop, but I kept the name Structuralist Workshop and applied it to all the work.

Given your emphasis upon structure, I'm interested in the fact that you use a realistic style.
    That's a really basic thing with me. Somehow theatre to me is realistic. I think we all understand realism. What I try to do isn't just realism, though, it's film acting. I've tried to do very intimate performances, to get the audience close to the actors so they don't need to project. It really bothers me to see actors pumping it out, as I would say — pushing it out. Often in New York in a small theatre you will see actors, realistic actors, working much too hard for the space. They think they're on Broadway. They think they're in a huge theatre and they're playing to the balcony. They're doing all of this big stuff, and I can't bear it. These things are related fundamentally. I think in terms of comparison to life, and that's what films are doing.

Yet you're focusing on are the formal aspects of the performance.
    Right.

I wonder if adopting a realistic style of performance is itself an effective way of making these patterns clear.
    I think so. I think there's a tension between them. And it might be that there's a pattern to things. That everything's structured. We may not perceive it, but it's there. I've said somewhere — though I didn't invent the phrase — that everything is related to everything else. And its just a question of how do you understand this? I think of myself as Zen or as Taoist. The Tao, the centre, is everywhere. If we don't see this, it still relates. I think maybe this is what I'm trying to say by working realistically, by drawing attention to real life.

In both First Signs of Decadence *(1985) and* Double Gothic *(1978) you appear to deliberately put a realism in tension with the structure of the play, revealing, it seems to me, the conventional nature of both.*
    I've never tried to work fourth wall in the sense of fooling the audience or suspending disbelief. Realistic acting style has nothing to do, for me, with suspending disbelief. Often the physical set up, completely apart from the structure, makes it difficult to suspend disbelief. To me it's

a marvellous thing in theatre if an actor acts realistically and you don't say 'Wow, how realistic!' You say 'Wow, what an actor!' I want the second one — not that it fools us, but that we realise it's acting and yet it's so real.

In some respects, doesn't this come close to a conventional idea of what realism entails? That a suspension of disbelief is an acceptance of a pretence?

Somehow it's more. I don't like actors trying to attract attention to themselves. One of the many reasons Richard Schechner and I are so opposite is that his actors are so pumped up, so aware of themselves and emotionally pleading with the audience to feel this, feel that, to love them. My actors are the opposite. The wind is blowing through. That's another Taoist attitude that I always look for when I act. It's just a kind of emptiness where you're completely open to the world — the world comes in and it goes out. It just passes through you. There's no modification, there's no change in this, there's no forcing yourself on it, it's just completely easy and natural. This is a goal to search for. It's tremendously exciting as an actor, for me, to reach that stage.

Isn't there a connection here between your focus on structure and the nature of the actor's performance?

Well, of course the actors don't focus on the structure.

First Signs of Decadence *continually calls for the actor to motivate actions which have actually been determined by an entirely formal concern, on your behalf, for pattern and rhythm.*

Oh, yeah. Definitely, sure. But that's only in *First Signs of Decadence.* That's one of the most difficult plays to act that I know of, because of that tremendous split between a realistic acting and justifying actions that are impossible to justify. But the more people do justify it, the more exciting it is. If they give in or don't even try — it would still be interesting, but I don't think it would be that interesting.

That particular tension may only be explicit for the performer in First Signs of Decadence, *but isn't it inherent within the work as the audience meets it anyway?*

I think there's always a tension between the representational aspects and the completely non-representational aspects. Always, they're being torn apart. But it isn't always in the actor. Most of the time the actor can ignore it. That's the other thing. In Ted Shanks' *Alternative American Theatre* (MacMillan, London: 1982), he claims that what I'm trying to show the audience are these structures and that it's a process of recognising them, of discovery, of finding out what these structures are, how elaborate they are

Double Gothic

When *Double Gothic* was presented at the Performing Garage, spectators sat on two opposite sides of the playing space. The two audiences were separated by a large, black, plastic-covered box-like construction, they could not see each other. Each group of spectators faced a blank scrim wall. When lights went on behind the scrims, they could see into the box and watch the play.

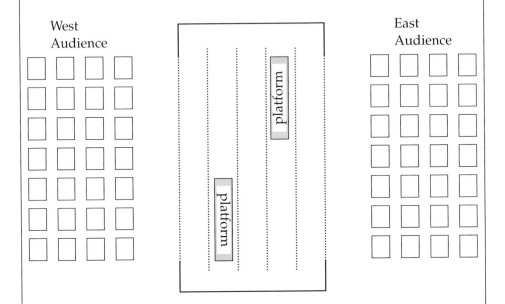

This arrangement is not necessary, however. Its purpose was to get as many spectators as possible as close as possible to the action. (The actors would not be speaking loudly.) *Double Gothic* may be done in a traditional proscenium arrangement with only one audience.

If there are to be two audience groups, six walls of scrim are hung parallel to each other, creating five corridors about four feet wide. If a proscenium set-up is used, only five walls of the scrim will be necessary to create the five corridors. Each corridor is lit by three hanging lights that cast their illumination straight down; all of the light is from above. When lights are turned on spectators can see through the scrim, sometimes looking through only one scrim and sometimes through as many as five scrims. All images are softened and blurred to varying degrees. (If all of the spectators watch the play from one side, the corridors might increase slightly in height, in a kind of step arrangement, as they move away from the audience.)

The space within the scrim curtains is empty except for two identical platforms, about six feet long and 18 inches high, arranged symmetrically in two of the corridors. Actors will stand and sit upon these low platforms: when bedding is placed on them, the platforms will become beds.

We will number the corridors 1 through 5. If there is only one audience, corridor number 1 will be the one closest to them. Action in that corridor will be seen through only one scrim. Corridor 5 will be the one farthest away; action there will be seen through five scrims.

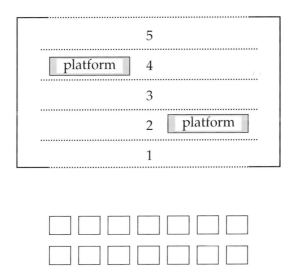

There are two similar, alternating stories in the play: Story A and Story B. Each is composed of six scenes. The first scene of the first story (A-1) will be presented in the corridor nearest the audience (or one of the audiences), corridor 1. The story will move scene-by-scene and corridor-by-corridor, away from that audience (or toward the second of two audiences). The second story will begin at the opposite side of the playing area and progress, scene by scene, toward the corridor in which the first story began. The two stories will 'pass through' each other, one getting progressively closer to the audience and one progressively farther away. The fifth scene of the second story (scene B-5) will be played in corridor 1, where the first story began. Scene 6 of each story will be played in the corridors with the low platforms that serve as beds.

Michael Kirby, from *Double Gothic* (1978) (courtesy of the artist).

and that this is the theatrical experience. I don't agree with that at all. I think that happens to some extent, but I don't do them for the audience as a game. I do them primarily for myself, which I'll talk about in a minute. I don't care if the audience sees them. They're there if the audience sees them or not. They function in the experience whether the spectator is aware of them or not. It isn't a game of awareness. Even if they don't recognise it, it's going to affect them. I don't want the same experience from everybody, and it isn't a question of 'do you get it or not?' — which to me is a very old fashioned idea. We've just shifted it from content — Do you understand it? Do you get it? What's the play about? — we've shifted it now onto the structure, onto the form. Do you get the form? I can't accept this at all. I don't want to do something which has one answer. I would like to do something that's completely open to many even contradictory experiences all of which are 'correct'. But this is not easy because I'm only one person — and the way to try and do it is to build in contradictions and not to tack everything down, building openings where it can escape and so on. So that's the best that I can do.

The reason that I started working this way is that I realised — thinking about John Cage and his chance work, which I didn't want to do — that I could give up making the decision, the aesthetic decision. This was tremendously important to me. That insight. To realise it was possible to give up. What I say to people is that I'm such a good critic that my critical judgement prevented me from writing. I can find fault with anything. Anything. The way really good critics can. So, if you try and write with a good critic working over your shoulder it's impossible. I was really unable to work. The only way I could work was through complete instantaneous creation. That was before I had this insight, before I really knew about Cage. I knew what everybody knew, but I'd never read him. It was this idea that you could give up, that you didn't have to go by 'taste'. I realised that by making rules for myself, which is basically what structuralism is to me, making these rules that I go by, they allowed me to write. This was a tremendous freedom. I didn't want to reveal my unconscious. My Bachelor's degree is in psychology — I did not want to spill my guts out, I did not want to show who I was. I did not want to reveal myself. Again, exactly the opposite of Schechner. So by making the rules, if something came out, and of course it did come out, if it fit the rule I had to keep it, if it didn't fit the rule it didn't come out. There was a kind of liberating feeling to that, because the only way I knew how to work before was to go into myself and see what was there and bring it out. This way I could concentrate on the rules.

Figure 24 Michael Kirby *Double Gothic*, the Performing Garage, New York, 1978 (photo: Michael Kirby) (courtesy of the artist).

When you say the rules what do you mean exactly?

Well, for example, in the piece that I just did in Israel, *Demonic Quartet* (1989), there were four stories about demons. And one takes place in Israel during the Crusades, one in 1900, one in the present day and one in the future. There's a kind of rule there about the patterning of time, progressing from the middle-ages to the future, spreading it out, making the decision to have the four stories — they could have all been from today, why not? Maybe the audience will notice that. But I make this rule and it forces me into certain other things that follow from that. There are seven people in each story, because there are fourteen actors in the play. Each actor is in two stories. Each story was told in five scenes. One scene in each story has seven people. One has two people. One has three people, etc. I don't think anyone noticed that one. You come to write the story, the dialogue, and you've got to have two people in the scene. Perhaps I would like to have four, but I've got to have two. And so that's very interesting to me. It provokes ideas that I wouldn't have any other way. I think that if there's any originality in my writing it comes from that kind of thing.

In First Signs of Decadence, *the characters themselves reflect on the formal tensions by which the piece operates and the questions an audience might ask of it.*

That was purposeful. I think the introduction explains something of that and explains the way the content comes out of the movement. That line about — I had to get somebody to the window to pull down the curtain or to raise the curtain, because I needed more light or less light or something according to the lighting plot. And the only way was to have someone there. The same with the door. Light is coming in the door — so I've got to have someone there to open and close the door at the right moment. The music is the same way. The blocking revolves around these technical things — it isn't a choice that I make.

Why did you choose that subject-matter?

I didn't plan to write about Germany until I realised that two of the five actors were German. All of it was built on this very practical thing of there being two German-speaking people in the cast. And since I was born in 1931, I set it somewhere around there — and that's when the Nazis are coming to power. Then this became the decadence. I'd no idea — I was not after that decadence. I may have been after this other decadence, because there's a little theme of homosexuality. And it might have been that decadence. Now I have to admit that I am sympathetic to that kind of decadence. I'm sympathetic to decadent art — and the Nazis used that word in persecuting the artists. So it all works out fairly neatly if you take it far enough.

And the idea of formalist art being decadent.

Oh, yeah. Sure.

One of the disarming things about the piece is that one could accuse such a formal play through these issues as being an obvious example of decadence in art.

That's right.

And yet the piece announces this possibility in its title, and in doing declares its own ambivalent position. In this way, it's rather disarming.

That's right. The title is bivalent. It can either be strongly against it or strongly in favour of it. Hopefully it's both at the same time.

There's another big influence that I really don't want to skip. There's a big connection with Minimalism, systematic work and visual art. I'm also a visual artist, and I think that makes for a big difference between my work and other theatre people. I'm trying to do something that's a work of art like the visual artists do, and not do a theatre piece like the theatre people do. Although I do have a degree in theatre and I do work in theatre, the

First Signs of Decadence

The play is set in Berlin in 1931. That is, the settings and the costumes are of that period. Not all references will be historically accurate, however. (The spectators should not be told the date in the programme; they should sense it.)

Act 1

A living room. There is an entrance at the rear centre, a window with curtains or drapes at the left front, a door (which will be used only as an exit) at the right front. At the left of the centre entrance, along the rear wall, is a cabinet with a telephone on it. To the right of the door is another cabinet that serves as a bar with glasses, a few bottles, etc. To the left of centre, almost touching the left wall and facing the audience, is a sofa with a small end-table. To the right of centre, against the right wall, is an easy chair with a small table alongside. In the extreme front centre is a trunk. To the left front, by the window, is a small table with flowers on it. At the right front, against the wall, is a record player on a cabinet that contains records.

Perhaps everything is in white, black, or shades of gray. Even the actors' faces and hands are gray. Perhaps a scrim fills the prosceium, dimming the image slightly.

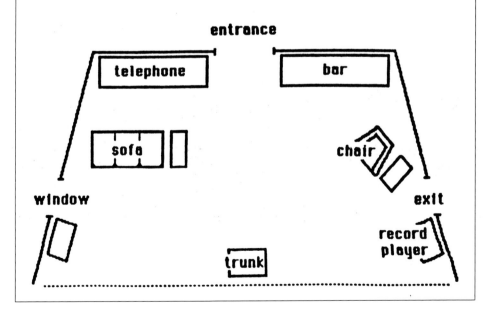

The room is, or can be, illuminated from four sources: a lamp with a shade at the left rear between the sofa and the telephone cabinet, a lamp with a shade at the right rear between the easy chair and the bar, light that comes in the window when the curtains are open, and light that comes in the exit door when it is open.

The actors will locate themselves in only nine spots in this setting: they will not use any other playing areas, except in passing from or to one of the nine spots. The nine locations, which should be limited as narrowly and precisely as possible, are: (1) the entrance (2) in front of the telephone cabinet, (3) in front of the bar, (4) centre, (5) on the sofa — seated or lying, (6) in the easy chair, (7) front centre, (8) at the window, (9) at the record player.

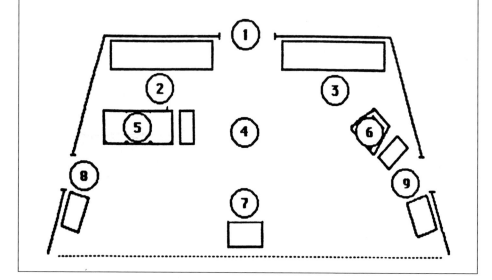

Act 1

In the first act, the actors are going to move every 25 seconds. Since there are 84 of these 25 second beats, each act will be exactly 35 minutes long. (The beginning of each beat may be cued by an off-stage sound and/or by small stage lights concealed behind the furniture.) The play is filled with a punctuation of very brief pauses as the actors freeze briefly, waiting for the signal to begin the next beat. Occasionally, they hurry slightly to complete the section in time.

Although it is not important that the spectator notice, there is a regular pattern in the appearance and disappearance of the characters in both the first and third acts. In the first act, three characters are on stage at all times, and each character appears with every other possible combination of two characters.

(There is also a pattern in the lights. Each of the four lights is on alone, paired with each of the other lights and in every combination of three. Once, in the middle of the first act, all four lights will be on. A single light remains on for 3:45 before there is a change in lighting. Two lights are on for 2:05, three for 1:40, and the four lights are on together for 50 seconds. Each light should have its own distinctive quality, helping to distinguish the various combinations.)

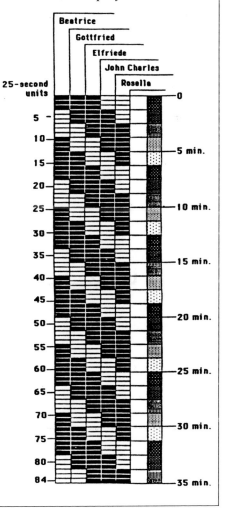

Michael Kirby, from *First Signs of Decadence* (1985). Reproduced by special permission of I. E. Clark, Publisher, P. O. Box 246, Schulenberg, TX 78956 U.S.A. Copies of the playbook and permission to perform may be obtained from I. E. Clark.

aesthetics really relate a lot to what Sol LeWitt and people like that were doing, are still doing.

Was Yvonne Rainer's analysis of her dance-work (Rainer 1974: 63–9) through what she takes to be the terms of Minimal Art important?

This was very important to me. It may be more important than Cage, because Cage was just one kind of insight that was crucial. Of course, my work has become less Minimal, but the early work, even *Double Gothic*, is much more Minimal. And that was intentional.

One of the things that seems to be going on with Rainer's correspondence of terms is an attempt to equate performance with object-work. Yet Cage explicitly opposes the notion of fixing the terms of a performance — of, in his terms, making the work into an object — and seeks instead to produce unpredictable situations and processes.

I think what I want to do is the object. You know I was working on sculpture, and that's why I was protesting earlier that I don't care about showing the process or having the audience figure out what I'm up to. To me it is an object and it should be complete in itself. I've directed other people's scripts, collaged Shakespeare and Chekhov into my own work, etc., and when I do all of the writing myself, as well as the staging, the lighting, the final piece certainly seems more like an object to me.

It's about its own presence.

Right. Sure. That's why a lot of people ignore my work — because they can't paraphrase it.

The other reason why I'm thinking in terms of 'object' and 'process' is because in making this tension between a structure and other elements....

The content.

I'm trying to avoid the word 'content'.

No, I accept that in terms of representing something — even if it's the genre of the work — *Double Gothic* is about Gothic ideas, the Gothic novel — *First Signs of Decadence* in theatre terms is about a drawing room play — that's content to me — although I'm not going to tell you anything about it. I'm not going to explain the content. I refuse to deal with content in one way of using the word, and yet I refuse to reject content in another way of using the word — content as references to life. I will not do a completely abstract piece. I want references to life. So many of our emotions come in there. And I'm not going to give up that. But I'm not going to tell you anything about life either.

This concern with the 'object' and your attitude toward content brings me to certain notions of formalism. One formalism might be an aestheticism — the kind of pursuit of autonomous form that I would associate with post-war abstract and non-objective painting. Another might be concerned with the effect of certain formal strategies that, in a way, admit the presence of an audience and deal with the effect of setting up certain structures in that place and time — with the experience of meeting or engaging those structures or rules. This would relate to Minimalism in its tendency to make the viewer aware of her presence before the object.

I think of affective form or expressive form — as opposed to what we could call 'aestheticism' or 'pure form' — as relating to content, that is to make the content clearer or more emotional. Those are the two kinds of form to me, and mine is neither one of those. It's not non-objective — it's not form for its own sake. And the form is not supporting the content.

When I worked Minimally, I think the impulse was to clarify the formal elements as you reduce them from out of all of this clutter. Remember, I'm coming to New York at the time of Abstract Expressionism. I'm here in 1957. And Pop Art is not in yet. And there's a tremendous clutter of detail in Abstract Expressionism. One of the things that Minimalism offered us was this chance to really focus on the relationships without any interference or static and that kind of thing. But now I feel the influence of Wooster Group after acting with them for six years. Now, I feel, let's go for it. We're not in the Minimal period any more — those days were tremendously exciting and active, and Minimalism was really comfortable. In active times quiet work is terrific. Now it seems boring. Now we need — because the times are quiet — work that is as active as possible. And let's go for the clutter and static and everything else, the way Wooster Group does. *LSD* (1983) is a maximum piece. You can never pin it down. Just when you think it's one thing, it changes completely. And it's so exciting. I did a play, years ago, called *A Style Play*. It was based on the idea of changing styles. But Elizabeth LeCompte does this without — you know — not intellectually. I did it very programmatically. She just does it. Then it takes you by surprise. The way I did it was predictable, the way she does it is completely unpredictable. I have no concern with the society, the way *Wooster Group* does, but their productions are very exciting to me.

ANTHONY HOWELL
(THEATRE OF MISTAKES)

Anthony Howell founded the The Ting: Theatre of Mistakes in London in 1974, following a one-year fellowship at the Iowa International Writers' Programme in 1973. Originally trained with the Royal Ballet from 1962 to 1965, Howell danced with the company in 1966, but left shortly afterwards to concentrate on his writing. As a poet, Howell has been published widely since the late 1960s, his most recent volumes being *Notions of a Mirror* (Anvil Press, London: 1983), *Why I May Never See the Walls of China* (Anvil Press, London: 1986) and the novel *In the Company of Others* (Marion Boyars, London: 1986). With the Theatre of Mistakes, Howell's performance work in collaboration with the artists Fiona Templeton and Mickey Greenall, among others, was seen widely in Europe and America. In 1977, the year in which the Theatre of Mistakes first presented *Going* and *A Waterfall*, Howell and Templeton co-edited and published a collection of exercises drawn from the group's work under the title *Elements of Performance Art*. From 1978 to 1981, Howell was a full-time director of the Theatre of Mistakes, directing pieces such as *Waterfall 3* (1978), *Orpheus and Hermes* (1979) and *Homage to Morandi* (1979). Since 1981, Howell has performed solo, while continuing to write and teach. He is currently Lecturer in time-based studies at the South Glamorgan Institute of Higher Education, Cardiff, Wales. This interview was recorded in July 1994 in Cardiff.

*   *   *

What were the starting points were for the Theatre of Mistakes?
     My interest in performance developed out of my interest in abstract writing. I had carried abstract writing to the extreme of writing 'instruction recipes' for poems under the influence of Sol LeWitt, who would write instruction recipes for wall drawings. Having started creating such recipes for poems it became obvious to me that one could also make them for actions. This idea occupied me while I was in Iowa city at the International Writers Programme, in 1973 and 1974. I came back and started a workshop in a studio of a friend of mine in The Dairy in Prince of Wales Crescent in London, a large vacant building where lots of artists were working — the Film Co-op, many groups. The initial workshops of our group, The Ting: Theatre of Mistakes, were based on the idea that we were making art by

creating instruction recipes and we were all the servants and masters of each other. In other words, anyone could suggest an exercise and we would all adhere to its rules as rigidly as we possibly could, on the understanding that the person who set that exercise would also be our servant or somebody else's servant in the event of another exercise being set. That idea of being servants and masters of each other created a body of exercises which we referred to for the next few years as a 'body of thought', a gymnasium of performance exercises, if you like — very many more exercises than were finally edited into *Elements of Performance Art*.

Was any of the performance emerging in the late sixties in response to Minimal Art important to the work?

We were very influenced by Systemic Art, Minimal Art — Sol LeWitt, in particular. Fluxus had been an influence on my own previous work, as had the Situationists: that general sort of condensation from the sixties. The performances that were influencing me at that time were the vast scale events of Robert Wilson. I'd seen *Deafman Glance* — or possibly one of the variations, like the *Homage to Sigmund Freud* or *Joseph Stalin* — in New York in 1972. This was a tremendous influence. At the beginning, although the idea of the instruction art was very 'Minimal', the performances were created rather like you order a meal in a Chinese restaurant — from a vast array of exercises — and they were quite baroque. We wore beekeeping hats and flying suits which would contain grey suits. So the performances were not really 'Minimal' themselves. They had a Minimalist dynamic organising the system.

Which would again relate to Wilson. Wilson pares things down, and the performance slowly unfolds over an extended period of time, but what is presented is usually visually very extravagant.

Yes, that had a considerable bearing on the work; particularly the idea of stillness and slow-motion. There were exercises which in their most primitive form might be simply 'stand still for an hour' or 'stand still until somebody comes and stands still behind you'. There was a general idea that if you moved things very slowly into each other, you could make anything merge, anything work. The idea of these slow collages was very important. That was all from the influence of Wilson.

In some respects, the instructions in Elements of Performance Art *(Theatre of Mistakes, London: 1977) also seem to recall Fluxus scores. A number of them present conundrums to which a reader or performer can respond, but which resist being exhausted by any particular response.*

Yes. I mean, the exercises collected together in *Elements of Performance Art* are at some degree of refinement. Certainly, there was an aphoristic tendency that probably came from the poetry. Equally, though, I think it's to do with trying to stimulate the performer's imagination. For instance, I think there's one of those exercises which says something like — 'Move so slowly nobody can see you moving, or move extremely fast and then freeze for as long as it would have taken you to have done your action moving so slowly nobody could see you moving'. Well, that sort of — if you like — conundrum — seemed important to stimulate the imagination. But the exercises were never written simply for the entertainment of a concept. Again, though, the Theatre of Mistakes evolved quite rapidly in the first eighteen months. For one thing, it became extremely popular within about six months of the workshop starting. There were something like 72 people coming along to it. When we did *The Street* (1975), which we first did on a street in Kentish Town for some six weeks, that had a performance group of at least 60.

That was a piece that involved participation.

Indeed. Everybody on the street, which was a sort of mixture of working-class and middle-class people, externalised their sitting rooms and put them out on the pavement. But it was all conceptual. It involved participation in concepts which we found that people of all walks of life immediately related to and enjoyed without feeling patronised.

Was the performance itself generated by rules?

There were a whole set of exercises which covered areas of the pavement and the windows where there were choruses of people. There were rules such as — if any passer-by walked up one pavement, all the performers in the street fell down dead. They remained completely motionless and prone on the ground until such time as somebody walked up the other way on the other pavement.

So the performers responded to triggers from the people who were ostensibly the audience.

Exactly. And a reverse trigger would also then open up the windows where we had choruses of people performing. It worked as a sort of mechanism. Also, the entire text was based on remarks made by anybody in the first five seconds of the performance — it came from whatever people in the windows heard. Whatever they heard they wrote down. What they wrote down was accumulated into a form of repetitive sonnet. And these sonnets were then performed out of the windows. It was very much a machine for expanding one small moment of the present, multiplying it and developing it.

Gradually, though, we became interested in swimming against the flow. So much of the late sixties had been concerned with dropping out and loosening up — especially, really, in England. The early performance associated with people like Jeff Nuttall always seemed to promote a looseness. For some of us, that became a mannerism, and we felt performance art could go much further. I think our stance was also antipathetic to becoming 'gurus' — to forming a tribe. That seemed to be manipulative — and, in our terms, incorrect. So, having gone through this preliminary popularity, there was then a group of six of us who really wanted to make the problems we were dealing with more difficult. We became more and more concerned with creating extremely difficult performance conundrums. And, because performance in those days was seen to be so much on the margins, it seemed intriguing to see if we could begin the job of establishing it. So in some ways we started moving against the general flow of being loose, of being revolutionary in a casual, 'drop-out' way, of being impromptu. I can remember a phrase I used to use — that the exercises might be so difficult that a ballet dancer would find them very hard to perform. Remember, I had that ballet training, so I'd had that idea of discipline. Indeed, I thought that where I could create a unique art-form was by throwing balletic discipline at highly conceptual areas of performance.

Looking at it now, I think there was also a sense that we were not really creating spectacle in Wilson's sense, we were making a dialogue. We did, in performances after *The Street*, wish to create conceptual performances where the essential notion governing the performance could be read by its audience. That seemed to be a really interesting opening. And, indeed, it was — from there it rapidly took us to the Serpentine, from the Serpentine to the Hayward, and from the Hayward to the Paris Biennale. Because it was unusual.

What do you mean by 'conceptual performance'?

Well, we were talking earlier about the development of *Going* (1977). *Going* began as a structure for spontaneous improvisation in which four performers watched the actions of one performer and then at staggered intervals attempted to imitate the actions that they saw as near-perfectly as they could. Then, in the second act, the second performer would create a series of actions and the other four would imitate that performer's actions. And the idea of copying each other's actions came from the philosophical point that we were performers not actors: we were involved in conditions of being rather than conditions of acting. And because we were involved in conditions of being not conditions of acting, the only way we could, in a sense, 'act', would be by being each other. So the idea of 'being each other' became a sort of behavioural performance concern. This led to a structure which evolved to order the possibilities of one person copying another.

Presumably, this notion of the condition of being demands that the nature of the behaviour which is being choreographed always remains functional.

Functionality was very important. Again and again during the evolution of the company the difference between dance and performance was stressed as essentially relating to the function of the action. A ballet dancer might jump up in the air with his hands lifted, but a performance artist would jump up in the air to pull down a coat that was hung up on a branch — there was a function to the jump.

How did Going emerge out of these concerns?

The precursor of *Going* was a performance called *Homage to Pietro Longhi* (1976), which was very commedia dell'arte in its actions. The

Figure 25   Theatre of Mistakes *Going*, Paris, 1977 (photo: Kirk Winslow) (courtesy: Anthony Howell).

performance exercises we were preoccupied with were concerned with moving one joint at a time, producing quite strange angular poses and positions. But more importantly, there was that conceptual, copying framework. And this became a very tight, almost fugue-like structure. We then debated a notion of an ideal *Homage to Pietro Longhi*, that is, we started discussing what would be the best functional actions we could possibly do, in terms of actions which could be copied. There was also the idea that it would be interesting to have moments of reversal. Therefore another aesthetic which came in was that actions could be reversed. And there are certain things you can do — get up from a chair and be called back by somebody else. So, at a certain point of realising we could do things like shake hands and wave and pull each other back on to a chair, this mini-scenario developed. And the more it developed, the more we demanded of the structure that it refer to itself. And *Going* then became a highly rehearsed version of what had been an improvisational structure.

And the concern with 'being', in this context, was a rejection of the representational nature of 'acting'.

Absolutely. But there is an irony there. Because as soon as you rehearse your ideal form of copying, you do really enter into —

— representation.

A form of representation. And, indeed, I think if you were to talk to Fiona Templeton, who created *You: The City* (1988), she would say, well, for her, ultimately, through that experience, she came to believe that *high* performance is indeed where acting should be at today. I think there's a lot to be said for that. So there's a twist to the whole thing. At the most *intense* level of performing *Going*, we were, indeed, acting. Equally, though, I think there are things to be said about acting's seeming inauthenticity. A really great actor will often approach a difficult emotional scene through some form of functional action, like straightening their tie or even tying their tie. Certainly, in cinema one sees this all the time. In as much as performance at its most intense may bend over backwards and become acting, I think the opposite is also true.

The notion of 'being' could be said to go somewhat further than this, though, especially when opposed to acting. 'Being', here, seems to look toward a core, it aims at a kind of purity of state.

Well, again, remember these are historical statements. I'm talking about something like an attitude held in 1976. Indeed, my attitude now has completely changed. For instance, I'm very much more interested

GOING

There are five acts in the play. Each of the five acts is a repetition of the first act, each is begun by a different performer. In each act a further element is introduced by the first performer to enter in that act. Each new element is repeated in all subsequent acts.

EXAMPLE: ACT 1.

Scene 2:   – Metronome.
             – Entry of the first performer.
             – First performer executes an action with words.

Scene 2:   – Metronome
             – Entry of the second performer.
             – First performer executes an action with words.
             – Second performer repeats all actions and words employed by the first performer in Scene 1.

Scene 3:   – Metronome.
             – Entry of the third and fourth performers.
             – First performer executes an action with words.
             – Second performer freezes — only turning in order to observe the actions of the first performer.
             – Third performer repeats all actions and words employed by the first performer in Scene 1.
             – Fourth performer repeats all actions and words employed by the first performer in Scene 2.
             – Exit of the first performer.

Scene 4:   – First performer as metronome.
             – Entry of initial metronome as the fifth performer.
             – Second performer repeats all actions and words employed by the first performer in Scene 3.
             – Third performer repeats all actions and words employed by the first performer in Scene 2.
             – Fourth performer freezes — only turning in order to observe the actions of the second performer repeating all the actions and words employed by the first performer in Scene 3.
             – Fifth performer repeats all actions and words employed by the first performer in Scene 1.
             – Exit of the second performer.

Scene 5:	– Metronome.
	– Second performer begins Tone Poem Chorus.
	– Third performer freezes.
	– Fourth performer repeats all actions and words employed by the second performer in Scene 4.
	– Fifth performer repeats all actions and words employed by the first performer in Scene 2.
	– Exit of the third and fourth performers.
Scene 6:	– Metronome.
	– Second performer continues Tone Poem Chorus.
	– Third and fourth performers begin Tone Poem Chorus.
	– Fifth performer repeats all actions and words employed by the first performer in Scene 3.
	– Exit of the fifth performer.
ENTR'ACTE:	– Metronome begins Slowed Songs while all other performers continue Tone Poem Chorus.

There are five performers in the play. Since Act 1 was begun by the first performer, Act 2 will be begun by the second performer, Act 3 by the third performer, Act 4 by the fourth performer and Act 5 by the fifth performer.

In each act another performer begins Slowed Songs instead of the Tone Poem Chorus — thus, by the end of Act 5, all the performers will be engaged in Slow Songs.

Anthony Howell, notes for *Going* (1977) (courtesy of the artist).

in improvisation, via my investigations into the relationship between psychoanalysis and performance art. So things have turned full circle. I also think there's another aspect that should be brought in here. It's not just a philosophical issue of 'being' not 'acting'. It's also a sculptural issue. We felt very much by the time we were creating the refined version of *Going* —

Over what period of time did it actually develop?
     All in all, I would say about two-and-a-half years. We felt very much by the time, say, that we had got to the Paris Biennale, that we were creating a piece of living sculpture. So you then have to take on board artists like Gilbert and George. That was a big influence, too. Antithetical to 'site-related' sculpture, it was the idea of producing something that was always the same wherever we did it. We had a notion of turning things through 90 degrees. Very important, because of that sense of a performance with volume, a

performance that was not proscenium-arch related, a piece that you could, in a sense, turn round in front of the audience and which would remain the same in its dimensions. That was all very much influenced by Michael Craig Martin, a great friend of Mickey Greenall, who was a member of the company. Michael was fairly engaged with the company. At the time of *Going*, he came to all our performances and many rehearsals — and often discussed ideas.

It's very important to remember also that in those days the theatre-world, especially in the UK, was absolutely opposed to performance art — ignored it — poured scorn on it. Performance art really only existed within the context of the visual art world. We related to the conceptual sculptors and visual artists, not to the theatre people or to the dance people.

At that time, of course, most fringe theatre groups were engaged with an explicitly political agenda.

That was another difference, indeed. But it wasn't that we were vapidly unpoliticised. We strongly believed that the politics resided in the structure. That phrase, *the politics resides in the structure*, was often reiterated. It was the idea that if you produced a piece like *Going*, which had five characters, each character was given an absolutely equal status. Nobody was a star, nobody was a subsidiary performer. That was where the politics lay. Indeed, we were very involved in the notion of mutual art, in the first instance, and the body of thought that we had developed from the exercises was seen as a shared wellspring of artistic activity. So our political notion was the idea of the democratisation of structures.

Going seems to be made up of performance elements that specifically direct the spectator's attention toward the structure. Because it is a 'copying', each new action explicitly refers the audience back to what has already happened and so to the developing pattern of events.

Absolutely. And the structure was always clearly apparent. Most of the early programmes would print the diagram of the structure. And the audience was specifically invited to relate to the work via its structure. That *Going* was about perpetually saying goodbye, was seen as something we really, in some ways, in the early days, hardly referred to. Indeed, we saw the content as a result that we had not predicted.

Was it important in Going *that the audience could predict what would happen next?*

Yes. But, equally, we were always very involved in an ironic relationship with our audience. And with considerations of surprise. I think these are important, because I see them as being very consistent in my work.

Art into Theatre

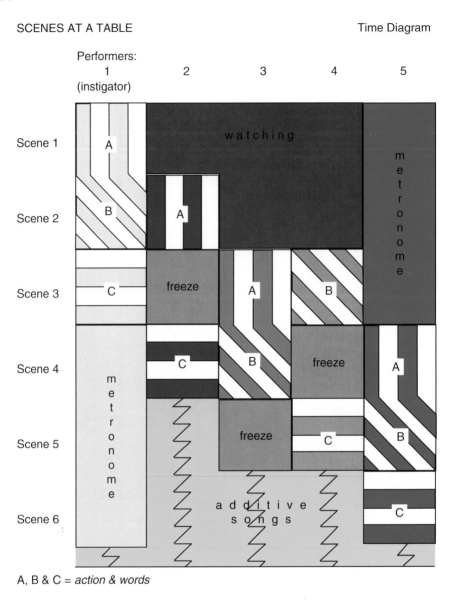

SCENES AT A TABLE   Time Diagram

Performers:
1 (instigator)   2   3   4   5

Scene 1   A   watching   m e t r o n o m e

Scene 2   B   A

Scene 3   C   freeze   A   B

Scene 4   metronome   C   B   freeze   A

Scene 5   freeze   C   B

Scene 6   additive songs   C

A, B & C = *action & words*

ACT ONE

Figure 26   The Theatre of Mistakes, selected diagram from *Going* (1977) (courtesy: Anthony Howell).

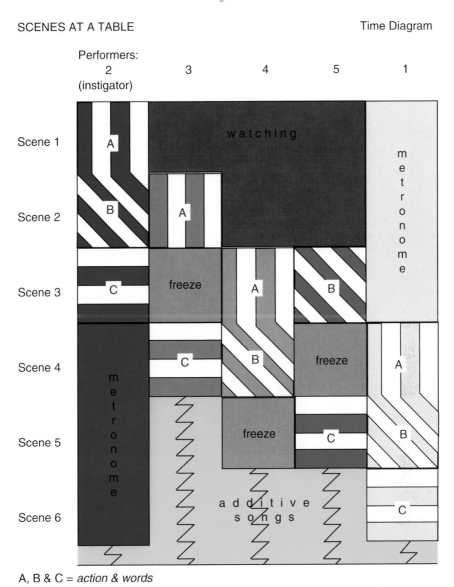

SCENES AT A TABLE   Time Diagram

Figure 27 The Theatre of Mistakes, selected diagram from *Going* (1977) (courtesy: Anthony Howell).

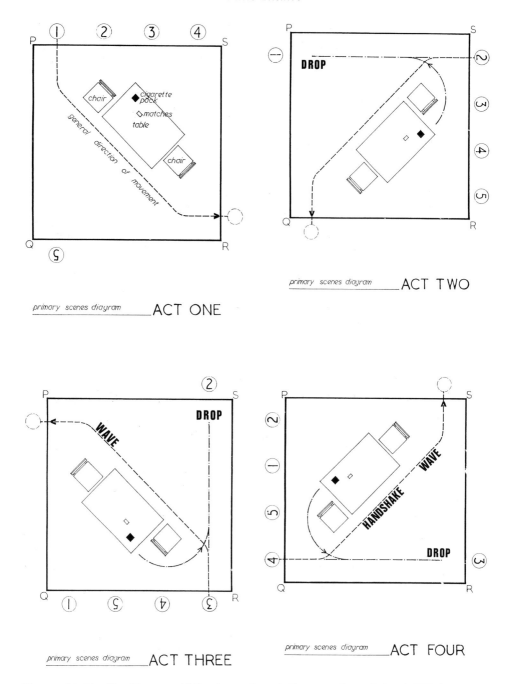

Figures 28–31 The Theatre of Mistakes, selected diagrams from *Going* (1977) (courtesy: Anthony Howell).

Although you could read the structure of a performance like *Going*, you wouldn't be able to predict where the mistake would occur. The mistake would act as the *punctum* to the performance. But, equally, you see, the mistake was highly rehearsed.

Was there ever a time when it wasn't?

Oh, yes. The entire structure had come out of a set of rules where accidents would indeed happen and mistakes caused forfeits and signals. But by the time it became the resolved piece, all those things had become set, had become sculpted. The mistakes were things like inadvertently forgetting to pick up your jacket from the back of a chair. So, in a sense, you could perceive what the mistake was. Equally, though, I think it's quite important in all performance that there is always a post-hoc comprehension that you could have predicted the inconsistency.

So in seeing Going, *the spectator sees a system generating a performance, even though it will always be repeated in the same way. When the 'mistake' occurs, and the system goes into reverse and corrects the mistake, the spectator sees the system more clearly.*

That's right.

So the mistake refines the spectator's viewing of the terms of the self-generating system.

Absolutely. I think that's absolutely right. You see the inexorable nature of the leitmotif.

In Going, *the performers signal the nature of the mistake to each other — so there's a kiss to the forehead, a signal, another kiss — then the performance reverses and repeats. It's clear signalling is going on, but it is unclear what precisely is meant by the signals.*

Again, there's a certain profound absurdity here. Yes, we wanted the audience to read most of what we were doing, but we were also concerned with the absurdity of the signals being the kiss on the lips, a kiss on the cheek, a kiss of the forehead and a warning finger held up in front of somebody's nose.

The signals also invite associations around 'mistakes' — comforting, admonishing —

Around mistakes and around a notion of a humour that was deadpan and always carried out with a mien of solemnity — which is very important — and often misunderstood. Less misunderstood in Europe and America, I have to say, than it has been in England. British humour is so often slapstick. What we're talking about here is a much more ironic, Eastern European notion of humour.

Despite the fact that in Going *the system is so rigorous and the product so 'sculpted', the notion of the 'mistake' suggests a rather ambivalent attitude toward the system. I notice that in one of your own commentaries on the work, you remark that 'we use systems to defeat their own logic and create something that transcends those systems. I think we use systems to defeat ourselves'.*

Yes. Again, this carries on through, say, to the solos I did after the Theatre of Mistakes, *Table Move Solo* (1981) and *Two Table Moves* (1983) in which I performed solos 1 and 2, as well as into the performance, *Homage to Roussel* (1993), which I did with Deborah Proctor at Chapter Arts in Cardiff. Performance may be an 'infernal machine', but that machine cannot run on entirely pre-ordained rails. I think that's a performance problem which is not a Minimalist artist's problem. Many of the performances that we've done have begun with a seeming repetition, but the repetition is like a long fuse to a series of very unpredictable fireworks which then start to develop with increasing force from the first third of the piece on. This relates, actually, to Hegelian ideas like the *rousing moment* in theatre. I actually feel that the sort of performance the Theatre of Mistakes was doing was very like Greek tragedy or indeed Greek comedy. Ideas like the pendulum plot you get in *Philoctetes*, for instance. There's always that moment where, having set up the notion in the audience's mind that it can predict the structure or can predict the story, you then pull the carpet out from under the feet of the viewer and say, ah, you couldn't really catch what was going on.

Even though the system itself produced it.

Even though the system itself seemed to be producing it. Or suppose that the structure that seemed so predictable is suddenly interrupted by a completely chaotic event which it attempts to cope with by adaption. This was a notion that was very important to me in the *Table Moves*. The notion that when an ant is busy about its own affairs, it may suddenly have a disaster occur to it and may lose a leg. Really, in the end, what the ant does is to carry on with one leg the less.

The Table Moves *consist of a series of moves of pieces of furniture which are repeated, but varied in each repetition.*

The arrangement shifts around, usually through 90 degrees, so that this little room of furniture which occupies a square is seen from four different angles. In the *Table Move 1*, at a certain point, a wardrobe falls

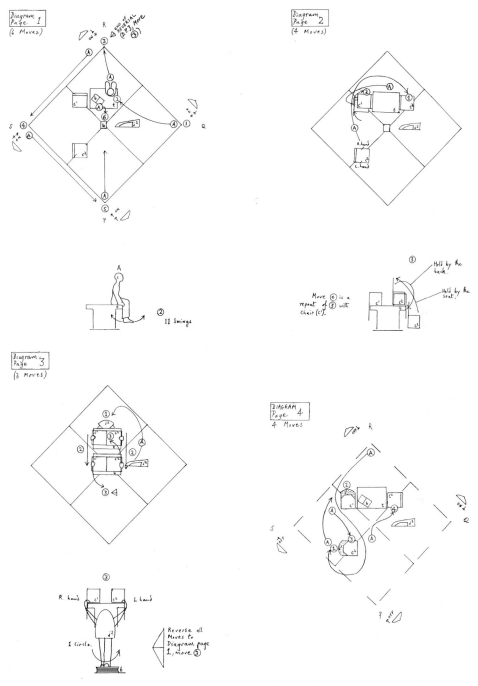

Figures 32–35 Anthony Howell, selected diagrams from *Table Move Duet* (1983) (courtesy of the artist).

down. At the very moment the wardrobe falls down, I jump on to a chair and from then on I have to keep producing the 90 degree configurations of the furniture, but I'm not allowed to touch the ground. So I move the furniture by moving from a table to a chair and carrying the chair over the table.

So in response to the crisis, the system adapts and produces something new. The system is still in operation and it's changing.

Yes. And the system may have some fundamental alteration imposed upon it. At a certain point, in *Table Move 2*, I must continue to move the furniture without being seen by the audience. From then on I hide behind the furniture as I move it. When the piece is totally reversed to the audience's view, what you actually see is me hiding behind the furniture.

So systems seem to be useful in setting up a predictability. It's not a piece of Minimal Art, though. One is not simply going to demand that the audience is witness to a repetitive predictability. One is constantly dealing with predictability and demanding that unpredictability be thrust against it or develop.

It would be important to say, then, that the transcendence of the system, in a sense, is linked to a mistake entering into it.

Absolutely. Some form of catastrophe occurring to the system. That catastrophe in some cases might be predicted. Yet there is also a notion of 'red herring'. In the *Table Move 2*, where I begin to hide behind the furniture at a certain point, one of the actions I have to do in each round is to change my shoes and socks to gym shoes and socks of another colour. At some point in a very early round, one perceives that I've got my socks wrong and that I'm wearing one black sock and one white sock. It's then, as I'm trying to resolve that and get back to wearing two white socks and two black socks, that I start to disappear behind the furniture. So the system is changing, but the audience doesn't quite perceive what the change is until it has occurred. That was fairly important. There are similar games of predictability and unpredictability going on in the *Homage to Roussel*. Again, Deborah is trying to carry on a system of moving the furniture around, while a grey suited character simply follows her, making use of the furniture. Then at a certain point her eyes shut and she has to try and keep performing the piece blind.

Was it rehearsed in such a way that when she was blind she always did the same thing?

Again, here's one of those difficulties between being and acting. Deborah knew that performance so well that she could indeed move the furniture through 90 degrees with her eyes shut. There was that usual problem that we had to almost develop a certain simulation of blindness. But then, of course, she is sabotaged by the other performer, because at a certain point the male performer moves the chair into the wrong position. So in the single move that the male does, he deliberately puts her into a situation which will, if you like, demand punishment. But this is perhaps moving on into areas of psychology. They all do have a certain psychological undertone, despite the fact that they are very much developed around structure.

Well, you are inevitably dealing with representations and meanings, even if a resolution or tying together of those meanings is off-set by an attention to the formal rigour of the system. It must be essential, though, not to give way to those meanings — that they are not overtly thematized, for example — because that would be to obscure the process that you've been talking about.

You're quite right. Remember that earlier in this interview I referred to people in *The Street* falling down *dead* on the floor? Well, actually, we only said that they should fall down horizontal on the floor. That was the sort of language we would use. We would talk about 'equipment' not props. The way of thinking was structural and sculptural, though, when we expressed it in a programme note, we always had an ironic consciousness of the absurdity of our own jargon.

I think now, though, that the interesting thing is perhaps what ultimately begins to get left behind in this sort of work, i.e., the relationship of the performer to the continuum of the present. I'm now very interested in returning to improvisation, improvisation within a pretty large vocabulary of exercises and previous structures and performance routes, that I can adapt and play around with. I'm intrigued by the idea of the audience acting as a sort of analyst and analysing the performance as an occurrence that is literally unfolding before their eyes in the present — and which is not something that has been entirely rehearsed and sculpted. I think if I could find two or three people who I could work with, I would now try and do a lot of what we used to call 'free sessions'.

When you say 'the continuum of the present' what precisely do you mean?

Well, I'm very interested in people like Derek Bailey and that group of improvising musicians that gather around him, especially during *Company Week* at *The Place* in London every summer, and in performance artists like Min Tanaka who I saw and was most impressed by at the Sidney Biennale many years ago. After all, we're no longer in a situation where hardly any work is highly rehearsed. Nowadays, almost everything is highly rehearsed. Everything is scripted. Nevertheless, we have performers of enormous experience and ability, such as Gary Stevens, Julian Maynard Smith, Fiona Templeton, several people who're in Clock who can work in a free way. And I think that in some senses having an excessively ironed out structure to a work is a young man's anxiety.

This issue is also connected to the whole notion of the performance being the composition of an individual. This is a problem for music. I don't really enjoy many of the modern composers like Fitkin, and so on. Somehow, that form of structured, predicted and predicated composition will only give you the structures apparent to any one individual organising the efforts of some five or six others. To some degree, again, here, we're talking about the politics residing in the structure. I would be very interested in a situation where the intense creative powers of people whose work I do admire — such as Julian and Fiona and Gary — came together in moments of great possible electricity, in situations that the audience was aware had not occurred before.

I mean, it is a matter of improvisation in the sense of the cadenza. I think it's interesting that in the highly structured music of the Baroque you do find this free area handed to the soloist. I think that's why some forms of improvisation by people who do understand structure, who do understand action and the functional type of action that performance has made its base, could be very exciting to watch. The audience would be witnessing a sort of electricity generated by performers as beings rather than as actors. We're back to this issue of being. Because what destroyed being was the rehearsals. I do think one notices in free sessions, and in those improvisational situations which are often not done in front of the public, very exciting moments where to some degree the psychology is bared. One is right on the edge of dealing with one's anger. That increases the danger, and one always has to be moving into a dangerous area. I also believe that it's the way for a kernel of new work to evolve, work which might have more structure eventually — but we need to return in our present work to a more flexible, fluid and immediate condition.

PING CHONG

Since 1972, and the presentation of his first performance-piece *Lazarus* in New York, Ping Chong has produced dance, multi-media theatre, and television, as well as installation, video, and film, both with his own theatre company and in collaboration with the director and choreographer Meredith Monk. In 1979, Chong separated from Monk's company, and has since produced a series of award-winning performances, as well as a wide range of visual arts and film works. Chong's performance work is often technically complex, and typically employs film, video, multi-track sound, dance and installation. Formally, the work often sets out a fragmented surface, making use not only of multiple channels of address but using found or quoted materials to create rich and complex visual and performance texts. Chong's many theatre works include *Nuit Blanche: A Select View of Earthlings* (1981), *Nosferatu* (1985), *Angels of Swedenborg* (1985) and *Noiresque — The Fallen Angel* (1988). Chong's texts for *Nuit Blanche* (1981), *Kind Ness* (1988) and *Snow* (1988) are published by Theatre Communications Group, while his work on video includes *Paris* (1982) and *Turtle Dreams (Waltz)* (1982), both in collaboration with Meredith Monk. This interview was recorded in June 1990 in Glasgow, shortly before a performance of Ping Chong's *Deshima* at the Tramway Theatre.

*   *   *

Was there a particular body of visual art that was important to the development of your performance work?
        No. I think that my first love — or maybe parallel with my love for the visual arts — was cinema. I graduated as a film major. I think that has had, in a way, a much more important influence on me than anything else. The atmosphere of the sixties was also very important. But the work always had a sense of cinema about it. It changed — with *Kind Ness* (1986), obviously. But even that has some of it because of the way time is played with. The physics of time is something that I'm very interested in. When I think of my Western visual arts training it's not people like Braque or Picasso that I feel any relation to. I think of people I like that influenced me. It's more — I'm very fond of Giacommetti — or — I don't love Francis Bacon but there's a connection. There's a connection with Magritte. Surrealism seems to relate.

So it's like a sensibility?
        It's a sensibility.

Was there a connection in the sixties with experimentations in the fine arts?
        Well, for instance, one of the early works I dedicated to Joseph
Cornell. It's not that he influenced me, but he's a kindred spirit. I find it very
hard to talk about who influenced me, except perhaps Meredith Monk
because I worked with her. Yet even from the very beginning when you see
my very first works and her work, it's not the same thing at all.

*I wonder how strong the connection might be between Cornell's collecting together,
juxtaposition and re-presentation of objects and your own approach to making
performances. You describe your first performance piece* Lazarus (1972) *as a
'bricolage'.*
        I thought of my early work as bricolage, but I felt that I never really
fully explored that. My early works had a much more home-made quality.
The later works are more polished and slicker and much more developed
structurally. I don't think it's a qualitative thing. The early works had a really
home-made aspect — partly because of the finances — but at that point I
liked that way of working. With *Lazarus* I re-edited an old fifties monster
movie and used it. I used old materials to give it a new resonance. That's
what I was thinking of as bricolage, recombining materials that were not
in those combinations before in order — as I remember it now — to create a
kind of luminosity. But as the years went on I felt that I didn't want to be
hindered by any kind of manifesto. I didn't want to bother with that.
Whether you have a manifesto or not, if you keep working it's going to
make a through-line. I felt I didn't want to limit myself by labelling myself
in that way. Even the term 'performance art' — I predate performance art
and some of the works are not really performance art at all. I don't think
Kind Ness is performance art, I just think of that as theatre. Even if certain
theatre people may think it's a little too radical. In fact it's relatively
conservative. The problem of being someone who doesn't fit in one or the
other form is that you get trashed from both sides. The visual arts people
say it's not hip enough, but the theatre people think it's too cold. Last night
I went to see Trisha Brown — and when you see something out of context
it's really interesting. This is not meant to be derogatory — that work really
comes out of the sixties. I was thinking, well, what's my relationship to
that? Well, for one thing she's an older generation. She really is part of that
process generation — Cage, Nam June Paik, the Fluxus folks. I'm after that.
I'm sort of between Meredith and them. Also, I'm Asian. So I'm a formalist.
In a way, I could never be that *process*, that open ended. Even saying I'm

Asian is not enough, because there are Asian people who did that and do that still. But they were a part of that generation. I really come out of something very specific to me. I do have a sense that I came out of the sixties, but ultimately I'm not a part of that thing.

Can you say something more about the connection between being Asian and being a formalist?

I think I should qualify that by saying that I'm a first-generation Asian. If I was a second-generation Asian I wouldn't be doing what I'm doing, I wouldn't be a formalist. Being a first-generation Asian, I could not entirely be a Wild-West American. I have been brought up with certain formality.

So by 'formalism' you mean —

Ritual, a sense of ritual. All those things are sublimated within me. By this time, the Asian influence is sublimated because I hardly speak Chinese anymore. But I feel that, in the end, I'm still of Asian sensibility. But I'm also modernist. So it's a strange mix.

Somebody like Richard Foreman, who also seems, in a way, to be attempting to see the familiar as strange, uses highly rigorous, formal strategies which would disrupt the way the material being presented is seen. Your work doesn't seem so concerned with overtly formal strategies.

Foreman is first of all an intellectual. I can't read his manifestoes. I've tried and I can't. And I like going to see Foreman. When I see Foreman I sit there in the same way as when I see the Wooster Group — I sort of get my brain washed out once a year. Foreman's work, to me, is kind of a brilliant babble of his inner mental state. That's very different from who I am. And when I say he's an intellectual, he's also utterly Western.

I find Angels of Swedenborg *(1985) powerful because it seems to reveal a kind of intuitive sense or recognition of meanings or possibilities that underlie a particular kind of empty technocratic culture.*

You see, for me, for example, Foreman is like Swedenborg, because it's like someone who's running around in his own head and can't get out. That's his achilles' heel, but it's also his gift. And that's where I step back because I will not completely accept being a Western person. That's why I would do something like *Swedenborg*. It could be read in many ways. It could be read, obviously, as what it says, or it can be read as an inner dialogue with myself — a dialogue between the tension between the Western, intellectual tradition and this much more fluid, primal kind of consciousness, whether it's Asian or it's Amer-Indian or whatever it is. It is that thing that makes Westerners so uncomfortable — the undefinable, the mysterious.

Both Michael Kirby and Richard Foreman — and it's drawn indirectly perhaps from John Cage — talk about reaching a point of what they describe as 'no mind' or stillness.

But there's an irony and a paradox there, because Cage and Foreman and Kirby — they want to get to *no mind* but they cannot escape the mind because they are Western intellectuals. So it's an irony, a paradox, because they can never get out of it. They are products of a mechanistic society.

One of their subject-matters, in that sense, might be their attempt to move toward it.

Right. That's why I say I'm related to the sixties but I'm not, because all of that is outside of me. I see it and I know about it. I read about it. I was in New York. But it's odd, because I'm always this person who is a part of yet not a part of. That's my metaphysical condition.

In this context, I'm interested in the sources of your imagery. Are the angels in Angels of Swedenborg *derived from Leonardo's* Annunciation. *Is the source that specific?*

Yes, it is that specific. And the Mephistopheles character — the stranger — is taken from an idea in a bestiary of T. H. White — an image of a bishop-fish. But the angels came out of Renaissance angels, definitely. In fact, Swedenborgian angels don't have wings. And the Swedenborgians were around a lot when the show came up — because I was the first artist to give them any kind of publicity — they even gave me money. And they said, why did you put wings on the angels? I said, well, who would accept an angel without wings? In the audience? In *Angels*, though, there's also definitely an Asian dance influence — not that I was trained in Asian dance.

Despite this sense of being 'a part of and yet not a part of' there seems finally in the work to be a sense of an underlying unity that belies the fragmentation which most critical responses to the work have emphasised.

I understand what you're saying, because the fragmentation is only a strategy. It isn't really fragmentary. I understand what you're saying, but I think that it's not understood, often, by the press. To me, while it looks fragmented, it's really three dimensional chess. It's all inter-related, but not in a linear manner. They are connected, but they're not connected A-B-A-B, that's all.

Figure 36 Ping Chong *Angels of Swedenborg* (1985) (courtesy: Ping Chong).

Given this, I wonder about the status of the imagery which is not, essentially, of the West or America. If the work is played to an American-Asian or Asian-American audience, how would they —

No, they wouldn't necessarily get it. Asian-Asians would find my work not particularly Asian, but that's because they can't see through the surface. Ironically, it's non-Asians who see the Asian aspect. Within the same week I had Asians telling me how my work is not Asian and then non-Asians saying how Asian it is. You know, you have to laugh.

There is a Western audience that has absorbed this desire for a spirituality, a non-Asian audience that has grown up in the atmosphere of the sixties.

But that's a specific generation, too. But right now it seems like just one big mess, I think. I mean the most interesting work that's going on right now at all is in the visual arts. Not in the theatre.

Which work in particular?

In installation work. Installation work is some of the most interesting work that's going on. Even though I'm still questioning it.

Is there a connection between the development of that work and your own?

Deshima is more installation. It's difficult. Apart from ideas you have to talk about economic realities — why things can't be done the way you'd like them to be. The other tension is that I never thought I'd get to a point where I'd make a show like *Kind Ness*. From *Lazarus* to *Kind Ness* is a very long distance and I fear at this point whether I've moved too far away from my essence or not. The tension with me right now is an extrovert-introvert thing. *Lazarus*, obviously, was a very introverted work, while *Kind Ness* was obviously not introverted or monastic. Right now I'd like to be more monastic.

Can you characterise the difference between conventional theatre design and design as installation?

The difference is that the mise-en-scene has more weight and moves itself from out of a theatrical context. It's not passive. It may have a metaphysical dimension. It's not just passively sitting there like so much theatre is. It's like, for instance, Japanese flower arrangement. Japanese flower arrangement has, I think, a very different weight than Western flower arrangement. I don't feel Western flower arrangement, as beautiful as it is, has a metaphysical dimension, while Japanese flower arrangement has a metaphysical dimension. I think that may be equivalent. The set is not just a set, it's something more than a set. It's also a statement that has its own weight.

This notion seems important to a number of the pieces. In Snow *(1986), the constant fall of snow suggests a lamentation —*

Snow is a kind of microcosm-macrocosm — the personal and the universal. Those two things as indistinguishable and inseparable. This is something very present in my work. When does history begin and when does personal history begin? In a way I've also been thinking that where I am also different from, say, Foreman, and those people, is that in a way, by not fully being that Western intellectual I feel the need to make a holistic kind of statement.

It's interesting to me that when you talk about art you talk about modernism, being a modernist, and you talked about Surrealism rather than contemporary American art. It seems to me that the European work at least attempts to be more holistic, to be much more of a statement about what lies beneath the surface, or to look toward something that might in the end provide a unity despite the tendency of the surface to break apart.

I talked to a Japanese concert designer — a friend of mine — about how, as Asians, we can't abstract in the way that Westerners abstract. Even when we abstract there's a context and a content level to it. You know, Japanese flower arrangement is not independent of meaning. So that's — that I am still Asian. I mean, I think it would be interesting to do but I've never been able to do it. I sometimes set out to do it. And there are some works that sort of seem like they have that. On the surface they appear to be like that, but they're not really. Not in terms of what supports it and the process of creating it.

It seems that the work has a strong element of alienation, but it is not simply a disruption or a denial of connections between things.

Right. They open you up to the realisation that your assumptions are not infallible, they're not absolute. But you can see all of that comes out of my own defences against the West. It's my way of constantly saying, in a way, 'No your system is not the only system, no matter how much you think it's the number one system going on, it lacks *a lot*'. But you don't see it, you know. I think that's definitely an underlying impetus for me.

And also the fact that you are implicated within this system, whether you choose to be or not.

Right. I mean, I'm an American. In terms of the last works I have been very interested in America. I call it the 'what's wrong with the picture' hypothesis. That's why I say sometimes I long for the *Lazarus* stage, because *Lazarus* was very uncompromising. I didn't know enough at that point to even think about the audience. It was the painter in me. You saw it and you responded to it or you didn't. Later I became more conscious of trying to make a bridge with the audience. But the visual artist in me sometimes doesn't want to think about that, it just wants to create whatever comes into my head because this has some kind of haunted thing for me and I want to do it. I miss that sometimes. But by not doing things the way I did in *Lazarus* I felt that I had this responsibility toward the audience. I think maybe other people would say, well, that's not important. The sixties certainly said, you know, it's not important whether the audience understands this thing or not. But for me, I feel the responsibility to give the audience some clues as to where I'm trying to go, where I'm trying to take them. But I'm ambivalent about that. *Kind Ness*, obviously, wanted to make a connection with the audience. In *Lazarus*, the narrative is much more sublimated than in a lot of the other works. It was closer to my visual arts roots at that time. It was 'purer' in a way because it didn't really have to deal with theatrical conventions. It wasn't trying to tell a story. It didn't have any relation to those kind of things. It was really an ontological piece. Very purely that. At the same time, you know, I could see myself doing a very small hermetic work and let the meaning come out of the subconscious — or whatever you want to call it — and organise itself. I think I'm missing that feeling, still. As long as I'm trying to make work that has a degree of accessibility I feel that it's harder to please the poet in me. I think the roots of something like *Lazarus* are very poetic.

But, you know, I don't believe that traditional playwriting theatre is legitimate anymore because of all the changes that have happened in this century. I think that regardless of how chaotic the experimental works have been or how uneven, they're the only thing that can be true to the times. It may be the end of live performance, maybe that, too, but nonetheless it has to happen. I think it's the only thing that makes sense right now. After Beckett and Ionesco you can't go back, really, I don't think.

RICHARD SCHECHNER

Since the early 1960s, Richard Schechner's work has engaged with the alternative theatre through theory, critical writing and performance practice. As editor of *The Drama Review* from 1962 to 1969, Schechner was instrumental in giving voice to the new avant-garde performance. In 1967, while teaching in the Drama Faculty at New York University, Schechner established The Performance Group, whose members came to include Spalding Gray, Elizabeth LeCompte and Jim Clayburgh, founding members of the Wooster Group. Schechner's work for The Performance Group included *Dionysus in 69* (1968–69), *Makbeth* (1969–70), *Commune* (1970–72) and *The Tooth of Crime* (1972). His account of the Group's working process and performances, *Environmental Theatre* (Hawthorn Books, New York: 1973), advocated a participatory theatre in which the transactions between audience and performer, and the relationship of performance to text, would be redrawn. In his subsequent and highly influential writing, Schechner came to define notions of performance theory and theatre anthropology, and his volumes include *Essays on Performance Theory* (Drama Book Specialists, New York: 1977), *Between Theatre and Anthropology* (University of Pennsylvania Press, Philadelphia: 1985) and most recently *The Future of Ritual* (Routledge, London: 1993). In 1986, Schechner returned to *The Drama Review* as editor, bringing with him a new emphasis on performance studies. While he publishes widely, Schechner's theatre practice also continues unabated, most recently with *Faust Gastronome* (1993) presented in collaboration with the theatre company, East Coast Artists. This interview, which concerns the developing relationship between Schechner's theory and practices since the 1960s and the various influences acting upon his work, was recorded in October 1988 in Leicester, where Schechner was contributing to the conference *Points of Contact: Theatre, Anthropology, and Theatre Anthropology*.

*   *   *

How has the recent development of your ideas, in Between Theatre and Anthropology *in particular, informed your theatre practice and work with students?*

Well, I'm of at least two minds. When I direct work from a very personal basis, I don't ask myself certain questions that I ask when

I'm theorising. I don't ask questions of overall logical systematising, or concerning the impact of what I'm doing on 'the world', or even concerning how people receive what I do. Later on in the rehearsal process I do: but what I start with is something I want to or must do. There's a kind of blurry edge between 'I want to do this' and 'I must do this'. The 'must' actually takes two forms. Usually when I direct nowadays, I've accepted a contract, whereas with The Performance Group I gave myself a contract. So at that very basic level I have a 'must'. Somebody is expecting me to show up and three weeks, four weeks, six weeks, eight weeks later they're expecting the public to see something.

Within that there's a second must or want. For example, the last full production I did — which was in 1987 at Florida State University — was a combination of *Don Juan* and *Don Giovanni*, and I realised that the Don Juan theme had been floating around in my mind and heart for many years. Megan Terry and I once worked on an idea of a female Don Juan — must have been the late sixties, early seventies — then we put it away, she moved to Kansas I think. But the idea of Don Juan as a middle-aged sexual reprobate who, in a certain sense, is able to forestall paying his moral debts until he pays them in one fell swoop was both ethically interesting and delightful. In other words I think all of us, whether we're sexual reprobates or reprobates in another way, would like to say, yes there's a moral universe but it won't catch up with us until the very end, and we're free up to that point.

I also enjoyed the contradictions in Don Juan's life — that is, he's an extremely logical atheist, and a humanist person who seems to oppose hypocrisy. He is also a theatre director and actor who knows how to use a false front, which is different from hypocrisy — in other words he doesn't ever fool himself. I think the hypocrite very often fools himself. Tartuffe is somewhere between being a hypocrite and somebody who is fooling himself, whereas Don Juan is very clear-headed.

Also, there were certain sexist themes in Don Juan which I wanted to run up against and then play their opposites, so there was a feminist 'counter-text' to Don Juan written by two women, one of whom played Sganarelle. I also wanted to have the Moliere story, which I thought was very acerbic and ironic, run against or be side by side with Mozart, which is extremely romantic. Whatever the words, which you only hear in Italian, the music itself is not the music really of tragedy and neither is it of melodrama — it's a kind of dancing lightly until you fall off the wire and you die, but that's an accident rather than a tragedy. So these are themes that felt I must and wanted to work on. Now your question was how does my theory, my theoretical work, connect to this, and the answer there is that I think the deepest part of me is both active and theoretical, both personal and theoretical. In other words, the theory connects in the sense that, first of all, working with actors is where I get my ideas of process from, so the theory stands on the practical work, yet the practical work does not illustrate the theory.

It seems to me that the notion you outlined in your talk, that the individual in fact consists of multiple selves, is something that was deeply within your work in the sixties and early seventies. Spalding Gray describes playing Hoss in The Tooth of Crime *in terms of taking up one role, dropping that role, letting go of it, and then taking up another. Also your idea that in playing a role the performer experiences being 'not me' and yet 'not (not me)' seems to be reflected in the relationship between performer, personal life and character in* Dionysus in 69.

I think that's true. Those are all theories which are also, if you want to put them in quotation marks, 'facts of my interior life'. But I don't think that they're just my interior life.

I don't mean that you illustrate your theory. I think it's inherent within the processes of what you're doing. I wondered how that had changed.

Well, it deepens, it doesn't change. In other words, the sixties are interesting because — I don't think I'm nostalgic in any sense, but I see people looking at them first with contempt and scorn and 'let's not remember any of that', and now with a great deal of interest. So I feel there have been some consistent themes in my thinking — ritual process, multiple selves, non-proscenium or environmental staging, audience involvement if not participation.

The participation in *Dionysus* was powerful, but suited only to that day. But I think there are certain consistent themes that I still believe in. I'm not a modish person, and neither am I stubborn. So those themes that I've just enunciated and those ideas are constant from that day but they've changed considerably in the sense that in the theory at least they have deepened and become elaborated. I think I'm deeper into some of those problems just for having thought them over and worked them over from the *End of Humanism* book through to *Between Theatre and Anthropology*.

Do you find you explore these ideas in a different way in workshop programmes or workshop investigations with students?

Yes. But I don't do workshops that much. I like to do performances. I don't do workshops because workshops for me are integrally connected with training and deconstruction and that's integrally connected with reconstruction. If you just do a workshop, if you do it effectively for five or six days, you take people apart but you don't put them back together again. One of the ironies is that people are always saying, are you doing theatre or therapy? Well, I believe that theatre can be very therapeutic but I'm not a therapist. So the kind of theatre that I do, the kind of workshop I do is not therapeutic. I take people apart or help them come apart in order to construct these actions and roles to make a public entertainment which hopefully will have some personal reverberation for the performers and the spectators and also some ideological content and a narrative content.

I do deeply believe that performance can be therapeutic and that drama therapy right down to the catharsis of an audience works, but it's not my personal interest. In other words, theoretically I recognise that dimension but I am not interested in doing a workshop that would, in a certain sense, help the individual. Now as far as helping individual performers, it takes more than a few days to give them a training technique. I have a good training technique, I think, in terms of voice especially, and movement in relationship to sound, but it takes more than a few days to do it. Therefore I feel kind of exhausted when I'm asked to do a one-day workshop or a three-day workshop because a lot goes out, people breathe and they learn, but I know a week after I leave they're not going to do it. I'm almost angry before I begin. But if I'm doing a production — and I've had enough feedback from people, coming back years later, saying, that production I worked on with you was important to me — if you carry it through to some kind of rhythmic conclusion, which is a public performance, then it sticks with people. So when I work at NYU I don't work in a workshop situation. There I'm teaching theory, and outside of the University direct performances.

Now sometimes when I teach theory there's a practical aspect to it — like I'm teaching directing theories in the spring, and students will be asked physically to reconstruct the styles of certain directors. In other words, they'll take a certain scene and be asked how Artaud would do it, how Peter Brook would do it, how Brecht would do it, and so on. But that's not to train directors so much as to allow a class, including directors, to see these different styles, to understand Brecht's theories and Artaud's theories.

I'm very interested in the way that you go about asking this kind of question about a performance that has gone and from which only certain kinds of structure are left...
How do you interrogate an event that's finished?

Well, there's a lot of interrogation of events that are finished that goes on in a conceptual way. The question is how do you combine that in theatre with a physical investigation of an event that's finished, particularly one that stressed a living process?
I know what you mean, but I don't know what you mean in relationship to what I do. For example, if I do a production the things that are

past that are brought back are certain techniques. The first thing l do with people is teach them a certain kind of stretch that I took from yoga and a certain kind of breathing with panting and all that: every time I begin that it's the n'th time I've done that because it tends, in my experience, to bring a group together — you know, if you breathe together you can begin to move together. Any amount of bullshit talk about being a group doesn't mean anything: because a group emanates from around the navel, and in the breath.

So I will do these breathing exercises using different resonators. Anybody who's worked with me knows that you have to sit on the floor and do this and you have to move. And there are certain exercises that are in *Environmental Theatre* — 'follow no leader' and some others — that I constantly do. But like any kind of physical activity, like dance training, or anything else, once you do it it is a repetition but not exactly the same. So in that sense the work is constantly recalling itself. But I don't try, like a ballet master, to do a performance again. Somebody will say, do *Dionysus in 69*, but I did it, I don't want to do it again. It would either be better, in which case I would feel bad about the original, or worse, in which case I would feel bad about this. In any case I don't feel like doing a whole performance again.

I'm not meaning a reconstruction. I'm talking about precisely that idea that there are certain perspectives and values and themes that recur, that are inherent within those techniques.

Right. Let's say that there are certain very basic things. I always start with taking the furniture out of a room. Sitting in a circle. Why in a circle? Simply because whoever speaks in a circle is at the head of a table, while if you're in any other configuration, rectangle or so on, there is a head of the table. In a circle everyone can see everyone else and also you're very close to the person next to you and you're face to face with the person across from you. So you're receiving a lot of impulses from the unconscious, perhaps, or non-conscious impulses. Why remove the furniture? So that the bodies begin to structure the space. You bring furniture back in later. I want a clean floor. I will very often ask the people, as the first exercise, to bring a mop and a pail and clean the floor. And they say, what are you doing, we're not janitors? No, but you're going to lie on this floor. Like in Japan, cleaning your space: this is our nest. I would often say, we're not going to use dressing rooms, you're going to use this room, so that the room becomes the living room. Here's a place for eating, here's a place for working, so the space itself begins to breathe the life of the particular group. This may carry over into the performance — where I did *Don Juan*, for example, was a space that had never been used as a theatre before, that had been a church. But there was still a low stage at one end of the room and I used that stage as the dressing room, even during the performance.

We put a few lights, the audience could either be watching the performance or if they glanced to the side they could see this little stage on which people were getting dressed and undressed, and it was the green room and they were chatting. It was a kind of strange ironic inversion that the stage was not used as a stage but as a dressing room, and the place that had been used for the congregation or the audience was now being used as multiple stages and the audience were on different platforms that were rearranged during the production. So I will, in that sense, take a page out of Brecht's book — make the familiar strange, make the strange familiar. But it's not like l come in with that in mind. I have to see what the room offers and what those people offer, and then select or generate whatever it might be that I would use in relationship to these themes.

Now that also relates to my theories and my fieldwork. In the most 'natural' kind of staging, when an event just happens, people tend to form a circle around it so far as they can. So circles seem to be a very efficient way, it's the way you get the most people in the least space. When people 'crowd in', they crowd in a circle. So I start with that.

Also, I find, for example, if I'm interested in movement, whatever culture I'm looking at, movement can be better observed from above.

The Greeks knew this: when they had their amphitheatres, you looked down on the chorus. I think that one of the bad things about the proscenium stage is that the orchestra seats are often below the level of the stage. So that this enunciated text dominates and you can't see the movement really, the movement is flattened out. So I also try to elevate the audience and work with these movement patterns, because then I feel that movement is received by an audience viscerally, just like sound, while flat movement kind of pushes an audience away. Robert Wilson overcomes this by slowing the movement down so much that flat movement almost becomes visceral because you become exhausted by looking at it and finally you stop looking at it to a certain degree and you go into your own thoughts, and then back and forth to it. You can't stare at one of those movements for forty minutes.

So there's a constant interplay between the theories which are generalisations based on experiences, and the experiences which are extremely specific about particular groups of people and particular obsessions of my own.

When I look back at the plays I've directed there are certain emergent themes, political and personal. The political themes have to do with who was in power and how power is dispersed. The personal themes are usually sexual themes and the two interplay. In other words, are power games really sexual games or are sexual games really power games? Then I respond to people like Pina Bausch who I feel in her own way is working on her own version of these things. I don't like simply pretty performances that mask all those deep human contradictions and conflicts.

In another part of your talk you suggested that performance created realities rather than imitating them, and that this process of constructing truths through performance was important socially and politically. It seems to me that there's a lot of work that through its form attempts to make an audience aware of this process — Wilson, for example, the Wooster Group, Happenings, a whole body of experimental American work including your own. I'm wondering if you feel that you are taking up these ideas in the form of work you're doing now.

To a certain degree. When l did *Don Juan,* — and I didn't have this in mind when I began, but as I cast, as I saw the people, I finally cast two Don Juans. An older man in his forties and a young man, a student, who was only eighteen or nineteen. And they each had their kind of good looks but there's no doubt that the young eighteen or nineteen-year-old had that certain flowering of late adolescence that's just very beautiful. So the way we did it was that the role was shared. Sometimes one was speaking, sometimes they were in unison. And the older man only wore the seventeenth-century Don Juan costume while the younger man sometimes wore an identical costume, sometimes was dressed in a suit, and sometimes was in drag and a dress — never in a dress that was attempting to look like a woman, but he would have lipstick and a crew-cut and a dress and high heels and silk stockings and a garter belt. On one occasion the two kiss, and you're not exactly sure — is this a homosexual kiss or is this a kiss with the boy in drag? I mean who are these people in relationship to each other? Does this occur inside the Moliere Don Juan or only in Schechner's Don Juan?

At the same time there was a chorus of the jilted, as I call them. It was a chorus mostly of women, but sometimes of men, sometimes in drag and sometimes not, who would always wear wedding rings on their left hand. And these were the women and people that Don Juan was constantly promising to marry. They also perform the chorus for *Don Giovanni*, and they follow him. At first there's just one or two and then there are more and more until at the end there is everybody in the play, except for Don Juan and Sganarelle, and they're going to chase him to hell. Their leader is the Commander, who in my production was played by a woman, Donna Elvira. And the basso profundo singer is singing 'Don Giovanni', but this woman is walking toward him as the statue of the Commander. And l made one change of the text — instead of saying the Commander is taking the form of a general or whatever, the Commander is taking the form of Kali, the goddess of revenge. But she's just a woman in an evening gown, and these women and men raise their hands, not in strength but in an almost crooked way with their wedding rings as they come after him.

So there's this multiplicity of jiltedness, a multiplicity of Juans, as it were, and he is kind of surrounded by his own images — even in that performance which would seem to be about such a singular figure. It also has two Sganarelles and I used them like sports people. In other words there were two Don Juans, and these were definitely two aspects of the character, whereas the Sganarelles were totally different. They were two women, one was very heavy and one was very slim and it was a long, long role and I just wanted the audience to get the experience of two interpretations. They would just, kind of, tap each other on the shoulder. They wouldn't know when, but one would substitute for the other, yet play the same character, like you'd have two quarterbacks on a football team or two left fielders. They each play their own way but it's the same position. We might see two interpretations of *Hamlet*, but usually we only see that in alternate productions. I wanted to give it in one production.

Then with the counter-text the whole text stopped, and these women enunciated their own objections to the Don Juan theme. Of course, that was to a certain degree co-opted by the production which a man was directing, but they were aware of that too, so they commented on that co-option. And we made the audience think, what were they enjoying here? We had discussions after the play and what people wanted to talk about mostly was not that I used *Don Giovanni* and *Don Juan*, not that I had a double Don Juan, not that there was gay kissing, not that there was another scene in which there was a lot of eroticism, but this counter-text — not the ideas it introduced, but how could I break the play that was so enjoyable and allow them to have their enjoyment challenged directly?

The audience, both males and females, often felt angry. And I said, that's good, I'm intrigued that you felt angry, that your visceral pleasure was broken and then you had to get back into it. Yet the production was very successful, we could sell as many tickets as we wanted to, it didn't break the pleasure so much that people weren't coming. To me that is the mark of a good production. That's not simply culinary, that is entertaining, and at a certain point also a little bit annoying, but still everybody wants to see it. That's the mark of a good production.

A lot of experimental American work opens up such possibilities by a sort of continual reinvention of itself formally.

Right. And a reflexivity. A consciousness of self to being itself. But, you see, among the experimenters I'm probably one of the more conservative in that way. I've always worked with classic texts. I like those texts and I like the Stories they tell, whether it's *The Bacchae* or *Macbeth* or *Don Juan* or *Oedipus*, to name some that I've directed, or modern classics like *The Balcony* or *The Maids*. It's ironic that people accuse me, mostly, of destroying texts, because I never just throw them away. I refuse to 'write my own plays', I refuse to not work with it. I like to take a text and deal with it, or as I could otherwise say dance with it, make it dance.

So you actually take things that have a certain value, a certain reverberation and strike up a radical dialogue with them.

I want to know that the people in the audience are replaying earlier experiences with this very story rather than getting away, as it were, free with a new story. From my earliest student days I was fascinated with that because I felt that the two greatest ages of theatre that I knew at that time (and it was confirmed when I went to Asia), namely the Greeks and the Elizabethans, always dealt with known stories. When Sophocles wrote his *Oedipus*, it wasn't the first *Oedipus*. We've lost the other plays but several people had told those stories in dramatic form and before that there was a myth that everyone new. Everyone knew the Trojan war stories which Euripides played with. Everyone knew English history — I mean they might not have known Shakespeare's exact version of it, but they knew who Henry IV was, they knew who Richard III was, they knew who Julius Caesar was, and I thought: why aren't these great writers writing their own plays like Eugene O'Neill does? Because I feel you get a double play, you get this blurred vision, you get this reverberation. The play is already being played inside the audience and then they have to see it again and like that. And you can rip the scrim and say, these objects that you thought were behind glass like in a museum are really in front of you. Not only that but they are being used in ways that maybe you think they shouldn't. And it's not simply an interpretation, it's not a slight tonal change, these are large changes, and yet the text and the story seem not to be uncomfortable. You're uncomfortable, but they're not uncomfortable. Don Juan isn't uncomfortable having a male lover. You may be. And what are you uncomfortable about? You're uncomfortable about having your expectations wrenched. But then as a director I have to be careful. I don't believe in wrenching too far, I mean not even in *Dionysus*. I like the thing to be a success.

But isn't that necessary? Because if you want to strike up a dialogue and a rapport with the audience you've got to strike up certain balances.

Right. And to me, again, I think it does relate to the theory in this regard, that the sister arts to theatre, not only dance but ritual on one side and sport on the other, are important. Sport is always a little bit antagonistic and it always arouses aggression, and the audience is not always in favour of everything: they're opposed to this side and they're in favour of that side, and ritual creates unity. So I play between the sportive, which is the disjunctive, and the ritual which is the unifying — and theatre and dance are in the middle there, but I want to make sure they, in a certain sense, reach out to their sister arts. Let's say theatre's great thing is narrativity, so I want the story, but I want to reach out to the 'we-don't-know-how-it's-going-to-turn-outness' of sport and the 'we-are-all-togetherness' of ritual.

That relates to another aspect of environmental theatre where you're using the formal language of the space and the relationship between audience and performer to create a certain sort of rapport, and that is in tension with playing with a form which the audience is familiar with and may be disturbed by.

Right. And it also takes, and this is another difference that I have — at least with the early performance art work and some of the Happenings — that I believe in trained performers, like I believe in trained athletes and trained ritualists, because the performer has to be really familiar with the space. The discomfort of the audience can't be through the awkwardness of the performer. If the performer is awkward it has to be a studied awkwardness, it has to be the awkwardness of the almost-error on the tightrope of the circus performer. It has to be the awkwardness of the clown, where you know that the awkwardness is intended. I don't like amateur performing.

So you're 'sharing with' the audience and at the same time you're challenging them.

Right. And the performer must be trained to be familiar with the space and with audience performer interactions. If one asks a question of the audience, of a spectator, you have to be prepared, really prepared, to deal with unexpected answers. You can't ask audiences rhetorical questions.

That raises the famous incident in Dionysus *when you continued the performance after Bill Shephard was kidnapped. Yet you had created a situation in which Shephard as Pentheus was attempting to leave with a member of the audience. Do you think that, given what you said, it was appropriate to continue the piece?*

You see this is where I live with history. It's what I did. I was in a buoyant mood that night, we all were, and the play at that point became a ritual whose logic had to be completed rather than an aesthetic event. And it just had to finish.

In a way you're talking about the fact that you've struck up a certain transaction with the audience.

Right. And they wanted us to finish, too. And there was somebody willing to do it. If I had asked, will anybody play Pentheus, and no-one had stepped forward, then it would have been a different situation. In other words, I wouldn't make a general rule of it. I'll say that is one of the contingencies. Like the other famous one, when *Commune* was stopped for three hours. But there was a general rule out of which we had set up a situation. You can't then break it. In other words, it's a kind of sacred bond. Otherwise you're made to look cheap. You've made this bond — unless there's a question of physical safety — and the only thing at stake was whether the performance would finish or not, so we had that bond.

That criticism, which is a very popular criticism, is arguably based on looking too closely at a single aspect, at the logic of the text, if you like, the performance score.
    And also the logic of the commercial theatre. We want to get home by the time the underground stops running, or this is not the way theatre 'should be', but it's really using a West End or Broadway model of the way theatre should be. It's not using a kind of ritual model of the way theatre should be. A ritual model would say that sometimes actions encounter obstacles. The action can't change, the obstacle must be overcome. Sometimes the only way you can overcome an obstacle is to sit by its side and wait for it to go away.

But there was something else at stake in that particular process, wasn't there? Which was the actor. Because Dionysus *was structured partly through rules and games, and the actor was actually going to pay a price if he was unable to leave the theatre. So, if he wins a way out...*
    Then he can get out. What I think people don't understand is that a performance can work according to several schemes at once. It can tell a narrative, but part of a narrative can be gamebound. So you can use game structure some of the time or in part of the space, and narrative structure at other times and in other parts of the space. You can play with all of these performative genres. Just like you could say *The Tooth of Crime* dealt with narrative structure, but also with performance in everyday life. That's what Spalding meant, that some of his 'real self' was engaged directly, not used as in character-actor training as a way to invest the character, but side by side with the character. Let's take Brecht seriously. You see, I always thought that Brecht had a theory but didn't live up to it. The self of the actor was also created by Brecht — in other words, there was Mother Courage and there was Weigel's comment. But it wasn't Weigel's comment, it was their agreed-upon theatrical comment. My only step was to be stupid in relation to Brecht. I said, well there's Hoss and there's Spalding Gray. But Spalding Gray is not going to be Richard's construction of Spalding, he's going to be Spalding's construction of Spalding. And in a certain sense that was the seed that led to these monologues, which is Spalding playing the multiple Spaldings.

*Which is apparent when you see a film of him doing it, but not from the monologue
itself when you read it.*

So that there I've reached out to the performative genre, the
performance in everyday life, role playing in everyday life, and brought that
into the theatre — without cancelling out the narrative, but to stand side by
side with the narrative.

In *Dionysus* there was the games. In *Don Juan* it wasn't performance
in everyday life, it was multiple personalities and quite a bit of audience
involvement because the space physically changed three times and the
audience had to get down off their bleachers, they had to move to certain
places. Some of them had to help shift the space, then they came back. Of
course, when I proposed this to the producers they were very, very hesitant.
They said, well audiences can't do this, they're paying money. I said, they'll
love it, they'll just love it, because they're constructing the very space they're
participating in. And of course they did love it. I mean, I wouldn't do it in an
old persons' home, but this was a college.

It has more than physical implications to do that, doesn't it?

Yes, of course. It has a ritual-communal, shared-work implication. It
also involves the contradiction that this physical labour preceded a selection
from *Don Giovanni* and Moliere, which is a very nice contrast. Because I do
believe that contrasting actions stimulate thought and feeling. I don't want
a big unity, I'm not a Wagnerian, I don't want a wash of unity. I know that
there is art based on that, but mine is based more on dialectical contradiction
and resolution, though the resolution is temporary, too. In life we're standing
on solid ground, but the ground is an iceberg and it's melting and moving.

*Doesn't this bring us back to this idea of a multiplicity — where you are on shifting
ground as you watch and as you go along with the process?*

Right. And you're actually creating the ground that you're on.

*And you become aware of creating the ground that you're on as you go along. Which
raises another issue. In* The End of Humanism, *you say that during the 1970s
American artists 'fell into a formalist deep freeze', that their work 'did not manifest
significant content' and that 'we are still waiting for the formalist experiments to be
turned into content'. I wonder if your feelings about this work have changed, given
this idea that it is important to reveal this kind of process?*

This is seven or eight years ago. I don't know if you know any of
Philip Auslander's writing as a critic. He's written about resistant and
transgressive art works. And talking about the Wooster Group, he said that
at the level of overt content there isn't content there, but that they are

transgressive in their very existence. That makes a political statement, and the audience, just like when they went to punk rock when it was around, knew that they were making a political statement which wasn't encoded in the words or the gestures but in the very existence and style of the mode of performing. I would agree with that. At the same time, though, I think certain formalist stuff has become even less contentful. Unfortunately, I think a lot of the later Wilson, and some Philip Glass, has apparent content, like *Satyagraha* (1980) or *the CIVIL warS* (1984), but doesn't have any real content. The scrim is even thicker and the politics is converted into beauty just like — this is an horrendous example — if you showed Auschwitz in slow motion, and you could look at its structure and in a certain sense be distanced from the horror. When we do a lot of stop action and slow motion in film technique what it does is aestheticize.

So I am still of two minds. For instance, I think that certain groups and people — Lee Breuer, Elizabeth LeCompte, Karen Finley, those three performance artists — have moved to making their work transgressive or at least resistant: and therefore it's not the overt content but the style that raises political questions. But others — Wilson's operas, Philip Glass's — have really been absorbed by their producing organisations, and their aesthetic or their political values are no different that those of La Scala or whoever is producing them. No matter how spectacular a Wooster Group production, it wouldn't be accepted by the patrons of the Metropolitan Opera. It couldn't be performed there. It's not just a physical thing, they're too transgressive of the values of the Opera, which are 'the values of beauty'. The Wooster Group is not beautiful. And in that sense they're political. Now at the same time there are emerging new forms of narrativity and content.

One of the things that has happened in the UK is that as performance has become more recognised you've had this coming together of theatre forms and the sort of questions that performance art raises. And with someone like Impact Theatre you find a play between narrative and image, which has that aspect of multiplicity.

Well, that interests me. The theatre I've seen here that most impressed me a few years back was IOU. I really enjoyed that kind of work which seemed to me to be both environmental — I saw the piece that they did in the railroad yard in Copenhagen — and extraordinarily powerful and beautiful, with a lot of social content and ironic content. It's not heavy-handed. I'm not talking about, you know, Brecht's Lehrstucke or something like that, which I enjoy in its own way, but about a much more subtle kind of content that is, let's say, socio-political. Neither psychological, as in let's say Tennessee Williams, the classic psychological naturalist play, nor a

Lehrstucke, but a kind of socio-political or anthropological drama which is
occurring.

Much of my work has been concerned with performance art, particularly looking at
Kaprow, Beuys, Vito Acconci, Ulay and Abramovic and a number of others. And
the work is so ephemeral. It's interesting to set up one kind of information against
another in an attempt to begin to ask questions about what it does.

  You see, when you talk about that work, I would say the emphasis
is on the aftermath. That work's emphasis is whether it gets documented
in *High Performance*, and who talks about it. You have a picture of Ulay
and Abramovic, they're standing naked in a door and you pass through
[*Imponderabilia* 1977]. Fifty people, two hundred people did it, and that's all.
But that has caused a great stir about body space and so on in its aftermath.
Similarly Kaprow's pieces, some of which nobody has seen, couldn't see —
the walk in the desert watching the footprints — it's the aftermath.

  A lot of that kind of performance art — the art-life thing, the
confrontation stuff — is really about its documentation and dissemination
and aftermath. It's kind of an example which becomes a concept. It's not a
performance. Like the opposite, where the performance is the thing, is a West
End or Broadway show, where if they could they'd like to have no rehearsal,
no training, no aftermath at all, just an endless run because then they make
the most money. So they do have rehearsals, of course, but they have them
in order to get to the run. So the emphasis there is on what I call the show.
Stanislavski's emphasis, on the other hand, was on rehearsal: he loved to
rehearse. One got the feeling he didn't care that much about what finally
was there.

Yet a later piece by Abramovic and Ulay, say Nightsea Crossing, *would seem to be*
a different kind of thing. There it's not such an ephemeral statement in the sense that
it's made, disappears, then you actually contemplate it later. The thing itself is an act
of contemplation, and if you see the documentation you actually lose the tensions,
which serve to draw you into the process of contemplation.

  There may be the other thing, too, of a complete ephemerality that
doesn't count at all. I don't know how I'd put that in my scheme.

But isn't there a concern running through this work which connects a lot of the
forms, which is to do with the experience of being there for the time of the piece, the
address to the fact you're there, and the way the rules of the piece are shaping your
experience.

  To a certain degree. But if that were true then you couldn't write
about it, there'd be no documentation. If that's really what mattered, then
you were either there or you weren't there. But since there's a good deal of
documentation it is obviously also aimed at the people who aren't there. You

could say that a Broadway play is much more only about the people who were there: the producers don't give a shit whether it's written about except in the form of reviews that bring people in. They really are concentrating on the event. And they want to keep the event running as long as possible. But this other stuff — the very fact that you can write a dissertation on it means that enough documentation exists that you can say something about it. If it was truly just a present moment thing we wouldn't know about it. I assume there are some such performances. I think Kaprow actually does do some such performances, we just don't know about them.

I would associate that kind of work in Kaprow with the game performances for performers only.
     But he does it when we don't know about it. In other words. he now does kind of meditative works and lives part of his life as a kind of ongoing meditation in that sense.

That is another sort of work again from the ones like Self-Service *(1967) from the mid-sixties.*
     Of course. It's different from *Self-Service*. But that is also highly documented. It's for performers only, but it's highly documented.

It exists in two worlds, then, doesn't it?
     Three. Because it actually has a pre-score too.

Right. But it does exist as a performance as well. A performance that was experienced by a group of participants. As well.
     But its emphasis isn't there, because you can repeat *Self-Service* again and again and again and get more and more participants. But really he didn't make much effort to do that.

No, but if you did do it again and again and again, if you do it with a different group of people it becomes a different experience. And the focus lies in the experience of each group of participants.
     But that's an if. If he did that it would be that kind of performance. But he didn't do that. The experience is still important to the people who did it, but it wasn't so important for Kaprow to give that experience to many people that he did it ten times. It was important for him to have it and see it and to let it go.

But only doing it once also has certain consequences for the people who are doing it.
     Absolutely. But among the consequences is that it's only a small group that gets to do it. In other words, although the show itself is not very widespread, it's reverberations are.

Yes. One of the things that strikes me about the kind of pluralism inherent within this work, is that none of these things necessarily has a primacy.

Well, no, no, no. Let's say that none of these things have what we would, philosophically, call an 'a priori' or absolute primacy. One may be primary for you, one may be primary for the other person. It's different to say they do not have primacy — this is this democracy argument again. To say nothing has a primacy means even for the person for whom it's primary it's not primary. I vote in the United States. I know that my vote 'doesn't count', and neither does yours and neither does yours and neither does yours. In some vague sense they all count but basically they don't count. That's different from saying my vote counts but only for me. These performance events absolutely count to the people who make them and go to them. But that primacy does not extend to the general public. In other words, they're not masterpieces, and in a sense designed to be not masterpieces. Artaud's influence has shown even there: No More Masterpieces. So that they have an immediacy and an experiential primacy which is what Clifford Geards would call 'local knowledge'. Local: very important. And in that sense they are primary in their local community, even if it's a community of one or ten or what have you. But they're not structurally primary elsewhere. In other words you can't still say that this performance is that much better than that performance because the two performances don't really exist in the same arena to be compared. They have stepped outside the kind of capitalist competition which hierarchizes everything and says this is privileged and this is not.

In that sense there's a politics implicit in this, but it's not a democratic politics, it's more a meditative politics, a kind of Zen illumination: for those who have done it, they're illuminated, for those who do it some place else, they have another illumination. But it's not that you have to meet and say, my illumination was better than yours. So it's neither democratic nor hierarchical. It's a third situation of intense local experience. Now I would say that, although I have no way of restructuring the whole world, that is not a bad model. That's not a bad education towards a world in which I would like to see multiple cultures and multiple values co-exist. And I would like to see some general ground-rules because I come from where I come from.

But let's take a really tough one, a really tough one. Clitoridectomies in portions of East Africa. Now, am I to go in and say, no, you're never to do that operation, it's hard for those women, which I believe it is? Especially as there are, as I saw in a documentary, certain women, Muslim women, saying we've had this for ourselves, and we want this for our daughters. And I could say that's barbarous, you know, people want to do a lot of things, the

Christian saints in the middle ages wanted to see themselves with arrows put through them. And yet at the same time I am wondering which is worse, the clitoridectomy or sending in an army to prevent it.

Now what I can do is send in an argument to prevent it. I can ask feminists to argue, I can ask other people to argue. but at what level does one intervene? Now, let's take another situation: apartheid in South Africa. There I would send in the army to intervene. Now what's the difference between clitoridectomy and apartheid? It's very hard for me to locate philosophically the difference: one is an obviously oppressed group of people who are fighting with stones, whatever they can, and an obviously offensive government and an obviously blanket racism. You don't have very many blacks coming out and saying we're for this system. While in the other situation there is a cultural habit in which those who are being operated upon, some of them, say, we don't consider this wrong, we consider this part of our tradition. So I'm a relativist only to a certain degree.

Isn't there the idea of a 'doubleness' in this? Because on the one hand you're a relativist, on the other hand you have to acknowledge that you are a member of a culture yourself.

Right. But I have to put a leash on my culture to a certain degree. I also recognise that the particular culture I'm into is one that has a history of violent intervention in other people's cultures, and therefore as a member of that culture I have to restrain my moralising. A lot of this intervention has been moralistic intervention. Indeed, I think that many British felt that it was a white man's burden, that they were leading India out of the Dark Ages. And there are still missionaries being sent out, many missionaries who think that unless you believe in the blood of Jesus you're really gonna go to hell. I think that that's a lousy intervention in other people's beliefs. So I have to say that before I will intervene the pressure has to be great. In South Africa it's great enough. In East Africa it's not great enough — for me — to intervene except by argument. So that's what I mean. So I'm not an absolute relativist, but I am a multiplist if you want to say that, and I want to be responsive to letting people — to get back to performance art — see a world where contradictory systems can exist without always being hierarchized with the supposed top one trying to influence, overcome, and change the supposed bottom one.

What I'm suggesting about looking at performance art is not simply that the performance is its aim. The whole point about that field of work is that it exists in a variety of forms. George Brecht's work is a good example of this, where the whole thing is a collection of interpenetrating fields and interpenetrating pieces. And you can examine certain things within it which you find in common with certain other things which themselves are parts of other interpenetrating pieces and fields. But to acknowledge the variety within the work means looking at the fact that these things have, at various points, looked toward an action and in doing so have questioned the primacy of the object or exploded their definition.

I agree, that's what they do. And in so exploding the definition liberate some other, later on, to look at the performance in some new and different way. Masterpiece performances tend to want to confirm a genre in such a superb way that one almost says, what's the use of doing another one of these things? I mean what's the use of directing another production after Chekhov's *The Cherry Orchard* has been directed by Stanislavski? You'd no more want to do that than you'd want to paint another Botticelli. While the work you're talking about, in a certain sense, liberates one from the masterpiece. Not by destroying it, 'a la Artaud' but by questioning the very basis of making art so that somebody else can also question the basis of making art.

Yes. And any work that embraces this multiplicity begins to confuse that kind of approach. Instead of the spectator being dominated by the work of art, it draws him in to become a part of the process of its definition.

Exactly. In other words, at a certain level I want an art-work to dominate, I also broadcast moods and so on — yet one of the cores of environmental theatre staging is that there is no privileged place. And the privileged place actually is the place that's also most submissive in the proscenium theatre — the place from which the view is best, which means it's the place from which you're going to be most dominated by what's coming from the stage.

Now I want a theatre in which there's no such place. In each place the spectator is constructing her own kind of performance — roughly the same as the one next to her, but still different enough that the balance must be mutual. We are each dominating each other, yielding to each other, and there's no single point of perspective, therefore there's no single meaning. Whether you watch *Don Juan* from up here or down here is much different, and it isn't better from up here than down here or over there. It's different but not better.

The other thing I wanted to ask you about was performance training. Obviously when you were with The Performance Group you developed particular ways of working and performers did train with the group. How do you find working with performers who have been trained in mainstream theatre?

Hard. In other words I know that in my life I've made a big choice. I could start another group, possibly, but if I were to do that the advantage, of course, would be not only to have trained performers but performers training the way I would want them trained. The disadvantage would be that I would be less able to do theatre anthropology, travelling, less able to focus a lot of my loving energy on my family. There are lots of trade-ins. So if I'm ever going to run a group again I won't until my children are at least in High School. Either you fold them into your theatre or you ignore them, and I don't want to fold young children into my way of working because they don't have any choice in that. It's just my own decision. So I've given up the possibility of actors who will be as responsive to my way of thinking as The Performance Group was, after all those years of training. On the other hand there are certain advantages. I don't have to worry about where the next meal is coming from for all the actors. I can experiment in other ways. But there's no doubt that I miss working with people with whom there's... not only a rapport, but also tensions, which are known tensions.

Wasn't it part of the vocabulary with which you worked?

Yes. And there comes a point where you can let them go. What you train people in, finally, are the habits of working, not particular techniques. Yes, they get some techniques. but basically it is the habit of working. You come in, you clean up, you do your warm up, you work with the other people. After working with people for a long time, when they kind of select themselves out, you come to a group where if I'm a half-hour late they're working for a half-hour. If it's this other kind of group, if I'm a half-hour late they're sitting round having coffee. They wouldn't think of beginning. So there's still the attitude of the boss and the labourers, while when you have your own group there's not that attitude. The other thing I miss is that when people really know each other they can very subtly play off each other. When people don't really know each other it's an interesting interaction but it doesn't have the same kind of intimacy, and you don't have time to wait to bring things out of people over the long run. In other words, there are certain performers who I was working with and I knew it would be two or three plays down the line before they would shine. I'm willing to wait, just like a sports coach. But if you're only going to play once with them, then little sins and little errors are very bothersome. You don't have that time to wait. So those things I miss, and I don't think there's any replacement for that. I mean the replacement doesn't come in the art work, it comes in the writing work.

Has working through towards Theatre and Anthropology *changed your idea of what a performance training ought to consist of?*

Not really. Because performance training takes place in different cultures. In other words, if you mean training in 'Euro-American performance', which is the one that I practice in, then, no, I think since we don't in theatre have codified forms as we do in dance you have to start with basic vocal and body work, and you have to do group work. In dance it's different, if you're going to be in a ballet school there's a shared codified vocabulary. In other cultures — the Guru Shishi relationship in India, where you work with one teacher, or the joining of a Noh school, a family — I recognise many, many different kinds of training. But I don't think that too many of them are appropriate for Euro-American culture except the kind we have and direct transmission. I mean I don't believe you can just go to a school and get training, it depends who is training there and who that person trained with. It's not the name of the school. It's the particular person. As Victor Turner would say, 'chaps not maps'.

Who are the individuals who were important to you in that way?

Grotowski foremost. Although I only actually physically worked with him for three or four weeks, they were a very important four weeks at the very beginning of The Performance Group. I used to take the work that I did with him in the afternoon and imitate it and vary it and give it to the people I was working with in the nascent Performance Group in the evening. Kirsten Linklater, who did a brief vocal workshop with The Performance Group and helped me and them learn a certain kind of vocal training and panting. A yoga master named Krishna Macharia in Madras, whose system is encoded in two books by one of his Indian students — the basic yoga breathing and yoga assonance I learned with him, and that entered into my life and into my performer training.

And into your philosophy?

You see, what's interesting is that yoga, hatha yoga, is not so much a philosophy as a daily practice. So it entered in as a practice and the practice itself is the philosophy — it's not that there's a philosophy that informs the practice. Breathing is the philosophy. You can philosophise about it but its essence is that thought is in the body, as it were, and in the breathing. So in that sense it very much entered in because I believe thought is in the body. I learned that in 1972, but I worked with Grotowski in 1967. Then, having said you only learn from people and not from books, there were some books that were important. *The Theatre and Its Double*, which I read early, was important to me. The Greek plays, the sheer emotional monumentality of those plays, and especially *The Bacchae* of course. Many others of Euripides' plays, and *The Oresteia*, and some of Sophocles, *Oedipus* and *Oedipus at Colonus*, and *Philoctetes*. I never directed *Colonus*, but *Oedipus* and *Philoctetes* I directed. So those are some of the key kind of people that I owe allegiance to.

Another person who was important to me was John Cage. I only had one extended conversation with him — Michael Kirby and I interviewed him in 1963, I think, and we published it in 1964. His influence was related to the whole notion of indeterminacy. The notion of a certain kind of, if you will, pluralism, in which silence has as much right to exist as noise. The street itself can offer spectacle if one is just open to it, and Cage's disciplined receptivity to that, which is usually repressed or not heard, is very important.

LINDA MONTANO

Linda Montano, Performance Artist, has taken a vow to not give any interviews for 7 years 1991–1998, while performing

ANOTHER SEVEN YEARS OF LIVING ART

Figure 37 Linda Montano, *POST-MENOPAUSAL 1991, Linda as Lenny & Linda as Dancer* by Annie Sprinkle, Collage: Linda Montano (1991) (courtesy: Linda Montano).

MARINA ABRAMOVIC

Following her training at the Academy of Fine Arts, Belgrade, from 1965 to 1970, and post-graduate studies in Zagreb, Marina Abramovic developed her work toward performance through highly innovative time-based presentations realised in Belgrade. In 1973, Abramovic took up a teaching post at the Academy of Fine Arts in Novi Sad, and, without direct contact with the Body Art being developed in the West, extended her work into performance and video. Following her presentation of work in Western Europe, Abramovic met the German artist F. Uwe Laysiepen (Ulay) in Amsterdam in 1975. As a consequence of their meeting, Abramovic and Ulay agreed to collaborate on all their subsequent work, and over the next twelve years their performances, videos, and films, were shown widely in Europe, America and Australia. Rejecting rehearsal, repetition, or pre-determined endings, these works presented an audience with moments of physical and mental intensity frequently developed to an extreme over extended periods of time. In 1981, Abramovic and Ulay began their performance of *Nightsea Crossing*, a piece in ninety parts completed over a five-year period. Their last collaborative work, *The Great Wall Walk*, was completed in 1988. Since that time, Abramovic has continued to present performance, 'transitory objects' and object-based installations, as well as video and video installation. More recently, Abramovic has made two theatre pieces, *Biography* (1994) and *Delusional* (1994). The interview-text that follows is in two parts. The framing text is drawn from a conversation with Marina Abramovic recorded in London in October 1994. Intercut into this discussion is an interview with Marina Abramovic and Ulay, recorded in December 1983 in Amsterdam, at the time of their performance of *Nightsea Crossing* and preparations for *The Great Wall Walk*.

*　　　　*　　　　*

What was it that brought you to performance?
　　　　It was very simple in a way. At the age of twelve I had already had an exhibition of work. Painting was very attractive to me. I know that I started painting the sky. First the clouds, then removing the clouds — just a kind of blue monochrome. At one point, looking at the sky, I saw the planes passing and leaving this white track, which was almost like a drawing. I was

so impressed with this that I wanted to make a kind of concert. What I was interested in was that you could see the process — you could see things happening and dissolving all at the same time. So I went to the military base and asked for fifteen planes — and they sent me home. They asked — do you know how much this will cost?

Then, for some time, I did projects on paper, drawings of the sky, using fire, ice, and water. None of these projects were possible, basically because of the restrictions on things. Then I started shifting my interests to the idea of sound — like putting the sound of a bridge falling down every three minutes with an actual bridge. As you cross the bridge you hear the sound of the bridge breaking. This kind of shift. I realised a piece with one house in the middle of Belgrade. I placed speakers on a house and played the sound of the house falling down. This installation occurred for only one day — because everybody in the neighbourhood reacted very violently. It reminded them of the war and they removed it.

What date was this?

This was all around '68, '69, '70 to '71. I was interested in changing visual and acoustic information. My last one was in the Cultural Centre in Belgrade. This was a place — a kind of hall — where people waited to go to the theatre, the cinema. They could have a coffee, sit, read a newspaper. It was a meeting place. I placed speakers there with the sound of an airport. It was a very cold, specific sound, telling all the passengers immediately to go to Gate 242 because the plane was leaving to Tokyo, Bangkok, and Hong Kong. I mean, at Belgrade there were only two gates at the time — and every few minutes there would be this information. So everybody waiting there became imaginary passengers, waiting for this trip. It was a way of going out. Yugoslavia during this time was really quite difficult. I was dealing with structures — socially, politically, culturally, you know, family. Everything was involved.

Did the work put you into difficulty?

Extremely. And that gives you a lot of energy later on. But its hard at the time, because you are rejected — to the point of questioning whether or not you should be put into a mental hospital.

After the sound work, there was a natural development toward work with the body. The effect on me from my first performance with the body was almost a state of shock. I had such a strong experience that I knew almost immediately it was the only way I could really deal with the public — because through it I could come to an ecstatic state. I could never reach this when I was just alone in the studio with my work.

What was the first performance?

The first performance with the body was *Rhythm 10* — the work with the knives. And — I don't know — the reality of the thing was a kind of immediate transmission of energy — the directness of the media and also the temporality, because it is only when you are there — the rest is just a memory. All this made such a strong impact. Painting, the illusional system, just didn't get to the point.

RHYTHM 10

The Content of the Action

1   I put a sheet of white paper on the floor
2   I put twenty knives of various sizes and shapes on the paper
3   I switch on the tape recorder
4   I varnish my left hand nails with blue nail varnish

The Action

I take a knife and stab it between two fingers of my left hand. Every time I cut myself I take another knife. When I have used all the knives (i.e. change of all the rhythms), I switch on the tape-recorder reproducing the recorded sound of the Action. Then I switch on another tape-recorder.

The second part of the Action consists of repeating the game while listening to the recorded sound-rhythm of the knives. Following the rhythm of the knives' stabs I bring myself into the tempo of the previous rhythm, stabbing simultaneously with it.

I switch on the second tape recorder where the rhythm of the stabs has been doubled.

Marina Abramovic, *RHYTHM 10* (1973) (courtesy of the artist).

Also, theatre was an absolute enemy. It was something bad, it was something we should not deal with. It was artificial. All the qualities that performance had were unrehearsable. There was no repetition. It was new for me and the sense of reality was very strong. We refused the theatrical structure. The performances were always in an empty space with no lights, and even the video recording was one-to-one. I would ask for the camera to be put in one static position, and then left.

Were you aware of performance work outside of Yugoslavia at this time?

Not at the beginning. A few years later at Edinburgh I met Joseph Beuys for the first time, as well as Tadeusz Kantor and Hermann Nitsch. Then, it was like — there's a family, we were the same tribe. So it was very, very good.

Were any particular performances by other artists important to the development of your work?

I like Vito Acconci's work very much. He was one of the first to propose that the body is a place. His works are aggressive, but not in a physical way. It is more mentally. And from this came the whole idea of the body as a material, the body as a material through which you can transmit something. In sculpture it is the stone or clay or whatever, and here it is the body — make a drawing with the body, cut the body, open it, see what pain is, what the body is. Just exploring all the possibilities — the mental, physical limits, everything together. So Acconci began this kind of research.

After that, there was a very important event with Acconci, Dennis Oppenhiem and Terry Fox in the seventies, when they performed in the same place [*Environmental Surfaces: Three Simultaneous Situational Enclosures*, Reese Palley Gallery, New York, January 1971]. Acconci turned around like a clock for one hour [*Second Hand*], Terry Fox was making bread from soap [*Celler*] — it was a kind of impossible, alchemical mystery. Oppenhiem had a tarantula moving toward his face down a tube and he blew little balls of hair in its way, keeping it from biting his face [*Extended Armor*]. It was really good work. Then Chris Burden — very radical. Like the shot to his arm [*Shoot* (1971)], the crucifixion on the Volkswagen [*Trans-fixed* (1974)], the piece where he put electricity and water on the floor and left it up to the public to decide what would happen [*Prelude to 220, or 110* (1971)]. To me, they're very important pieces. Then with Gina Pane, the milk piece, when she drank milk and spat it out, irritating her system until she actually spat out a mixture of milk and blood — like the two liquids in the body [*Le Lait Chaud* (1972)]. Then Charlemagne Palestine and the *Body Music* [*Body Music I* (1973) *Body Music II* (1974)]. It was absolutely charismatic, shamanistic. Even now — and even though the tapes of this period are of such bad quality — they give you more energy than many live performances.

What was it that brought you to the work with Ulay?

It was very much to do with love. Also, I'd come to a point in my life when I was going very far in my performances. I was always considering — really — going to the point of playing Russian Roulette in the performance situation. I could see the chance that I'd kill myself, that I'd die. So it was, I

Figure 38 Marina Abramovic and Ulay *Nightsea Crossing*, documenta 7, Orangerie, Kassel, June/August/September, 1982, 21 days (courtesy: Marina Abramovic).

MARINA ABRAMOVIC AND ULAY

How long will a performance of Nightsea Crossing be on any given day?

U: By preference seven hours a day. We adopted a seven hour day because most institutions would be open for seven hours.

MA: 10.00 am until 5.00 pm. The seven hours was also important because we wanted to avoid people seeing the beginning and end. When they come to the gallery we are already there, like any other piece. And when they go at 5.00, the gallery is closed and the guard comes and tell us it's the end. The public only see one image.

U: Which is a motionless image. They do not see us sitting down or standing up. You see, the main interest is the process of being motionless for a long, long period of time. The fact of sitting on the chair is not as interesting as the process. After sitting for two, three or four hours, something happens. And that process is only possible for the audience or the spectator, again, if they are willing to sit too.

MA: I think the public wants to see a beginning and they want to see an end.

Did you state that you would be sitting motionless for the duration of the performance?

MA: No. So people are always waiting for something to happen. But when they finally come to realise that that's the reality of the thing, they start making contact with the piece itself. In *Nightsea Crossing*, after ten, fifteen, forty-eight hours, the whole space is charged with energy. And that energy affects you. To charge a space with energy needs a long time. After ten or twenty days the energy in the space becomes so dense from the repetition of the same thing that people get really affected. Something has changed — and it's not of the material world.

U: We never rehearse performances. In fact, the beginning of the performance is when we enter our own physical and mental construction. It's the first time that we've experienced that — as it is for the spectator. And it is an experience that can go in very different directions. You see, we are very aware of the spectator, and we work with the spectator. We work for the spectator, through our consciousness. We don't sit and daydream, we are not in a trance. We just sit.

Is it important that the spectator is aware of the context of the particular action they meet — that the performance is extended over 90 days and will occur in so many different places?

MA: They can know this or not know this. It's not important. It's just the presence, the feeling for each of them. The idea of our sitting is that we're present in that moment with the mind and the body. What you see is exactly what is happening. And that is *the* reality. There are very few who can actually sit and just be without putting a story into the mind. In that moment, when you sit with the body *and* the mind, you manage to make contact with us, because you're taking the reality as it is without any projections. It's like *now*, it's *now*. And that's what the sitting is about. It's very difficult to be present, because your mind is thinking all the time, every second.

suppose, also at that time a lucky solution. I just treated my body as if it was without limits. In my life there was a very strong male aspect. In all the performances there were a lot of strengths — the force, energy, or whatever.

And meeting Ulay — at one point it went back to a female energy because he was the male. Then there was the idea of the hermaphrodite as the perfect human being, you know, who has both sexes and is self-sufficient. And of the two bodies coming into one. To me this was one step farther than just doing your own work. It was very important. Then, we absolutely stopped doing any of our own work and for twelve years we only did the work together. So when we finished our relationship, it was a big problem for me to go back to my own work, because I felt it was a regression. It was going back again.

What were the contexts out of which Nightsea Crossing *arose?*

MA: The change in our work came when we went to Australia and lived in the desert. The heat was enormous, like 50, 55 degrees Celsius. Physically, you could not walk. We were in such circumstances that, actually, only our minds were functioning. And that completely opened another world to us. That connected straight into certain functions. It's almost physical, the mind. In our performance we had just reached the point where we could not go farther with the body, and now we have the whole other part of the mind.

I'm interested in the use of objects and symbolism in the performance.

MA: We are very impressed by the rituals of certain people, like the Aborigines, because they have a certain pattern of doing things, of using symbols in a way that they really function.

U: We have been trying to integrate certain symbols into our work. You see, the symbols natives use all have a very practical function. They're very practical. I think the symbols — the material, the colour, the shape, the placement of the symbol, and the approach to the symbol, has to be perfect. Then the symbol will be able to generate power. But only if it is perfect. If it is placed in the right time and the right place, and if the symbol itself consists of a certain kind of material and shape and form and colour. Then it can work. I mean, if you abuse a symbol it can bring harm.

MA: Yes, very much.

In what way?

U: I think, if you are exposed, if you are seriously busy with symbols and like to place them and like to give them function and you respect that function in a certain way, then you should be very serious about it. I have respect for symbols, because I have witnessed natives operating with symbols and how powerful a symbol can be.

MA: You see, the natives are completely connected with the earth's energy and the flow of nature. And from that they generate the whole thing. And in the simple way that we work, we work to be receptive to this.

U: I think that certain faculties which we call 'supernatural' in natives are faculties that are dormant in us —

MA: And for them they're natural.

U: For them it's a natural reality. It's a part of their daily existence.

MA: We feel, as performance artists, that we can't paint any more, because we really believe that objects are an obstacle. If you make an object, you put all your generating energy into the object. In the past, that was why many objects had this radiant energy, this power. But now, for many people the work is personal, because we don't really know the source, so the object simply becomes an obstacle. It's much more important to transform yourself first. Work on yourself. And afterwards you won't need the object to transmit the real idea — or whatever you want — the truth. You can do the work with just the power of your mind. You can transmit certain things, just directly, mind to mind. We don't have anything between us.

And your work and relationship with Ulay ended at the culmination of the Chinese Wall walk.

That was that. Saying goodbye.

Was that conceived of as an ending?

We wanted to have two separate experiences come together to make one work. But the problem was that it took eight years to get permissions from the Chinese Government and in this period our relationship changed completely. We were at the end of our relationship when the Chinese said yes. So the only way that we could do it was to end. It was like the perfect form for this scenario, for ending the relationship. It was dramatic and it was painful — everything together. And then, after this, the only way I could find things out was to create work which was actually directly to others.

So has the way you consider the audience changed? Or the way you consider the work?

The work. Now, the product that I give to the audience is for them to use. Before it was one-to-one, and now it's me and everybody else in relation. It is not closed.

Does that take you back into installation work?

No. I have two functions. One function — I'm always working with transformation. I have to transform something. So, the performance is one way of transforming work, in certain stages, psychologically, and going to another type of reality. Really, performance is to do with change and transformation. And some of those witnessing this could go with this. But the public always, until now, have had this role of being voyeurs, of not actually participating. They are always at a distance. But it is a time, now, especially at the end of the century, for the public to take a completely active part. So I'm building these kinds of objects. I don't call them sculptures, I call them transitory objects. They are almost like scenography, like a kind of floor, like a platform on which one can experience the quality of the material simply with the mind and the body, and go through this transformation.

Figure 39 Marina Abramovic *Wounded Geod* 1994. Iron/Geod. (courtesy: Thomas Adel).

It always seemed to me that that opening up was implicit in Nightsea Crossing *whereby, in watching, the viewer was participating — the viewer was actually doing what you, as the artists, were doing in the performance.*

    Yes. Exactly. That's the seat of the thing. It's really interesting — but I want more from the public. Duchamp always said that to understand the work of art, the public has to be creative as well. We always forget this part. The public have to go with it. The more participation, the more energy there is, the farther I can go. The public's understanding is crucial. If all you have is distance, it is like an impasse.

MA: We are now engaged in the biggest project of our lives — which is the walk of the Chinese Wall. And the walk in China will deal with the exposure to the elements.

U: You know the concept?

That you will walk towards each other, from each end of the wall, over a period of one year — photographed by satellite —

U: And we will collect materials, using the oldest technique of copying reality, of imprinting. And satellite photography is the most advanced technology of documenting. So we will use this too.

MA: The Wall is 5,000 kilometres long, from the Gobi desert to the sea. So it is exactly between the elements of fire and water — one part of the Wall starts in the sea and one finishes in the desert. And the start of the wall is called the Dragon-Head and on the door to the wall is written 'The First Path on Earth' and on the other one is 'The Heroic Path to the Sky'. So Ulay will start at The Heroic Path to the Sky and I will start at The First Path on Earth and we will actually meet in the middle, going through the four seasons like four stages of life. The idea is that we are going to be exposed for one year to those forces. And with that will come a certain mental and physical transformation — through that walk. And that is the experience that we will give to the public afterwards. You see, you must work on your own change in order to give. And the walk is actually such a preparation — for that change.

U: I think it's very important that after the Chinese walk, we will be exposed again to an audience — an audience which will be invited for talks and discussions. I think the whole model of this relation between the initiator — a person of particular experience — and an audience, the whole concept, is of a very special kind.

MA: We have been working a lot with the male and female principle — not just presenting our egos or our real relationship, but acting as a kind of example for the principle itself. So, you see, the Wall represents the female principle — the female as it is materialised at the Dragon-Line is water, while the male principle is represented as air. The Dragon-Head is the male and the Dragon-Tail is the female. So that, actually, I will be walking as a female on the male part, and Ulay will be a male walking on the female part of the Wall, and the coming together is the unifying of the principle of the mental and the spiritual.

So, again, it's a taking on of a ritual function.

MA: Yes. Not to be the 'I', but just to be part of the natural principle and to make that exchange. It's a de-personalisation. That's why they use masks in ritual — so that they leave the person behind and become *the* element.

U: I look for so much in art. But I think it's important to subtract.

MA: If you subtract you come to the point where you can really see the essence of the thing, where everything starts. You can see the roots of what you're doing. To me, the experience of Rothko paintings is really very, very strong. He really worked with essence.

U: Maybe not too many people have the courage to take away. It feels almost natural to all of us living in a time of a materialistic philosophy to add. We only have respect for goods, for cargo, for objects. I don't think too many people have the courage to renounce, because by subtracting you're making more space for other people. So I think by being very quiet, no action, that it is a good thing.

MA: And the Chinese Wall is, you know, it's a pioneering — it's just a very small step to count, maybe, in this lifetime, I don't know — but this is what we're trying to do.

U: You see, for non-English speaking people, as we are, the term 'performance' exists only in the visual arts context. But I think, besides an art-work, 'performance' can indicate a great moment of behaviour or concentration. The point is, if you do the performance for an extended period of time, then its effect is much greater. Art is nothing but a vehicle. It has its limits. And often it is very limited. But still it may be — Kandinsky would say — a mighty agent. And I agree with that. In the earlier days, I approached art as the realisation of art. I was looking for a focus, and once I had a focus it would absorb me. There's a process in which you're totally involved, and then there's the product. Later on, though — actually it was in the desert — I started to become much more interested in the art of realisation. Rather than the realisation of art, the art of realisation.

So the time passes, and after all this time I find I'm fascinated by the theatre structure.

How do you mean?
I've made two theatre pieces. The first is called *Biography*. In it I play my life in the theatre, with all the performances I've done and video clips in one hour and twenty minutes. The second piece is called *Delusional*, which I play with 400 rats live on the stage.

Biography is the perfect structure — artist, performer, plays her own life. Why should I trust anybody else to play my own life? So in the piece I mix real performance art with the theatrical. It's a very interesting structure. Like the star that I cut with a razor blade, I cut one more time, in the theatre — and it's real. It's not fake blood, it's the real thing. The public is in total shock because they're so used to this symbolic language of the theatre. With the knife piece, *Rhythm 10*, I play it live, but I play it for five minutes, and I reach an incredible intensity. I have to shrink the performances in time and play one performance after another like a video clip, but with real intensity.

It took a great deal of courage for me to do this. When I played *Biography*, it was like a cleaning process, because I could not talk to Ulay at all for six years after we split. There was a lot of pain. And when I say goodbye to Ulay in this *Biography*, I really mean goodbye. It is a public statement too, that I have finished with this period of my life. And then I called him and I told him, you know. It's fine — but now he will come to Antwerp to see it.

Then there's the second piece, *Delusional*. This is another kind of cleaning process. This is to do with my time in Yugoslavia. The basic point of this piece was the notion of shame, shame of what's happening right now. I was thinking of what you don't show in public because you're ashamed — it's the most vulnerable and the most difficult and incredibly heavy kind of pressure on yourself, to show what you're ashamed of in front of the public. So the whole piece is about that. And I think those events are for me a kind of metaphor for the ending of this century, the rights over protecting territory — I mean it's really hell in our society.

Figure 40   Marina Abramovic *Biography*, performance, Hebbel Theatre, Berlin, 1994 (Courtesy: Kristina Jentzsch).

Looking at your performance, there seems always to have been a tremendous flow between your life and your work. The performance appears to be a kind of revelation of disciplines and experiences you're in any case engaged with.

Yes. But every true artist is like that. I think that you have to come to a synthesis. You always have to start from yourself, but in the process the product that comes to the public has to be, kind of, transcendental and general. It has to become everybody else. But it starts with the personal, always. There is no other way. That's what you understand the best. You can't go from somebody else's problems. It's just not right. So the deeper you go into yourself, actually, the more universal you come out on the other side.

What happened to me was — I always wanted to leave. I had an obsession with travelling, in moving from place to place. Right now, I'm getting to the point where people say, well, where are you staying? And I can't tell. Every five or six days it is somewhere else. I have spent the last fifteen years like this, and I'm not going to change. That's the reality. I'm not fixed in one special place. And I think I keep with me all this Yugoslavia, you know, whatever this thing is, because you can't go away from those things. Wherever you go you bring these things and you add something else because of the interaction with other countries. Things change, and I'm not afraid of things changing. I absorb it into my work. I am going to Oxford next year, and I will give four lectures. Four different things. And the last one will be on art and travelling. Just this idea of the artist as a nomad, a modern nomad who doesn't belong to any nationality or any particular culture, but is a mixture of everything. And my main concept is the 'space in-between'. You know, the time when you leave one country — you've called everywhere, you take the plane, you go to the train station, to wherever. And then you go somewhere else. But before you arrive, that space in-between — that's the space where it is most intense. It's the space where you're open, where you're sensitive, vulnerable — and anything can happen. And another space I propose is the waiting space. We always consider waiting as losing time, but waiting is extremely important. It is where we need to put emphasis, because to wait is to deal with doing nothing. Doing nothing is exactly what it's all about. Cage says, we have to go to boredom, only through boredom can we come to another side. So the space in-between and the waiting space — that is where it happens.

JULIAN MAYNARD SMITH
(STATION HOUSE OPERA)

Julian Maynard Smith is a performance artist. Previously making solo work, as well as performing with the Theatre of Mistakes, he formed Station House Opera with Miranda Payne and Alison Urquhart in 1980 in order to develop a practice which combined sculptural, architectural and theatrical elements. Following their performance of *Natural Disasters* in London in 1980 and Amsterdam in 1982, their work was seen throughout Europe and subsequently in Japan, Australia and the USA. Since 1980, the company has made more than twenty performances for galleries, theatres and numerous outdoor sites. These include *Drunken Madness* (1981), in which performers were flighted within a system of interdependent platforms and pulleys, *The Bastille Dances* (1989), in which a breeze block edifice was built and dismantled by a company of forty over a period of nine days, and *The Oracle* (1993), which was presented in theatres and an outdoor site. This interview was recorded in May 1994 at the offices of Artsadmin in London.

*   *   *

Did Station House Opera's work come out of an art school background?
      Yes. We were all at art school. Nearly all. When we started we knew nothing about theatre.

Did you think of the work you were making as 'theatre'?
      We called it opera.

Why?
      Partly because, although it was not a theatre company, we realised it was *nearly* a theatre company. We definitely wanted to make a distinction between what we were doing and theatre as we perceived it. There was a valid distinction to be made — the aesthetics which guide the decisions we make are often not 'theatrical' at all.

What were the specific concerns that took you from visual arts practices into performance?
      I was doing the usual things that art students do — making little films and videos. I was introduced to performance art through the Theatre of

Mistakes. Fiona Templeton came and did a workshop at my college and there was something about it which intrigued me. I couldn't understand it. To me it was very strange at that point. It used very abstract and minimal rules for action which I found disturbing but physically liberating. We were doing extremely gruelling endurance performances, repeating the same thing over and over for hours on end. It was a sculptural way of dealing with performance, a sculptural way of dealing with bodies in space and time. And the time-structures were all fairly conceptual in the way that music is. There was a piece that was constructed exactly like a fugue. The actual material was improvised within that structure, but it was repeated, inverted, done backwards — all the kinds of musical procedures which give a plasticity to time and space which in theatre doesn't really apply. I was very involved in that from 1975 to about 1981. I was working with Miranda Payne in the Theatre of Mistakes and we left together to start Station House Opera.

Were you aware at that time of the 'structuralist' performance work in New York or Robert Wilson's 'operas'?

Well, Wilson is a funny case. Deeply influential, but I never saw it (laughs). So it was in exactly the same way that you read or look at a picture and imagine what it's about. Obviously, some of the Theatre of Mistakes structures were identical to the ones being used by Philip Glass. Also, there were connections with Yvonne Rainer and Trisha Brown, with the Judson Church Theater. Theatre of Mistakes had a very American, New York-based aesthetic, in one sense. But it had a curious English public school touch to it as well. I was always wearing cricket clothes or something daft — grey suits.

What was the first Station House Opera performance?

Natural Disasters in 1980. We did it at the Acme Gallery in London, which was where I had done previous solos. A year later it was at the Mickery in Amsterdam, with a big budget. But really that wasn't funded. It didn't tour.

The narrative thread in Natural Disasters *is passed to different people at different times, as if the piece is game-bound.*

Well, I think that is the difference between Station House and the Theatre of Mistakes. Theatre of Mistakes, although it had things called 'inconsistent' behaviours, was extremely tightly ruled. We wanted to do something a bit looser and freer. Theatre of Mistakes would never take into account the vagaries of the system. There would be certain cases where you would do something, where you'd hold a position until, you know, you physically couldn't do it any more and then you'd fall over. It's still tied in to a very kind of dance-oriented idea. Station House would take on much more of a natural system — extracted from something that already existed in the world. So it was more flexible, more descriptive. We would take something which is used for a particular kind of thing in the world, but which nobody really knows how to look at, and put it into a different context, in a sense making it visible by translating it into a different form. And we use the system in a 'non-moral' way, not making judgments about what we're taking. We're not making political points, but we're not just using it blandly. It's taking the real thing and dealing with it in a different way — and therefore fairly loosely. That was true right the way through from *Natural Disasters*, which was hung on a text written in scans ion. It repeated, so that you got the rhythm coming through, yet it would go from person to person — and to thing, person to thing, thing to person. That was a thread, and bouncing off that everything else would be improvised. In the breeze block pieces, you would accept the breeze blocks — accept their physical nature, not pretending they're something else — but translate them into something more gestural, by wearing them, by being expressive with them.

So there's a greater sense of play within the Station House work?

It would play with narrative much more. But the narrative is inevitable in a sense, because the phenomena we choose to work with are much more recognisable. They're not rigid abstract systems. They're located in the real world, they're just taken out of context and turned round. So, however you deal with this, it's going to be understood. Therefore it's going to be referential.

Watching the work, there always seems to be two things in play, and some of your notes on the work and comments point to that. In relation to Bastille Dances *(1989), you talk about seeing the material, seeing the work with the material, and so seeing the image of the building arise and disappear. This seems quite distinct from actually building a building — to use the materials for what they are but to allow the image of a building to alight upon them.*

And the crucial thing in all of the Station House work is this instability. Ideally, the physical construction of *Drunken Madness* (1981) should work perfectly, but it doesn't. You have to move, and then it goes out of kilter. This beautiful image is in fact not at all stable. It's the same with *Cuckoo* (1987). The stability you normally associate with furniture is taken away, as well as the floor.

Figure 41   Station House Opera *Drunken Madness*, Waterloo Studios, London, 1981.

In Cuckoo, *as the objects descend and both performers and objects are in the air, the performers become in some ways interchangeable with the objects. You begin to see the performance from all kinds of strange angles, as the performers, the objects, and their interactions are turned from the vertical to the horizontal, or turned around. And it's a process the performers are subject to rather than simply being in control of.*

Well, there isn't an objective point of view. It's lots of subjective situations, and as such it's not an appreciation of a totality. The audience can sit back and laugh because they see something the performer doesn't. The performer is — as you say — physically interrupting the chain of events, he's physically involved in it and influencing what's happening. I suppose people don't often see the body having a two-way relationship with the physical world. Either it's narrative-based theatre or, if you get people hanging up in the air, they do it without any sense of danger. There's no sense of interdependence. I always liked the idea of the physical set responding to the performer and the performer responding to the set.

Drunken Madness *looks extremely precarious.*

It is.

The fact that its precariousness is so clear must affect the way in which the performance is received. It must resist being seen simply as an image.

There's a danger in that, though. It's precisely not simply an image. We did *Drunken Madness* in New York, under the Brooklyn Bridge, and that was so scary for the audience that it detracted. I remember comments from people saying they were so fucking scared they couldn't sit back and enjoy it. We weren't wearing safety belts or anything like that.

When you're on the chairs you're just on the chairs.

Oh yes. In fact that was the most dangerous thing I've ever done, but mainly because of the way it was connected with wires against the wall. It was attached to the wall with bolts, glued in with acrylic glue — which is what the architect told us to do. When we were performing we could see these bolts coming out. We also did that piece in Amsterdam off a tower crane. It wasn't dangerous, but it was so high — and the whole thing took off. It was on such a large scale that the figures were just a little too small. It didn't have the physical immediacy of seeing someone actually in front of you doing something.

Could Drunken Madness *be described as 'site-specific'?*

A piece like *Drunken Madness* obviously needs a particular kind of place to do it in. It was first done in the Waterloo Studios in London, which

1: A (Dave) is heavier
than B (Jonathan).
A brings bottles
down from Table 1
and distributes them
to other tables.
B brings glasses
up from tray at
bottom. B then puts
on weights at
Table 1 to take him
down. He collects
empty bottles on the
way, depositing bottles
and discarding weights
at Table 5. The process
is repeated.

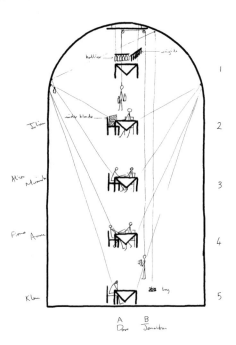

3a: When all the weights have been
used and are on Table 5, they are
taken back to the top. Firstly, 12
are taken to Table 4 by B, jumping up
and giving them to Anna: 12 jumps. A
bobs up and down between Tables 1
and 2. At Table 3, Ali and Miranda,
being unemployed, swing about: the
first irregularity. Then A takes a
cinder-block from the chair at Table 12
which brings him down to the ground,
taking B and the weights to the top.

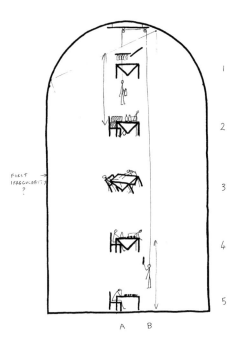

Figures 42 and 43 Julian Maynard Smith, pages from the working script for *Drunken Madness*, Brooklyn Bridge Anchorage, New York 1983 (courtesy of the artist).

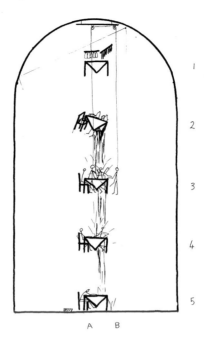

4: A waterfall,
tipped from Table 2.

6: When the weights
are exhausted, the
same procedure is
followed to get
them up again. A
takes the second
cinder-block,
tilting Table 2
even more extremely
(there is nothing
to counterbalance
Julian's weight).
Meanwhile Ali and
Miranda are changing
from their dresses
to b/w
trousers/shirts etc.

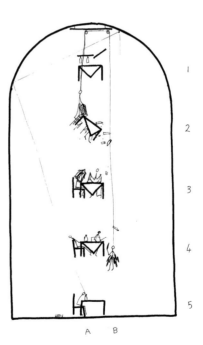

Figures 44 and 45 Julian Maynard Smith, pages from the working script for *Drunken Madness*,
Brooklyn Bridge Anchorage, New York 1983 (courtesy of the artist).

10: (Dave and Jonathan
are at Tables 2
and 4; A and B are
now Ali and Miranda.)
Table 3 comes apart,
taking A and B out
to the walls. The
pieces hang against
the walls, A and B
swing in space. Klem
at Table 5 becomes a
dog and runs off,
while his chair flies
up to join Table 1.

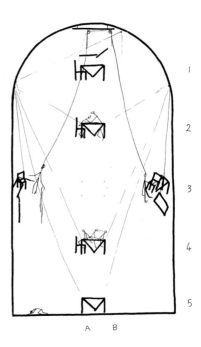

16: Wet clothes
and table cloths
are hanging out
on the upper wires.
Performers are in
a state of semi
undress, singing.

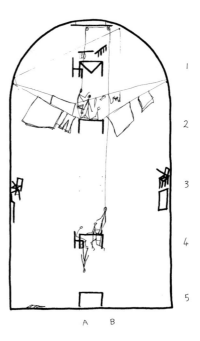

Figures 46 and 47   Julian Maynard Smith, pages from the working script for *Drunken Madness*,
Brooklyn Bridge Anchorage, New York 1983 (courtesy of the artist).

was an old abbatoir. It was derelict — two or three stories high with a broken glass roof, shit all over the floor. But in the middle there was this very beautiful recess. But we didn't look at the space and think, what shall we do for this space? If one only approaches the site with — what can we do for this site? — it becomes a very empty exercise. We did *Drunken Madness* in between the first performance of *Natural Disasters* and its performance at The Mickery in Amsterdam. In the Amsterdam version there was a table which floated around at about 45 degrees with someone sitting at it. We were just looking at this table and had fancies about table-cloths flying around space. So we were working in the space in the Waterloo Studios — just as a studio — and Miranda suggested we do it there. Just a flash of inspiration, looking at the most unpromising space in the whole building — a really horrible, difficult place to do it. But, of course, once she said — you know — do it in there — the idea of having tables one above the other just came automatically. And then, the whole thing of people going up and down in harnesses came pretty easily. It came together very, very quickly in response to the site, but coming out of something else. That's the way to work. I find it very boring to be commissioned to do something for a site, without anything else. If you're working anyway, sometimes the site will suggest something precisely because it stimulates again. But with Station House, you could expand the notion of site to include other things which are given. A site is just a physical given — and it's not necessarily the building in which you're doing it. We tend to work with lots of givens, because we take things from the world and work with them. The breeze blocks are a similar sort of given — it's 'site' in a sense. It's where you locate your body in relation to how you manipulate it. And how it manipulates you, as a physical thing.

Which means that you must pay attention to its identity in your use of it.

Yes. That's the crucial thing all the way through. The table remains a table even when it's 100 foot off the ground. It's still a table. They're not 'made up' worlds, they are an assemblage of system bits, but translated, somehow, into a different — I don't know how one would describe it, but it's a magic sort of change — when you use them in a different way, when you put them in a different place — that's what I mean by translating them.

Why the concern with flying?

One reason was that I was extremely interested in Tintoretto, a Venetian painter of about 1550. Tintoretto was painting at a point moving out of the Classical Renaissance, but before the Baroque. Baroque is characterised by this idea of infinity, which is what theatre deals with as well. You walk off

at the wings, you're out of sight. You just disappear. Tintoretto uses deep
perspective, but there's always an end to it. So he liberated his figures from
the usual Renaissance conventions. They occupy the most extraordinary
parts of the pictorial space. They're also occupying all the weird parts of the
physical rectangle of the painting. So I thought it would be great to use every
square inch of the performance space. We wanted to occupy every part of the
theatre — if it was a proscenium, every part of that rectangle, every part of
the whole space, equally. To use the theatre as just a floor, with a figure, is so
hierarchical in its arrangement of space. But theatre has always been very
conservative. It never takes into account its own physical limitations, which
is one of the things we've always tried to do — to make theatre out of the
physical limitations of the form. So we don't walk off in the wings. We're
always physically stuck in that space. It's like a whole world we're
describing, with no infinity. I mean, theatres are never really very pleasant
places.

Why not?
          Well, they don't know what they are, do they? And the black-box
theatre is the worst. The fact that they think that by painting it black it
disappears. Where did they get this idea from?

*I'm interested in the fact that while you pay such close attention to the architecture
and nature of a space, you also talk about creating a 'whole world' within it.*
          Well, it needs something else. It's not enough just to use the
technology, either. You have to transform it into something else.

So, again, there's a kind of double there.
          All the way through. To go back to *Natural Disasters* and the flying.
All this escaping by flying — all the hanging tables — is precisely using the
dual nature of what one might imagine is the ambition to fly. It's like the
mental world of fantasy or ambition, and what happens when it comes
crunch up against the physical reality. Once you get someone off the
ground they're incredibly heavy, which means that you have to use all this
technology. You find yourself with all these lumbering bits of cable and
pulleys. And it's precisely that each of those informs the other. However
you work on it, they need each other. And gravity, obviously, becomes a
central part of everything. That's why if you change the site the performance
changes. I mean, it's inevitably going to change.
          We've found it productive, in a sense, to inhabit a kind of theatrical
milieu while putting in this other stuff. Except that the theatrical milieu
has not given enough back to us to make it worth while in the perfectly
practical sense of money. But to play with representation, with narrative —

Figure 48   Station House Opera *Cuckoo*, The Mickery, Amsterdam, 1988 (photo: Bob van Dantzig).

in a kind of fractured sense — to deliberately court that, to use those sorts of ambiguities. That's going to give you the duality of the performer as ordinary bloke and the performer as someone who is going to be read as being somebody. A lot of performance art does not really accept that as soon as you stand up as a performer in front of an audience, you're kind of acting. It doesn't really deal with the fakeness of it. An awful lot of performance hovers on the edge of acting without really taking it into account.

One of the things that comes out of that for me is to see the performers working with the performance material, to see them working with actions or roles, to see them picking up and putting down both materials and images.

I've got a two-year old now and she plays games and even though she's really serious — when she's crying or she's really into something — if you switch it slightly she'll laugh. She knows it's a game. In a sense it's like a game that you play. You take on a role and then you drop it. But that has the consequence of it often not being taken very seriously. We have tended to fall between two stools, between people who want to see theatre and people who want to see performance art without any wry self-consciousness. The expectations of the audience are terribly important. That's why for us working in theatres is often very difficult. Also, I think people tend to — we're talking about the theatre-world I suppose — people tend to assume that if it's not about something, if it hasn't got a moral, then it's trivial. Well, go and see the Picasso show at the Tate. That tells you all about what it is just to do things — playing with things, playing with the material and with representation. Playing games, but playing them in a way that might raise questions about how you judge it.

Flying seems to be important to a whole run of early pieces, but then with Split Second of Paradise *(1986), the focus begins to shift toward the process of working with a limited set of materials.* Split Second of Paradise, Bastille Dances, Piranesi in New York *(1988) and* Piranesi in Tokyo *(1990) all use large numbers of breeze blocks.*

Well, we did that because they basically worked.

There also seems to be a continuing element of risk. In Bastille Dances, *the structures are constructed from piles of loose breeze blocks. Watching the work of making the edifice, I had a fear they might fall down.*

Yes. So did we. The *Bastille* outdoors was immensely tall — nine metres high or something. We were afraid of it blowing down. We never had any accidents, though, partly because we designed it to allow for collapses. It wasn't our intention to make those performances dangerous.

When you extend a performance over the sort of period of time that Bastille Dances *was extended, it must foreground the sheer work involved in the building and rebuilding of the breeze block edifice.*

The mental block is something to get over as well. When we first started the breeze block pieces with *Split Second of Paradise* there were 500 breeze blocks. It was very hard to come to terms with that many blocks. We found it very difficult to really comprehend, accept and actually be willing to get them all out — and it seemed such hard work to actually build something out of them. Yet by the time we did the *Bastille* we had 8,000.

Did Bastille Dances *change in the course of doing it in different places?*

It was adapted to different sites, to fit the different spaces. In general, we didn't have to do a major re-structuring of the piece. At the South Bank

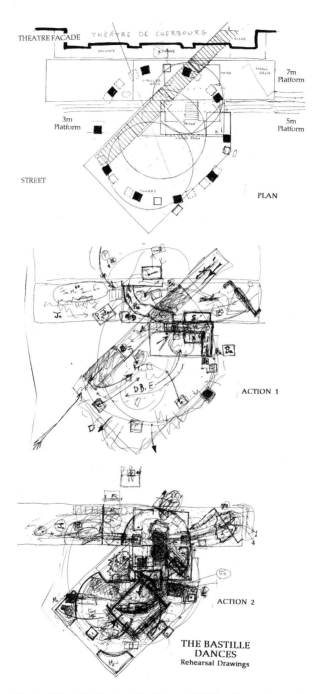

Figure 49 Julian Maynard Smith, *The Bastille Dances* (1989), rehearsal drawings (courtesy of the artist).

in London it was totally free-standing. At most of the other places it was integrated into the structure of where we were. We did it in Salzburg with fewer performers and fewer blocks, which allowed us to re-think the whole thing. That was really interesting. It was recognisably the same performance, but it had changed sculpturally. It had really come together. It was much more of a solid mass which sprouted rather than being in layers. At the South Bank it was built on separate platforms. It might be disguised in various ways, but essentially the actions were very separate. At Salzburg we had fewer platforms and a more integrated use of the blocks. Originally my initial idea was that we wouldn't have platforms at all, it would just be one massive great pile of breeze blocks. And of course that becomes structurally unstable.

This work still carries over notions of process —

Well, the processes became overemphasised the more we got into materials. I think we got a bit caught up in that, particularly with the last one we did, *The Oracle* (1993). Our materials have become a kind of counter-productive starting point. You just end up moving them about instead of having something else. It's one of the most difficult things to get right. The

Figure 50 Station House Opera *The Bastille Dances*, Gare Maritime, Cherbourg, 1989 (photo: Bob van Dantzig).

same could be said about our images. Some of the images are very strong, but in performance you start seeing other things — you start worrying about other things — things which operate in time. You don't have that distance of just looking at the sculptural mass of what's happening.

Do you have any projects currently underway?

I don't know what Station House will be up to in the future. It depends whether or not it makes financial sense. We're doing all these performances with headphones and walkmans — in the street. All a matter of passing information on — of trying to create an organism that will live. We've been doing it in workshops for a couple of years and want to develop it. We want to get some research money, now. It's the idea that you can translate performance into a set of instructions, into a descriptive system that can be stored on tape, and then posted to someone in another country and recreated.

I did this workshop with a guy who teaches in Switzerland. He sends me packets of tapes with a ground plan and says stop there, there, and there, and see what happens. And it's all really kind of weird. And you send one back. And that idea has real, physical — it's almost like a traditional Station House piece, only we're dealing with a primitive information technology, where the human being is having to take this stuff in and then translate it into action. There's an aspect to it that's quite strange — quite how it exists in the world.

It sounds like a disembodied performance that is dispersed — that exists as an experience, or as different sorts of experiences.

Because you can send information to each other you can keep up a dialogue — it's quite tangible. But there's a sort of cybernetic quality of programming these tapes against each other, or these languages against each other. And then there's the people, who're living with a dual consciousness. They've got their own thoughts and they've got the other thoughts. And the idea of how you actually could make a performance event grow and change independently of any external directions or external decisions is one that I've — it's like biology — you might evolve something, without having to write it — you set up the system and then see how it grows, according to conditions.

Earlier, when we were discussing documentation, you talked about a documentation of decisions — good and bad decisions — in the making of a performance.

Yes. I've a feeling that really decisions should be things that are taken very, very easily. They're not always like that, but one characteristic we always had was to hold off making decisions for as long as possible —

in terms of what it's about, what it's going to use, what it's going to have. It seems like feeling your way towards a process. And by considering the various aspects of the idea — physical aspects, the structural aspects of it — if you're thinking well or you're working well, the decisions that you actually have to make about what happens probably come quite easily. Obviously, they're the most important thing. But it's like playing music, if you've done all the preparation, the tune comes.

CLIFF MCLUCAS AND MIKE PEARSON
(BRITH GOF)

Brith Gof was established in Aberystwyth, Wales, in 1981 by Mike Pearson and Lis Hughes Jones, following their departure from Cardiff Laboratory Theatre. From 1981 to 1988, the company purposefully operated outside of the prevailing theatrical orthodoxies, creating their own circumstances for performance and relating their work to specific locations and occasions in West Wales. In these circumstances, their work became increasingly, and overtly, political, drawing on aspects of Welsh history and addressing experiences of cultural and economic decline and disintegration. In 1988, the company collaborated with the industrial percussionists Test Dept. to create *Goddodin*, a large-scale site-specific performance presented in the disused Rover car factory in Cardiff's docklands. Since then they have completed two more large-scale site-specific pieces. *Pax*, of 1991–1992, based on a descent of angels and concerned with the environmental plight of the planet, was presented at St. David's Hall, Cardiff, the Harland and Wolff shipyard in Glasgow and in the British Rail Station in Aberystwyth. More recently *Haearn*, meaning 'iron', was conceived both as a live work and a television record, and performed at the Old British Coal Works in Tredegar, Wales, in 1993. Brith Gof's work extends across large-scale, site-specific· performances, touring theatre performances, installation, video, television, and music, and the company is currently involved in several publication projects. Mike Pearson and Cliff McLucas are Joint Artistic Directors of the company. This interview was recorded at Brith Gof's offices at Chapter Arts, Cardiff, in January 1994. The short texts and statements which punctuate this interview are drawn from 'The Host and The Ghost: Brith Gof's Site-Specific Works', 60 interleaved texts by Mike Pearson and Cliff McLucas concerning the company's approaches to site-specific performance. These extracts are reproduced by permission of the authors.

*   *   *

What was it that brought about the first large-scale site-specific piece in 1988?
      MP: Well, I think it's within the history of Brith Gof not performing in theatre spaces. That's for a number of reasons. One is that there aren't a large number of theatres in Wales. There's a limited circuit —and almost all of those theatres are problematic in one way or another. They were all built

within three or four years of each other, but actually nobody had thought about what theatre might be in Wales. Coupled with that, right at the end of our life within Cardiff Laboratory we went to live and work in a small village in West Wales, and began to think about manifestations of theatre that were not theatre-bound. We were making performances for farmhouse kitchens, for the Post Office counter, and so on. That built somewhat as we began — as Brith Gof — to settle our activity. I think we went in two directions. One was to be increasingly working in non-theatrical spaces — barns, churches, chapels, what-have-you. I think it would be the venues in which a Welsh, particularly a Welsh rural audience, would feel more at ease in — rather than sitting in rows in the dark in a theatre. There are cultural manifestations, like the nosen Lawen, which is an evening get together, which might present easier models to work with. Lis Hughes Jones did a performance for chapel pulpits — an extremely restricted space to address. That was one strand of the work. The other was to build staging units, so performances could come as a unit with their own floor, seating, lighting, which could be put in anywhere, and which would concentrate activity in some sort of way, leading to a perfecting of conditions for the performers. That, equally, was quite unusual. I think we did learn a lot. Things like *Rhydcymerau*, which we did in a disused cattle market in Lampeter, with the audience sitting on two sides where farmers would have looked down onto the beasts when they went through, seemed entirely natural. It didn't seem 'site-specific'. I think that term was only appearing at around that time that we did *Goddodin*, anyway.

CM: I wasn't in this work, but for me the cultural placement of those theatre pieces, that cultural specificity, was exemplary. And the work that Lis did in those chapels — I never saw it, I decided not to go and see it because I was not of that congregation, that audience.

This notion of 'naturalness' seems important.

CM: Yes. In one sense. But it wasn't congruent. Doing a performance of *Rhydcymerau* in Lampeter cattle market was in the grain of the place, but not. And it's the gap between those two that was exciting about that work.

MP: I used to share with Lis Hughes Jones the idea that you're actually working with a congregation — like an aggregation of people with no theatrical expectations at all, but actually a religious one. And using religious subject-matter, but looking at that obliquely, was extremely interesting.

CM: In some of the work there was this tension about who the audience was. In the cattle market show, for instance, there would be the local farmers, who would have sat in that place and bought cattle. But there

---

MP 2 (SITE)

site specific performances are conceived for, and conditioned by, the particulars of **found** spaces, (former) **sites** of work, play and worship. They make manifest, celebrate, confound or criticise location, history, function, architecture, micro-climate… They are an interpenetration of the **found** and the **fabricated**. They are inseparable from their sites, the only context within which they are 'readable'.

---

would be other people who would come along, who'd heard about the company from Cardiff or wherever. So the company's audience has always been this hybrid. Hybrid is a key word in all of the practice. In other words, you shouldn't go away with the idea that these pieces of work were in some kind of sense 'natural' in a 'natural' environment.

MP: I think it's mainly only in the past year or so that I felt strong enough to admit that I'm an immigrant. And that, actually, Welsh society will have to take me warts and all. And they can choose to ignore me or embrace me. But I think for a long time there was a feeling that — not least because it's a minority, it's a culture under threat, it's a language under threat — that you have to slip and slide and hide underneath a prevailing orthodoxy, which you mustn't damage. There's a way, if you're not careful, that Welshness presents itself to you as this facade which you have to gaze at and get mesmerised by. But in fact it's not true. Most of that is a middle-class invention, which is no different from an English one, in a way.

CM: The other thing to stress is that, certainly in places like Aberystwyth where Brith Gof was first based, it's a bi-lingual culture. I think in any culture that is bi-lingual you'll find negotiability — hybridisation — as central elements of daily practice. So we're not talking about a Welsh language culture which is one thing. It itself is fractured, and there are people who are disenfranchised from that who are Welsh speakers. So it's very fluid. Because both Mike and I are immigrants — if you like — we've learned to speak the language and to negotiate our path amongst all of this. I think it's a very fertile environment within which to make work. It's apparent what needs to be done here — and that bi-lingualism, that discontinuity within the culture, gives rise to all kinds of political energies. The first large-scale piece came from that background of cultural site-specificity.

MP: I'm not even sure that we ever sought to do 'large scale' — that came from the venue that we found and the way Cliff decided to engage with that particular building. However, it was political. You have to remember

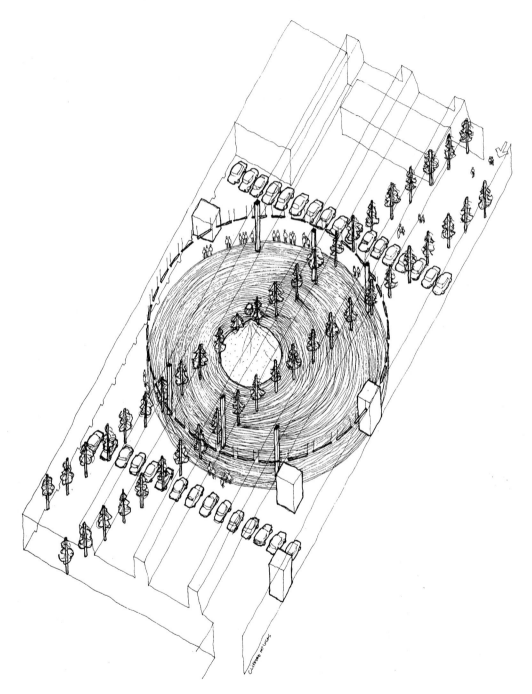

Figure 51 Clifford McLucas *Goddodin* (1988) in Cardiff at the old Rover car factory in the docks (courtesy of the artist).

what it was like in 1988. I felt that Test Dept. were amongst the few people within the artistic community in Britain who were willing to stand up and be counted about what they thought was going on in society. And I wanted to be associated with them. I think scale came in through the door when we started to work with them. Test Dept. wouldn't be content working in a small space. They expect in their concerts the number of people that eventually came to see the show and they had already done a number of events of some scale.

CM 13 A host site might offer a number of things

a a particular and unavoidable history
b a particular use (a cinema, a slaughterhouse)
c a particular formality (shape, proportion, height, disposition of architectural elements etc)
d a particular political, cultural or social context
c a particular kind of 'halfway house' for event and audience to meet (a workplace, a meeting place, a street, a church)

In other words, deciding to create a work in a 'used' building might provide a theatrical foundation or springboard, it might be like 'throwing a six to go', it might get us several rungs up the theatrical ladder before we begin.

CM: I think also the subject matter must have been in your mind. *Goddodin* is an epic poem about the slaughtering of Welsh warriors. And all kinds of metaphors are carried within it about cultural decline.

MP: Cliff uses the word epic, but there's no narrative in *Goddodin*, so it's an elegy. There's no story being told. You can construct a story out of odd details of the poem, but if you take a slice of *Goddodin*, it's the same as any other slice.

CM: In the docks in Cardiff there's this whole 'regeneration' of post-industrial areas of South Wales taking place. We did *Goddodin* in the building which had been the Rover car factory. Just by doing it in that building — by doing it in a place where there were no longer cars being manufactured — all kinds of resonances about cultural, economic and regional decline are brought in. That was what excited me about the site, apart from the actual building itself. It was in a wasteland. When people came they caught a bus at Chapter Arts and were driven down into this wasteland. They would get dropped off in the middle of a rain-swept car park and directed over to this industrial building that's kind of falling down, then in through the door to this really quite unique environment. All those things were charging the event up aesthetically and politically.

MP 4 (NARRATIVES)

site specific performances **recontextualise** site: they are the latest occupation of a location where occupations are still apparent and cognitively active. They are extremely generative of signs: the **denotative** and **connotative** meanings of performance are amended and/or compromised by the **denotative** and **connotative** meanings of site. Such performances are a complex overlay of **narrative**, historical and contemporary, a kind of **saturated space**, or a scene of-crime, where, to use forensic jargon 'everything is potentially important'.

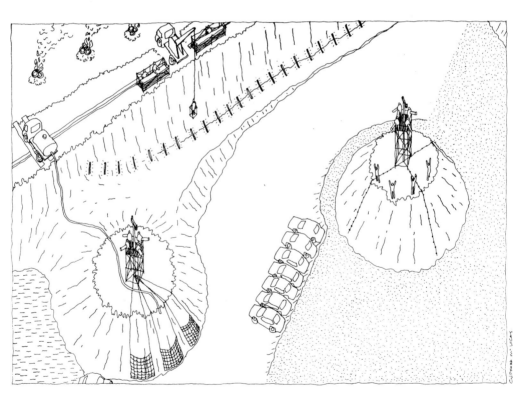

Figure 52   Clifford McLucas *Goddodin* (1988) in Polverigi, Italy (detail) in a working sand quarry (courtesy of the artist).

I'm very interested in the emphasis you place upon 'found' materials and the politicising of work through the attention to site —

CM: You can either use the word 'found' or 'chosen'. We choose these places.

There are two things I mean by that. One is to do with the idea of the 'found', conventionally, as an element which resists being perceived as something represented.

CM: Yes. That's right.

The other is to do with why you chose those spaces in particular.

CM: Well, I mean, first of all *Goddodin*. You know, things to do with the Rover car factory no longer being there. I think also it's worth saying that by that time Brith Gof had moved to Cardiff. We felt that there was a kind of Cardiff audience that we hadn't engaged with and which was quite different from the West Wales audience. After that, when we did re-stagings of *Goddodin*, the sites chose us. At some points we were simply given a site — and asked, can we do it here?

Where did you do it?

CM: First of all we did it in a quarry in Polverigi, Italy, then in a crane factory in Hamburg. In Frisland in the Netherlands it was in an ice hockey stadium, and then in the Tramway — the old tram depot — in Glasgow. Each time with all the problems of an interface with a new place. I think the word place is important rather than site.

MP: The interesting thing that Cliff does, is that within the materials that he's chosen to work with he makes an incredible negotiation with site — and in a way in which the work can begin to remake itself. In Frisland in the ice hockey stadium, we had 8,000 sandbags. We built sandbag islands for the audience to stand on, then flooded the whole arena. You can put a lot of water into an ice-hockey stadium. Curiously, the one place that the show didn't work — for all sorts of reasons, I even think on a conceptual level — was in Hamburg. Cliff did a design — a concept — for *Goddodin* in a large hall. Then at three weeks notice we weren't allowed to do it and we had to do the show outside, in a different site. But the problem was that when you get semi-naked men and fire in Germany it means one thing. And that's really where our problems lay.

CM: It was all touching on very sensitive things in Germany at the time. We were simply unaware of the potential for those readings of the piece.

MP: I don't know. One must have been aware — I think.

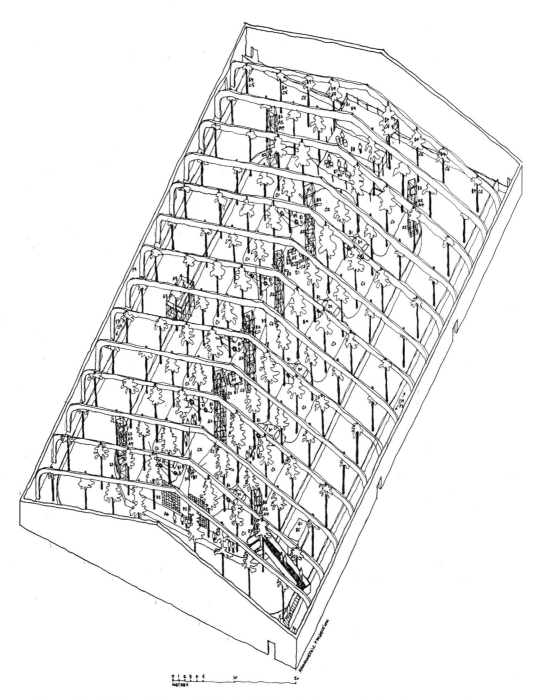

Figure 53   Clifford McLucas *Goddodin* (1988) in Frisland at the Ice Hockey Stadium in Leeuwarden (courtesy of the artist).

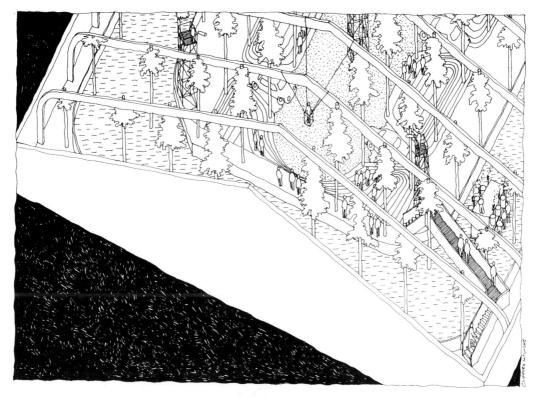

Figure 54   Clifford McLucas *Goddodin* (1988) in Frisland at the Ice Hockey Stadium in Leeuwarden (courtesy of the artist).

CM 17 Real architectural sites (hosts) such as British Coal's Tredegar Works encourage us to think formally in 3 and 4 dimensions, as well as, or instead of, 2. This has major implications for the concepts at the heart of the work, and the contracts at the heart of theatre. It may rewrite or problematize the nature of the relationships between all components of the event:

a between audience member as individual and audience as mass
b between audience member as individual and performer
c between audience as mass and performer
d between performer and performer
e between performer and architecture and so on

This inevitably broadens the deep, structural possibilities of theatre.

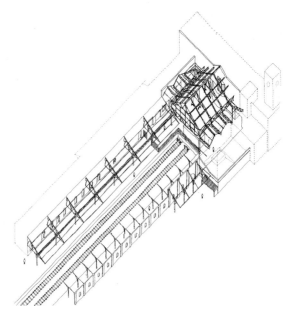

Figure 55   Clifford McLucas *Pax* (1991–1992) in Aberystwyth at the BR Railway Station (courtesy of the artist).

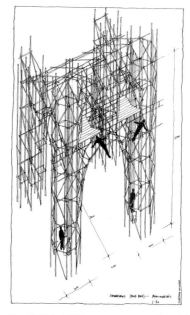

Figure 56   Clifford McLucas *Pax* (1991–1992), component of scaffolding cathedral with angels (courtesy of the artist).

CM: Even now with hindsight it would be interesting to speculate on what we could have done to foreclose that reading. It would be quite difficult. The central problem is that a piece of work within Wales which is about 'nationalism' takes on entirely different meanings when transported into Germany. It's a different kind of nationalism. If we're talking about a defensive nationalism, a kind of nationalism which comes from centuries of abuse and move that into a place where there was actually an expansionistic, destructive kind of nationalism — it's the same word, but not the same thing.

For me, an important part of my experience of Haearn *in Welsh was one of becoming aware of my otherness from what I was watching and who I was sitting with.*

CM: Absolutely. I'm pleased about that discomfort. I'm pleased about the fact that — Well, that's the problem. If we go to France or to the Netherlands, people accept that we are other and they are other to us. It's not really a problem. Within the dominant discourse of theatre in the UK, though, it's, well — why are you using Welsh? A lot of our pieces have Welsh and English in them. A piece like *Patagonia* (1992), which is a piece for a proscenium-arch auditorium, carries with it aspects of Welsh culture which we take for granted and are engaged with. How an English audience is engaging with that is very difficult to judge. It's very difficult to construct the work in such a way that an English audience is getting this thing but at the same time another audience in Wales — which is a bi-lingual audience — is engaged enough with its sophistication. One way of overcoming it is to drain pieces of work of any kind of cultural or political specificity or issue.

MP: I do think that this cultural specificity means that our work is often very problematic in, kind of, 'Euro-theatrical' terms. I think we often consciously use naivete and all sorts of 'non-U' techniques which are problematic in relation to air-brushed 'Euro-products' that can move anywhere.

With Haearn, *and although not following the Welsh text, I had a strong sense of the different elements clashing against each other in a way that would be challenging for any audience. To me there seemed to be a resistance within the piece to a reading which would synthesize its elements into a single statement.*

CM: I suppose it's my interest in trying to make a kind of Frankenstein work with an arm from here and a head from there and a brain from here. That emerged from wanting to do a large-scale piece of work that had an audience extracted from the middle of it. With both *Goddodin* and *Pax* the audience had to be in amongst it. That was very exciting, but by the time we'd done *Goddodin* in five places — and we did four performances in each place — I wondered what it would be like to make a piece of work which was slightly more formalised. I am interested in taking that a stage

---

CM 19 The Ghost — the large scale site specific theatre work **Haearn** — was conceived as a fractured (and incomplete) work. Like Frankenstein's creature, it was constructed from a number of disparate vital organs and parts.

Like all ghosts, **Haearn's** body is not solid — the host can be seen through it.

The Host and the Ghost, of different origins, are **co-existent** but, crucially, are not **congruent**.

---

further. I think what excited me about that was precisely materials sitting next to each other but not being embedded into each other.

MP: I also think Cliff's idea of the 'host' and the 'ghost' is interesting. That there are a number of narratives attached to the host building — economic, cultural, political, and so on. Then within that we're constructing at least seven architectures of narrative in one way or another. Within those two the performers are then almost guided into what they should do, because there are ways to move in all of that stuff. Equally, I think for an audience — to answer your question — there are all sorts of ways to move around in that material. From time to time you may suddenly be leaping all over the place and it may seem very confusing, but equally you can find orientations.

What is the place of text within these architectures?

MP: Lis Hughes Jones and Paul Jamrozy could use text quite freely within *Goddodin* because there wasn't a lot of information to be given. So the grain of the voices was as important — and where their voices sat in the music was as important — as what they were talking about.

CM: *Goddodin* was a very singular piece of work for me. It was very big — it was like a great boulder, and that was its strength, that was its power. It bowled you along emotionally. When we did *Pax* I think Lis, particularly, was concerned that the text should carry information, meaning, idiom, politics, all the rest of it. The way which she did that was to develop four voices within the text. Now, in seeing *Pax* I suspect most of the audience probably wasn't aware of that. I think it's a pity they weren't. It's our fault for not making it obvious. But there were four voices for four different characters who were all either sung or spoken within the piece. I think that really excited me — that you're coming at a set of issues from four points of view. In the small eleven-minute video that we made, those four voices were represented on screen — their texts are kind of

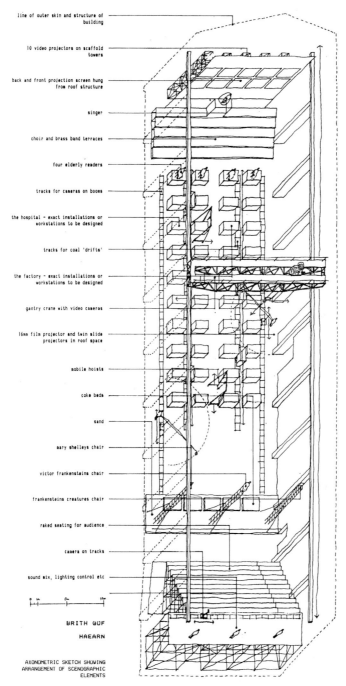

line of outer skin and structure of
building

10 video projectors on scaffold
towers

back and front projection screen hung
from roof structure

singer

choir and brass band terraces

four elderly readers

tracks for cameras on booms

the hospital — exact installations or
workstations to be designed

tracks for coal 'drifts'

the factory — exact installations or
workstations to be designed

gantry crane with video cameras

16mm film projector and twin slide
projectors in roof space

mobile hoists

coke beds

sand

mary shelleys chair

victor frankensteins chair

frankensteins creatures chair

raked seating for audience

camera on tracks

sound mix, lighting control etc

BRITH GOF

HAEARN

AXONOMETRIC SKETCH SHOWING
ARRANGEMENT OF SCENOGRAPHIC
ELEMENTS

Figure 57 Clifford McLucas, scenography for *Haearn* (1992) at the British Coal Tredegar Works (courtesy of the artist).

CM 23 The first of **Haearn's** architectures is **The Valley/The Mirror** and is composed of two reflecting components:

a the audience — from Tredegar and South Wales
b (i)   the Choir and Band — from Tredegar and South Wales
   (ii) the Steel Industry's historical film archive of men and women at work in the steel works of South Wales

The Valley/The Mirror marks the architectural parameters of, and contains, the work.

---

rolling across all the time. I think what I was interested in doing in *Haearn* was taking that a stage further. So you've got stuff from the industrial revolution, you've got Mary Shelley, and in it — well, somewhere in the middle, hovering in it — there's this hologram. You take a chance because you fabricate things, these architectures, these elements, and you try to make this thing live in the middle.

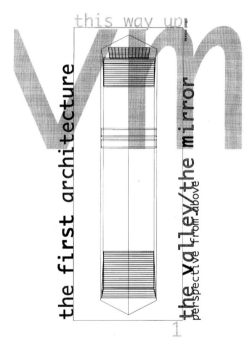

Figure 58   Clifford McLucas *Haearn*, the First Architecture, *The Valley/The Mirror* (courtesy of the artist).

CM: I don't know if it's the same thing, but I went to see the Wooster Group's show in London — *Brace Up!* — and it was wonderful the way that *Three Sisters*, this 'conventional' piece of theatre, hovered in the middle of this matrix of stuff going on. I don't think I'd seen that anywhere else. It's a wonderfully exciting artistic strategy. It was as if no individual invested any energy in bringing this theatre-piece, this play, about, yet somehow through the composite of what they were doing this thing started to emerge.

The emphasis on 'found' site and 'found' materials raises questions about how the performer might effectively find a place amongst such elements.
MP: One of the things that I'm interested in is trying to draw out the idea of an 'active' environment, which is barely possible in auditoria. The idea that you should use materials like wind, rain, which we're currently doing, so that the environment itself is an active one. And when one is watching the performers one may not be watching the conventional theatrical sign — you may be watching their symptoms — simply their symptoms. If they overblow it and try to turn their symptoms into a sign, then that doesn't work. If they're cold, they're cold.

This kind of engagement by performers can affect an audience in a very direct way, can't it?. But it can also be quite disturbing.
CM: Absolutely. I think from *Goddodin* — I can remember discussions Mike and I had about *Goddodin* — I came up with these scenographic ideas. You know, at some point the water will start filling up — first of all you operate on this sand area — and sand is a certain kind of material, you can run on it in certain ways, you can do this, you can do that. Then it starts filling up with water — it turns into mud. Then it fills up with more water, and everything you're doing is in six or nine inches of water. That agenda — that physical agenda — avoids a whole load of problems in one sense. It means the performers don't have to pretend to be exhausted, they are exhausted. They are cold.

In Haearn *the performers seemed to take up some of the overpowering aspects of that place — the freezing cold, the impact of the industrial machinery — by the sheer extremity of what they were doing.*
MP: That's absolutely right. I do think, though, that the physical engagement of the performers with place is not necessarily on the performing level. It's the technical levels which emplace them. They need to know what speed this crane is going to move at and where they're going to end up. For the performers *Haearn* was a strange experience on one level, because for acoustic reasons we were in a sound blackout. All of the

---

CM 25 The second of **Haearn's** architectures is **The Two Women**.

The two prime 'solo' voices are given to two women — one, **The Actress**, 2 metres from the audience; the other, **The Singer**, 100 metres from the audience.

Their two voices, and the narratives they deliver ride over, and are supported by, all the other materials. They are the first voices the audience hears.

The Actress, during the work, plays the parts of **Mary Shelley** (reading materials from her diaries, letters and journals written during the years between 1814 and 1822 — when she miscarried, lost two of her children, and wrote her novel, Frankenstein), Mary Shelley's creation, **Victor Frankenstein**, and her creation's creation, **The Creature**.

The Singer relates the stories of Greek demigods, **Hephaestus** (the crippled god of the forge, who cast golden women assistants) and **Prometheus** (the god who created man from clay) and their godly project to create a man and a woman.

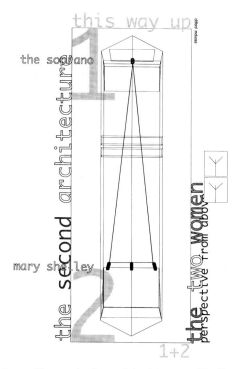

Figure 59 Clifford McLucas *Haearn*, the Second Architecture, *The Two Women* (courtesy of the artist).

> **CM 27** The third of **Haearn's** architectures is **The Narratives**
>
> **a** The Mythical (the stories of Hephaestus and Prometheus)
> **b** The Historical (first person accounts of the Industrial Revolution)
> **c** The Novelistic (Mary Shelley's novel Frankenstein)
> **d** The Personal (Mary Shelley's letters, journals and diaries)
>
> Each of these four operate within significantly different narrative architectures, and constitute significantly different audiences.

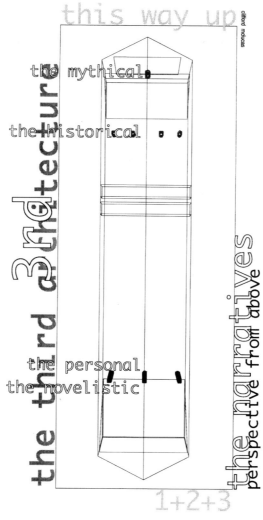

Figure 60 Clifford McLucas *Haearn*, the Third Architecture, *The Narratives* (courtesy of the artist).

CM 29 The fourth of **Haearn's** architectures is **The Body**

The parallel emergence of 'medical' and 'industrial' sciences during the Industrial Revolution represented the body in new ways:

a the biological/mechanical set of components — pumps, circulatory systems, hydraulics, heat engines etc

b the 'body of man' — in particular 'the work force' or 'the working classes' — monolithic servicers of the Industrial Project

Scenographically, these are represented by **The Hospital**, and **The Factory**. The man's body is consitituted in the hospital, and the woman's in the factory.

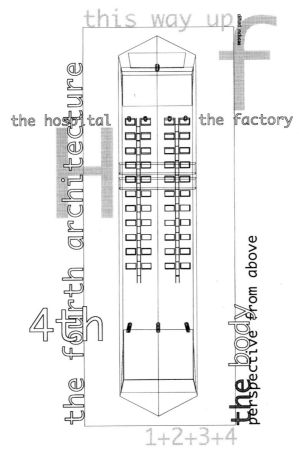

Figure 61 Clifford McLucas *Haearn*, the Fourth Architecture, *The Body* (courtesy of the artist).

amplification was in front of the performers, so there was this great sound thing that was coming at the audience but the performers could talk to each other. There was an unearthly quiet out there. That was actually very difficult.

CM: In these pieces of work, any one of the components doesn't necessarily know what other components are doing — and that often causes a kind of anxiety. Because that sound wasn't bowling them along, I suspect the performers in *Haearn* felt kind of naked and exposed, more than they did in, say, *Goddodin*. For me, sitting out the front, for instance, it's OK — it's good. They're really difficult pieces to make work — really difficult. We've done three now and whilst I think they've moved forward as a kind of artistic form, they are more and more difficult to pull off. You've got to rely on so many other people and so many technologies.

In writing about the form of Haearn *you've referred to a 'field' of activities and set it in opposition to the notion of an 'object'.*

CM: I think there's a question in our work — it's something that Mike and I have talked about — at the end of the day we make a theatre show that's an hour-and-a-half long and that an audience pays for, comes and watches, and goes away again. That form brings with it a number of things that we've either got to go with or deny. I can remember at one point we were talking about *Pax* and we talked about doing it as a twelve-hour performance in order to break the back of that kind of hour-and-a-half, you know, you do this, the graph goes like that, and then it goes like that. In· these pieces of work which have all these aspects of — 'field' — and 'hybrid' — and all of those kinds of words which are not about narrative, not about lines — there is a kind of conflict between the form that we've chosen — the hour-and-a-half show — and the materials we're addressing.

Some long performances seem to be tyrannical in their use or abuse of the audience's time, but some manage to create a sense that members of the audience can leave and come back.

CM: Yes. Well, you see, if you can leave and come back, if people are kind of dipping in to this thing and dipping out of it, then the whole structure of how these moments are tied together internally within the piece goes out of the window.

Is there not also a connection with certain archaeological practices? You've written about the approach to site in terms of reading clues, reading signs, of 'forensic evidence', 'scene-of-the-crime', and so on.

MP: I think it's something I'm thinking a lot about at the moment, largely through being in contact with archaeologists who question the whole

---

CM 31 The fifth of **Haearn's** architectures is that of **The Climate**

a temperature
　　(i)　the environment — all-over cold
　　(ii)　the coke beds — localised intense heat
b rain
c snow
d wind

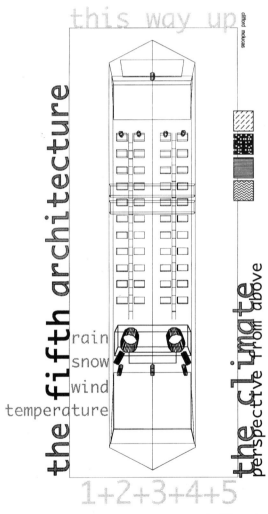

Figure 62　Clifford McLucas *Haearn*, the Fifth Architecture, *The Climate* (courtesy of the artist).

CM 33 The sixth of **Haearn's** architectures is that of **The Grid**.

In contrast with the sophisticated and continuous 3-d space generated by contemporary robotics, the key mechanical components of the Industrial Age such as the wheel, the track, the pulley, and the lever all generate limited and reduced movement in three dimensions — up and down, left to right, forwards and backwards.

All movements in **Haearn** arise from this mechanical agenda.

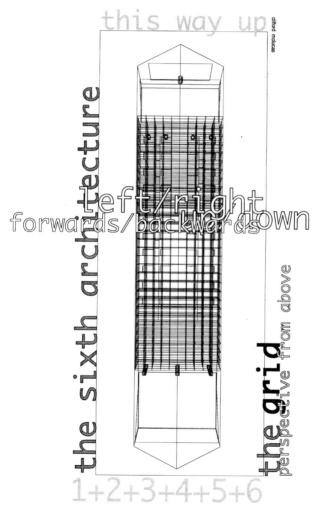

Figure 63 Clifford McLucas *Haearn*, the Sixth Architecture, *The Grid* (courtesy of the artist).

notion of the 'material record', of the archaeological record as a text that can be read and from which meaning is self-evident. That was the tradition I was brought up in. I think that the so-called post-processual thought about archaeology is really throwing that away. And exciting things come out of that. I even heard my great friend John Barratt in the Theoretical Archaeology Group conference (Newcastle, December 1993) saying — well, let's play around — let's think of the neolithic as a kind of playground. I think that the whole question of excavation itself and what diggers are doing is also extremely interesting.

One issue which both excavation and site-specific performance raise is that of the nature and value of 'documentation', of precisely what you can take away from a 'site' and the purposes such 'documentation' might serve.

CM: The interesting question about documentation for me is whether it's actually the recording of something you've done or something else, another thing. Or whether, actually, it can be both. I'm playing around with those things at the moment. If somebody reviews a piece of work and that's the only material that exists about a show, it seems a bit odd. Nobody else would do that. An artist would photograph their work at the very least — so I think we've got a responsibility to be taking care of documentation which is arising out of our work.

MP: I think the documents we pass on have to work. And they may need to be completely other to the performance itself in order to be useful.

Are you in the process of documenting work?

CM: Yes. The University Press in Cardiff wanted to publish a series of plays written by Welsh playwrights. They came to us and said, look, we'd like to do a *Brith Gof* one. I suggested *Haearn*, but I also suggested we'd like to do it graphically. To try to make a score of a piece like *Haearn*, which is a large-scale, symphonic kind of work — how do you do that? Neither the music nor the text nor the physical actions alone kind of carry the piece. So we've been thinking about a kind of A3, A4 width, so you can read the music off it and the text is kind of placed accordingly, with technical and background information.

So it would consist of a notation of the materials necessary to a remaking of Haearn.

CM: Absolutely. That's the conceit. That someone could pick up this book and go and make *Haearn*. And to do it in that way is exciting — it's a very dense and complex score.

CM 35 The seventh of **Haearn's** architectures is **The Times**

Four distinct time scales are stretched or compressed into the same span:

a Mary Shelley's personal and novelistic writings from 1814 to 1822
b first hand accounts of key developments in Industrial Science and Medical Science during the century 1760 to 1860
c the 'never never' time of Greek Myth
d the 90 minutes 'real time' of the event

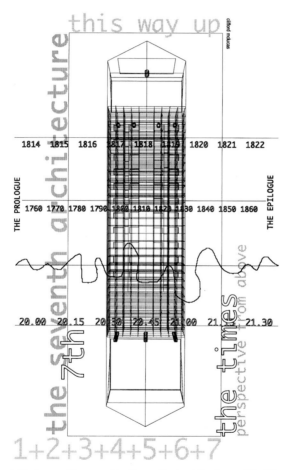

Figure 64 Clifford McLucas *Haearn*, the Seventh Architecture, *The Times* (courtesy of the artist).

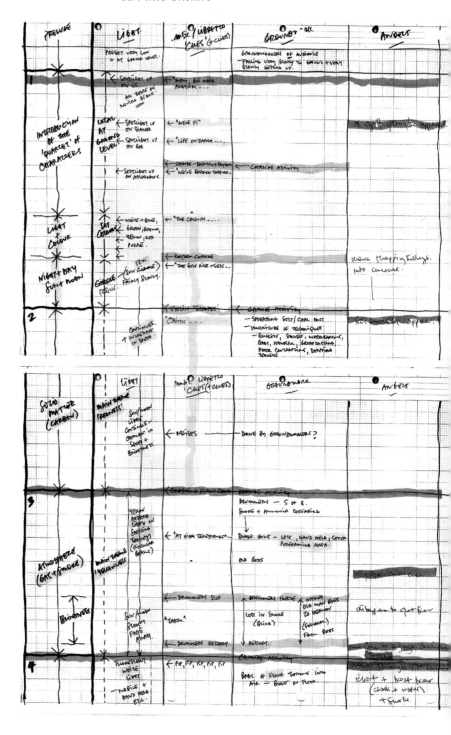

Figure 65   Clifford McLucas, working score for *Pax* Aberystwyth (courtesy: Brith Gof).

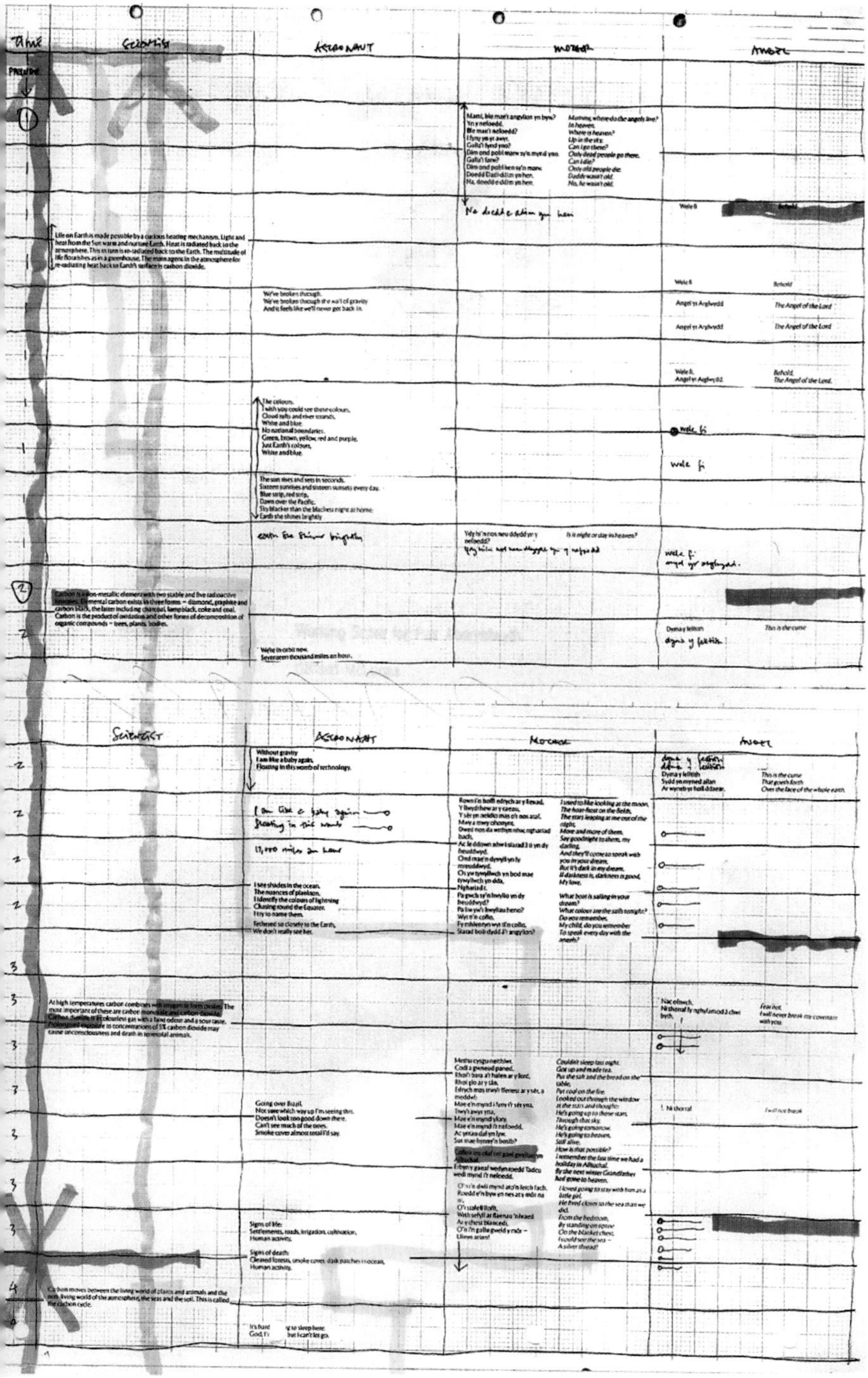
TIME
SCIENTIST
ASTRONAUT
MOTHER
ANGEL
PRELUDE
Mami, ble mae'r angylion yn byw?
Yn y nefoedd.
Ble mae'r nefoedd?
Lan yn yr awyr.
Galla'i fynd yno?
Dim ond pobl marw sy'n mynd yno.
Galla'i farw?
Dim ond pobl hen sy'n marw.
Doedd Dadi ddim yn hen.
Na, doedd e ddim yn hen.
Mummy, where do the angels live?
In heaven.
Where is heaven?
Up in the sky.
Can I go there?
Only dead people go there.
Can I die?
Only old people die.
Daddy wasn't old.
No, he wasn't old.
Life on Earth is made possible by a curious heating mechanism. Light and heat from the Sun warm and nurture Earth. Heat is radiated back to the atmosphere. This in turn is re-radiated back to the Earth. The multitude of life flourishes as in a greenhouse. The main agent in the atmosphere for re-radiating heat back to Earth's surface is carbon dioxide.
We've broken through.
We've broken through the wall of gravity
And it feels like we'll never get back in.
Wele fi
Behold
Angel yr Arglwydd
The Angel of the Lord
Angel yr Arglwydd
The Angel of the Lord
Wele fi,
Angel yr Arglwydd.
Behold,
The Angel of the Lord.
The colours.
I wish you could see these colours,
Cloud tufts and river strands,
White and blue.
No national boundaries.
Green, brown, yellow, red and purple.
Just Earth's colours,
White and blue.
wele fi
wele fi
The sun rises and sets in seconds.
Sixteen sunrises and sixteen sunsets every day.
Blue strip, red strip,
Dawn over the Pacific.
Sky blacker than the blackest night at home.
Earth she shines brightly
Ydy hi'n nos neu ddydd yn y nefoedd?
Is it night or day in heavens?
Carbon is a non-metallic element with two stable and five radioactive isotopes. Elemental carbon exists in three forms – diamond, graphite and carbon black, the latter including charcoal, lampblack, coke and coal. Carbon is the product of oxidation and other forms of decomposition of organic compounds – trees, plants, bodies.
Dyma y felltith
This is the curse
We're in orbit now.
Seventeen thousand miles an hour.
Without gravity
I am like a baby again.
Floating in this womb of technology.
Dyma y felltith
Sydd yn mynd allan
Ar wyneb yr holl ddaear.
This is the curse
That goeth forth
Over the face of the whole earth.
I used to like looking at the moon,
The hoar-frost on the fields,
The stars leaping at me out of the night,
More and more of them.
Say goodnight to them, my darling.
And they'll come to speak with you in your dream,
But it's dark in my dream.
If darkness is, darkness is good,
My love.
What boat is sailing in your dream?
What colour are the sails tonight?
Do you remember,
My child, do you remember
To speak every day with the angels?
I see shades in the ocean.
The nuances of plankton.
I identify the colours of lightning
Chasing round the Equator.
I try to name them.
Tethered so closely to the Earth,
We don't really see her.
At high temperatures carbon combines with oxygen to form oxides. The most important of these are carbon monoxide and carbon dioxide. Carbon dioxide is a colourless gas with a faint odour and a sour taste. Prolonged exposure to concentrations of 5% carbon dioxide may cause unconsciousness and death in terrestrial animals.
Nac ofnwch.
Fear not.
I will never break my covenant with you.
Couldn't sleep last night.
Got up and made tea.
Put the salt and the bread on the table,
Put coal on the fire.
Looked out through the window at the stars and thought:
He's going up to those stars,
Through that sky.
He's going tomorrow.
He's going to heaven,
Still alive.
How is that possible?
I remember the last time we had a holiday in Alltuchaf.
By the next winter Grandfather had gone to heaven.
I loved going to stay with him as a little girl.
He lived closer to the sea than we did.
From the bedroom,
By standing on tiptoe
On the blanket chest,
I could see the sea –
A silver thread!
Going over Brazil.
Not sure which way up I'm seeing this.
Doesn't look too good down there.
Can't see much of the trees.
Smoke cover almost total I'd say.
I will not break
Signs of life:
Settlements, roads, irrigation, cultivation,
Human activity.
Signs of death:
Cleared forests, smoke cover, dark patches in ocean,
Human activity.
Carbon moves between the living world of plants and animals and the non-living world of the atmosphere, the seas and the soil. This is called the carbon cycle.

It's interesting that the score deals with all those materials that you used in the place, but not the place itself.

CM: Absolutely. It's unavoidable. You've got to accept the fact that a site-specific work is site-specific. I think it's quite a challenge for those of us working in this field, where the work exists in real time, in real space — the work doesn't exist on the pages of a script. And because of that kind of reaction away from pages of a script we've left ourselves empty handed in terms of the work existing in any other media or in any other context. And that's where the whole impulse of — what is documentation? And you suddenly start thinking of sliding things along cultural strata and of having an effect which is quite disconnected, I think, to the original kind of event. I suppose the thing about the *Haearn* publication and the *Haearn* score is that it will be all of the materials that were there, but with none of the life or the live*ness* of the event. It can then only be brought to life by somebody else doing something with it. In principle it would be possible to do a site-specific work like *Haearn* in somebody's bathroom — and to take that score and to do that would be very exciting. We always used to talk about *Goddodin* as being — well, we could do *Goddodin* — it doesn't have to be *big*. And so you've got to loosen your grip on that actual event — there are all kinds of ways in which you have to do that.

MP: At the Theoretical Archaeology Group conference, it was interesting that in her paper Heike Roms pointedly said that the German word for 'theatrical presentation' and 'conscious memory' is the same one. I'm actually quite interested in the way that a score like this can help to create performances in the imagination. Not necessarily physically, but you can create pictures, or extended, enormous pictures for people to work with. In a way, it doesn't actually need a physical manifestation of the event itself.

TIM ETCHELLS AND RICHARD LOWDON
(FORCED ENTERTAINMENT THEATRE
CO-OPERATIVE)

Founded in 1984, Forced Entertainment Theatre Co-operative is comprised of a core group of six — Robin Arthur, Deborah Chadbourn, Tim Etchells, Richard Lowdon, Claire Marshall, Cathy Nadan and Terry O'Connor. Since their inception, the company have produced eleven full-scale performance works, including *(Let the Water Run Its Course) To The Sea That Made the Promise* (1986), *200% and Bloody Thirsty* (1987), *Club of No Regrets* (1993) and, most recently, *Hidden J.* (1994). Developed collaboratively over extended periods of rehearsal, through improvisation, writing, research and discussion, Forced Entertainment construct performances in relation to 'found' material from television, film, theatre, popular culture, and visual art. Increasingly, the company have come to extend their work across a variety of means, including installation and site-specific performance. In collaboration with the photographer Hugo Glendinning and performer Will Waghorn, the group presented the installation, *The Red Room*, at the Showroom Gallery, London, in December 1993. In 1994, Forced Entertainment were commissioned to devise a site-specific performance for Manchester Central Library, *Dreams' Winter*. This interview with Tim Etchells, who directs and writes for the company, and Richard Lowdon, who performs and is responsible for design, was recorded in Sheffield at the company's offices in April 1994.

*   *   *

You first incorporated television monitors and video into your work in 1987 with 200% and Bloody Thirsty, *and went on to develop this through* Some Confusions in the Law about Love *(1989),* Marina and Lee *(1991) and* Emmanuelle Enchanted (or A Description Of This World As If It Were A Beautiful Place) *(1992). Why did you choose not to use either video or closed-circuit TV in* Club of No Regrets *(1993)?*

  RL: There was a conscious decision early on in *Club of No Regrets* that we were tired of the monitors as objects. The monitors are so formal, one always has to think of where to place them.

  TE: We had two more ideas, really, that we've half tried. We wanted perhaps to work with a single monitor that was placed within the *Club of No*

Regrets room, so it becomes a television in a fictional frame. We also talked about — but had limited success with — in some way encroaching on or vandalising the monitors as objects. In *Club of No Regrets* we talked about having monitors in the 'outside' space around the set that would be wrapped in polythene. They would become these things that had been brutalised, encroached upon. We had various ideas about burying them in soil, of wanting to shatter that nice, square, matt-black box.

RL: We were also very aware of them as an element supplying another layer. It feels like everything has to stop so the videos can be used to supply that layer. Part of our desire was to let things on stage run their course.

What were the concerns that led you to an incorporation of the monitors in the first place?

TE: Initially, we did a whole lot of single-genre based work, such as *The Set-Up* (1985) and *Nighthawks* (1986), which were deconstructions of particular filmic genres. So there was already an interest in the imagery that one would associate with film and television. Then, in *(Let the Water Run Its Course) To The Sea That Made the Promise* (1987), we began to deal with Sheffield. And we found that bits of graffiti that we'd seen here, or notes that we'd found in the street, or gestures — that the feel of the place became manifested in the work. *200% and Bloody Thirsty* was an extension of this, of taking things from the urban everyday, of trying to get as much of that in as possible. We've talked a lot about growing up in a house with the TV always on in the corner of the room. On *Let the Water* and *200% and Bloody Thirsty* we talked a lot about cities and the media-scape — they were touchstones.

What do you mean by media-scape?

TE: I suppose one of our interests as a company has always been — where do you live your life? We live in Sheffield, in the city, and our immediate landscape is what we can see out of the window. But we have so many other landscapes. So where does our visual image bank locate itself? The space that we really live in is a kind of electronically mediated one. And it feels like one's landscape — the source of one's images, the things that haunt you — are likely to be second, third, fourth-hand. Also, in the early shows, like *Nighthawks*, and even *Let the Water*, we had taped voices that framed what you saw on stage. Because they were on tape the voices had an omniscient, body-less quality. They were exterior to the world. We wanted to put the narrator's voice in the world — on video — so that it would become more questionable and visible.

Could you talk about how your use of video and the monitors has developed since 200% and Bloody Thirsty?

RL: The visual world in *200%* located two angels, each on their own monitor, looking down over the scene as sort of 'not seen' or half-noticed presences. The angels spoke to one another and appeared to observe what was going on below. But the two worlds — the stage world and the video world — remained separate except when there were apparent looks toward the angels or apparent references to them in the text. When we get to *Some Confusions in the Law about Love*, the characters on the monitors talk directly to Robin on stage, so the vocal channel is opened up. In *Some Confusions*, the monitors were also positioned *within* the set, couched within the frame.

TE: So the monitors are dragged down into that world. In *Marina and Lee*, the video material takes on a framing function, giving the titles of individual sections. At the same time, it runs an ambient track of people running about and shows clips which shadow the quotations and appropriations from film that occur on stage. Finally, it's used for another

Figure 66　Forced Entertainment Theatre Co-operative *Marina and Lee* (1991) (photo: Hugo Glendinning).

conversation — like those in *Some Confusions* — between Marina on the stage and Lee on video. In *Emmanuelle Enchanted*, we firmly placed the camera on the stage and all that's shown on the monitor is what's happening live. All you see is what's there anyway, reframed. Interestingly, in *Emmanuelle Enchanted* and *Marina and Lee*, there is also a notion of performing to camera. When, in *Marina and Lee*, Cathy and Terry scream with the guns at the audience, every ounce of focus that's going on is towards some fictional other — and it's into a camera, it's a close-up. Repeatedly, in *Marina and Lee*, there's a sense of playing this moment intimately to camera.

RL: To pick up on that, I think *Club of No Regrets* posits the camera somewhere out in the audience.

TE: They're still performing to camera.

RL: The camera that was on stage in *Emmanuelle Enchanted* is now imagined to be somewhere in the audience. In *Club of No Regrets*, I put my arm in through the window and I look out to check whether my arm's in shot — find it's in the right place — then read my book. So there's a sense in which *Club of No Regrets* is still dealing with that, it's just that the monitors have disappeared. In the performance, I'm concerned with this framing.

TE: So we got to the point in *Emmanuelle* with the camera where we were saying — actually, we're not prepared to use the camera anymore to bring in extra material from another place and another time. We're only prepared to use it to show you what's there anyway. And at that point, you realise that your interest, your faith in all the pre-recorded fictions that are in *Marina and Lee, 200% and Bloody Thirsty* and *Some Confusions in the Law about Love*, has dwindled. I think at that point you say — well, are we going to do another piece where we show with the camera what's there anyway?

I'm interested in how these concerns with mediation inform what the performers themselves are doing, because it seems related to this sense that the performer's actions and texts are somehow second-hand or being re-phrased or quoted through the performance. It's as if the performers engage in actions, each of which they sooner or later wake up from.

TE: I think that metaphor of waking up — certainly in terms of the live performance — is right. The way we think about that is of 'dropping down' from. The performers do something and then they 'drop down' from it or they 'drop out' of it. They come to gaps in which they've stopped and they're thinking — what was that again? Why was I doing it? Yeah, maybe I'd better — and then they're off again. I think that's a strategy used on all levels within the pieces.

Figure 67 Forced Entertainment Theatre Co-operative *Emmanuelle Enchanted (or A Description Of This World As If It Were A Beautiful Place)* (1992) (photo: Hugo Glendinning).

Don't you as a consequence see them using the material?

TE: What you're watching is in some ways the task of these people using, dealing with, exploring these texts and their conjunctions, their collisions. And we dramatise that task.

And, in Club of No Regrets, *the sense of a 'film' framing, of playing to the camera and 'getting it right', of framing and re-framing, is one of the means by which that task is exposed and dramatised, despite the fact that no cameras are present.*

TE: Yes. In a sense all of what Richard and Cathy are doing is special effects and continuity straight out of film-making — 'Better just move that a little bit to the left'.

RL: 'We'll have to re-shoot that scene'.

TE: But it's not a 'pure' task, it's not 'work' in the way that some of Station House Opera's performance can be.

Figure 68   Forced Entertainment Theatre Co-operative *Club of No Regrets* (1993) (photo: Hugo Glendinning).

CLUB OF NO REGRETS is the tenth theatre project by Forced Entertainment.

In it a figure Helen X orders a series of enactments of scenes by a pair of performers inside a tiny box set, centre stage. To facilitate or perhaps hinder these enactments a second pair of performers function as stage hands or captors who, having tied the other two to chairs and threatened them with guns, proceed to bring them the texts and props they might need. The enacted scenes are replayed many times as though Helen is unsure as to their true order or correct arrangement. The scenes are framed by a further text from Helen, a confused narration of her fairy story/history which she calls CLUB OF NO REGRETS.

Tim Etchells, from *Club of No Regrets* (1993) (courtesy of the author).

What do you mean by that?

RL: With us, you're watching something that has been formulated to work within a dramatic shape. There's a difference between, say, the eleven-hour cardboard signing performance — the installation, *12 am: Awake and Looking Down* (1993), which we did at the Institute of Contemporary Arts in London — and the way the cardboard signs operate in *Emmanuelle Enchanted*. *12 am: Awake and Looking Down* acquired a completely different kind of dynamic, operating with only the five performers, the clothes and the signs, it was much more like *work*. You were watching these people working in a small space, and because one is working continually over such a long period, at times one's sense of presenting things dramatically dipped. What we were doing — as the clothes got more piled up over the floor — was just picking up any pair of trousers I can wear, any sign I could possibly be. It's a simple task that has dramatic resonances. But in *Emmanuelle Enchanted* those things came round in a particular order.

TE: The point is that we often work — not to that sort of length — but certainly to two hours in improvisations, just watching a person do things. And there'll be lots of things that are interesting in that. It may even be a completely fascinating two hours, but what we'll then end up doing for a theatre-piece is saying, right, that was two hours, let's condense that to a twenty-minute section. In doing that, though, you're replacing the original architecture with a theatricalized version of it. *Club of No Regrets*, now, is almost all fixed. The performers know exactly what scene's coming next and Terry always calls the scenes in the same order. Pretty well the same objects are used — and gags are played about interruptions and so on. But when we rehearsed it Terry just used to call any scene she wanted to and Richard and Cathy would put in any object. We videotaped it and worked from the videotapes.

One of the things 'task' work has been associated with is challenging or throwing out 'fictions'. Club of No Regrets *is obviously organised in a very different way from* 12 am: Awake and Looking Down, *but nevertheless it exposes the performer's 'task' of dealing with the 'fictional' scenes. As the scenes are repeated, you see the performers working with the fictions, you see the effort in their attempt to create and re-create these moments.*

RL: Yeah, sure.

I wonder how important this notion of 'work' and the exposure of fictions is to the earlier work — to Marina *and* Lee *for example? I find* Marina *and* Lee *a more difficult piece to watch than either* Emmanuelle Enchanted or Club of No Regrets.

TE: I think it's a more difficult show because, for one reason, the work of people dealing with things is more hidden. In *Marina and Lee* there's a notion of 'off off' as we call it. You go off and you stay off and you change your costume — and you come back totally committed to 'now' screaming with the gun, where two seconds earlier you were an opera singer. The process of transformation from one text to another isn't shown in *Marina and Lee*. I think that makes it a very aggressive show. It's very bracing. The process is hinted at a couple of times, but in *Emmanuelle Enchanted* and *Club of No Regrets* you are watching the process of transformation all the time. That's very much what they're about.

RL: *Marina and Lee* is also about entering the stage. It's about coming on to a stage. It's about presenting yourself in front of that audience.

In my watching of Marina and Lee, *it seemed that another reason why the piece might be more 'difficult' is because the audience is repeatedly denied access to what, apparently, one is supposed to be hearing or seeing. Performers whisper to the audience and they can't be heard, the person who is gagged is asked what it's all about. If they're not whispering or mumbling, they're shouting. And while the material you're actually being given is the displacement or obscuring of the various texts, the piece, in this way, presents itself as curiously out of reach.*

TE: Yes. In *Marina and Lee* there is a kind of blanking out of bits of text by one strategy or another.

RL: Even their confessions are obscured from you because it's too loud or they can't stop laughing — Cath won't speak up. And the moment when the stage floods with white light, and the performers are in their underwear, and it's as if — OK, well, this show may be Marina's fiction — but Marina's gone off for a break. You feel like — they're really going to tell me something now, they'll let me in on what it is they've been doing. But it's snatched away from you.

Why Marina and Lee Harvey Oswald?

RL: We became interested in them when I read the book *Marina and Lee* by Priscilla Johnson McMillan. It was constructed through interviews with Marina Oswald. Their story is quite fascinating, because it's this cultural icon and because so little is known about Marina. She was a Russian woman who Lee married in Minsk and then returned with him to America. He didn't want her to learn English. He refused to teach her English — he would speak Russian to her. So she was incredibly isolated in America. I think we were interested in her because her understanding of the world was only through him.

TE: And through a language that she didn't understand, which we thought was iconic of the way our characters operate —

RL: — are disenfranchised.

TE: It was kind of reading things through an inappropriate set of screens or frames. Marina seemed like a really interesting figure in that respect. I think also from *Some Confusions in the Law about Love* we had an interest in using historical figures — in *Some Confusions* it was Elvis Presley. With Elvis, I suppose, it was the way everybody uses him as a blank sheet of paper on which to construct any sort of religious, sexual, mystical, political theory. 'Elvis Presley Killed by The Mafia' was the last book that I saw on the subject.

There's also something distant about these figures. They seem unapproachable as 'real' people, and the audience is given very little information about them.

TE: A joke for us early on in *Marina and Lee* was that Lee would only appear on video and that when he did he would say: 'I didn't kill him'. And Marina would say: 'Who?' And he would say: 'Kennedy'. And she would say: 'I know'. And that would be it. Those were the only references to the real lives of those people that would feature in any way. It was a joke about taking real lives about which you know nothing, who are, sort of, very difficult to take as real, and doing something odd with them. Doing something that didn't belong to them. There was one other thing, really, which is that in Minsk, Lee and Marina had long suspected that an electrical device on the wall — probably a central heating thermostat — was a bugging device.

RL: When they moved out — when they eventually got a visa to go back to the States — they packed up all their stuff, sat on their suitcases and confessed to this thing on the wall. Confessed a whole load of things that they'd done and revealed things about people — not by implicating them, but by saying exactly what they thought of them. Like a way of ridding yourself of one bit of your past before leaving. And I always imagine them stood on the suitcase — that the thing is high up on the wall and they're sort of shouting up at it. That was very much what was going on behind the piece, that was what we started working from and where the idea for the confessions came from — the idea to confess your crimes.

In the piece, there's a strong sense of Marina being lost.

TE: Yes.

And of a series of events being filtered through these torn-up moments from television programmes that neither the audience nor Marina herself have any proper access to.

RL: She's lost in a landscape that she doesn't understand.

You keep on coming back to landscape.

TE: There's something about 'landscape' — in the way that we use it — which might include extremely dissonant possibilities. In Sheffield you will get the ruins of Attercliffe, the old steel production area, and in the midst of it there's the huge Olympic standard velodrome. The landscape is a mess, usually. We're working with collage and bringing things together from different places — and you can do that in such a way as to make connections. An audience will connect more or less anything to more or less anything else, but you can help by making the connections and textual similarities or dissimilarities work in particular ways. That will happen whether or not there's any propensity towards fictional cohesion. It's very important in *Marina and Lee*, that when you look at it a little bit more closely you see that all these fragments are of performative moments — a fragment of a TV movie, an opera, a Sex Act. There is nothing that's done that isn't a fragment of a performance of one kind or another.

And, in keeping with the other work, there is to some extent a synthesis of these fragments on an emotional level, which is primarily to do with tone. John Avery's music is obviously important to this — and the fact that the collage itself is organised, if you like, musically, rather than through a narrative.

TE: I think tonal similarities play a large part in the selection or rejection of materials. Also, there's a levelling when you bring everything onto the stage anyway. The material is going through these five bodies.

The 'work' you've talked about seems to be an important part of this tone — this unifying sense of displacement or loss.

TE: There's no first order utterance. There's no utterance from anybody that isn't somehow a quotation of something else.

To me, Club of No Regrets *seems very important in this respect. The re-playing of scenes in* Club of No Regrets *appears to be going somewhere, it seems to be moving toward the performers' 'possession' of the scenes. In other words, even though you are very aware of the repetition, of the 'quoted' nature of the scenes, the performance seems to arrive somewhere.*

TE: Well, it's odd, isn't it? The way *Club of No Regrets* actually works is that, on the one hand, the attempt by Terry to manipulate these scenes begins chaotically and — we could say — gets nowhere. It fails to the extent that Robin and Claire, who're meant to be acting the scenes, even stop doing them. They end up just holding each other for dear life in the middle of the set, while Richard and Cathy run around madly, doing the special effects in a completely out-of-synch way, and Terry, who's supposed to be directing it, ends up trying to do the voices. In a way, the whole thing spirals round for ages and then gets nowhere. It just stops. But there's something about them stopping and the way the accumulation of the material goes, that makes that stopping feel like *something* rather than nothing. You do feel that the whole project has worked — but at the same time as it clearly hasn't worked, because it's stopped.

I think it's not simply to do with the playing of the scenes, but with the work of playing the scenes. After all, the scenes don't 'add up', there isn't a 'right order' in which they would make sense.

RL: Absolutely. The other thing that happens when Robin and Claire embrace and stop doing anything is that you see them do something of their

---

A PROCEDURES SCENE

A: Half of my officers were themselves arrested this morning due to some administrative blunder in the East Side of the city. Can you imagine that?

B: It's terrible.

A: I had some thoughts about procedure I thought I'd run them past you. That OK?

B: Yes.

A: We're agreed that during the search attention should be paid, not only to all details but also to trivia. Those carrying out the search need to understand, instinctively, that everything in the area has its own intrinsic importance.

A SHOOT OUT SCENE

A: Ahhh.

B: What is it?

A: I think I'm hit. I'm seeing colours. I'm thinking in shapes. Hold me. Talk to me.

B: Oh god.

A: Talk to me, speak to me.

B: What do you want to hear?

A: Anything, I'm dying aren't I. I'm going down, just tell me something.

B: It's... It's OK. You're not dying. Just... Listen...

A TROUBLED SCENE

A: Queen of Nothing we call upon you to help us...

B: Today I am troubled, cease to speak, cease to walk. I am troubled by
     voices. I call on Our Lady of Carparks to help me. I summon her, help
     me break loose from these bindings.
     Prince of Lie-Detection and Broken Promises, I am coming dressed
     in rags to meet you. Queen of Nothing, mistress of the air and of
     satellites we have not seen you, it has been long since we've seen
     you. Oh can't you see I have no skin and no bones. I am dressed in
     rags just to meet you.

A QUESTIONS SCENE

A: When did you first discover that the world was magic? When did you
     first discover that you caused magic in the world? When did you first
     discover that there was magic in the world?

A LOOK HOW I'M CRYING SCENE

A: Look how I'm crying. Don't you care at all? Look how I'm crying.

B: I don't want you to leave.

A: Where am I going? What am I going to do?

B: I have pretended for so long that everything is fine.

Tim Etchells, scenes for *Club of No Regrets* (1993) (courtesy of the author).

own volition. And that's really the first time in the show — which is why one
feels like it's got somewhere. Up until then everybody has been forced to do
one thing or another. By the same token, Cath and I, outside the room, almost
become the people that care more about the thing in the centre than they do.

*Yet the repetition of the scene doesn't drain it of its meaning in a way that one might
expect. It's as if through their repetition the scenes threaten to become almost what
they should be, despite the fact that their repetition is so visible. It may be because the
performing of the scene, the work of the performance itself, becomes more intense, as
though the performers* will *take possession of what they are doing.*

     TE: I don't know about this, but my question is that — when can
we say that we 'own' something or 'are' something? I'm speaking now — but
the way I'm speaking, the phrases I use are all borrowed, either consciously
or not. I was having a conversation with Lloyd Newson of DV8, who was

saying, you know, he wants to find this way of being honest, of speaking truthfully, from himself. In a pure way. I just don't believe that's possible. I don't believe that anybody ever does it. I think that everything we say is already borrowed from somewhere, even when we're not aware of it explicitly. Within the work that's usually pretty obvious — that the characters are speaking in tongues.

One might say, then, that the sense of 'mediation' lies within the fabric of the performance itself rather than simply being a matter of the presence of televisions or the use of video. It's to do, perhaps, with the inability of the performers to fully inhabit the gestures and texts which they perform, which constitute what they do.

TE: It's as much perhaps that those borrowings or quotations or second or third-hand things that these people have got are to them probably the only language they know. As such, it's the language they use to try to define and to construct and come to rest about themselves and their world. I think in that sense the metaphor for us is 'rag-picking' — of going through the ruins and getting these bits and trying to do something with them. We sometimes talk about speaking in tongues, about possession. There's a line in *Ghostdance*, a film by Ken McMullen — it's a story from some African tale or something — in which a woman goes into a trance, and the voices that come out of her are the voices of the dead. That's really — I think — what's going on. Voices are coming out of these people and yet they aren't theirs — but in a subtle sort of way they become theirs.

Did you write the scenes for Club of No Regrets *or find them?*

TE: They're written, but they're written in the way that I write, which is that I have a notebook full of fragments of TV, conversation, books, bits out of the newspaper. Probably a lot of those lines individually are from other things, with some 'original' writing. I did a writing workshop a while back with some people — and one of them in particular was very disturbed by the idea that the writing was 'only' a copying out and bringing together of bits from all over the place. She was saying — but there isn't any of you put into it. This is the question we're discussing — what does that really mean — 'any of me'?

You said in the programme to Club of No Regrets — 'Club of No Regrets *is a performance about the work of seeing'. Can you elaborate on this?*

TE: I think that we're familiar with that idea that when an audience sees this work they are responsible for completing it — filling gaps and making connections between texts. As you said earlier, in our work the final synthesis has been staved off. I think that's true, but I think the truth is that

Telegram Scenes

Telegram One
DEAR NO-ONE I HAVE WALKED TO THAT BIT OF THE PARK WHERE THE TAPE SAYS POLICE LINE DO NOT CROSS AND I HAVE CROSSED IT STOP DO NOT TRY TO FIND ME STOP COS I'M A KIND OF HOMEMADE BOMB, DESTINED TO EXPLODE PRETTY SOON STOP BETTER FOR YOU IF YOU AREN'T NEAR ME THEN, BETTER FOR EVERYONE STOP OH YEAH AND I SUPPOSE IT'S NO SURPRISE I'M PREGNANT STOP FOR THESE THREE YEARS I HAD NO SEX WITH ANYONE, I TRIED TO FORGET I EVER HAD A THING CALLED SEXUALITY THEN ONE LITTLE FUCK AND I'M PREGNANT STOP IT'S GOING TO BE A GIRL I'M SURE AND SHE'S GOING TO BE PERFECT AND I'M GOING TO CALL HER GRIEF...

Telegram Two
DEAR NO-ONE I'M SO UNHAPPY I'M GOING TO GET INVOLVED IN BAD PEOPLE TO TRY AND GET MYSELF MURDERED STOP YOU KNOW WHAT IT'S LIKE THESE DAYS — YOU WAKE UP EMBROILED IN A GREAT ADVENTURE AND THE NEXT THING YOU KNOW YOU'RE THROUGH THE FUCKING LOOKING GLASS INTO WEIRD WORLD STOP OH YEAH THINGS ROUND HERE HAVE CERTAINLY CHANGED STOP IN MY DREAM I'M NOT SURE WHO I'M SUPPOSED TO BE STOP YESTERDAY I FOUND A NOTE BY THE BEDSIDE TABLE BUT IT WASN'T IN MY HANDWRITING STOP THE NOTE SAID I'M OLD, OR GETTING OLD STOP THE NOTE SAID I'M HIDING BUT I'M NOT SURE WHO FROM...

Telegram Three
DEAR NO-ONE STOP THE VOICES AND NOISES IN THE NIGHT ARE SCARING ME NOW STOP I'M INSIDE A CITY OF LIVING FAINTING BUILDINGS AND NOW IT'S GETTING DARK STOP DO YOU THINK THAT A ROOM CAN BE HAUNTED BY THE GHOST OF ITSELF? DO YOU THINK OUR BODIES KEEP THEIR GHOSTS STORED DEEP INSIDE THEM? IN MY DREAM I HAVE BEEN GIVEN A JOB AND I'M GOING TO KILL TO DO IT: TEN THOUSAND IN CASH AND A CAR AND FRIDGE FREEZER TO KILL SOMEONE WHO NO-ONE WILL EVER EVEN MISS SURELY THAT ISN'T SO MUCH A CRIME AS A MINOR BENDING OF THE RULES HA HA OH YEAH AND BY THE WAY DON'T CALL HERE AGAIN IT'S DANGEROUS...

Telegram Four

DEAR NO-ONE STOP I HAVE RENTED A ROOM IN A GOOD PART OF
TOWN STOP IT'S BIG AND CLEAN BUT THERE IS SOME NOISE FROM
THE ROOMS ABOVE AND BELOW STOP OH YEAH I HAVE FOUND A
KNIFE BENEATH MY PILLOW STOP AND I THINK I MIGHT HAVE
USED IT STOP WHEN I LOOK INTO THE MIRROR I CAN SEE MY LIPS
ARE MOVING BUT I'M NOT SURE THE WORDS ARE MINE OH AND
BY THE WAY I MISS YOU, THE WALKS WE'D TAKE IN THE WINTER
GARDENS, THE PEACE THAT WE HAD WHEN WE SLEPT EASY IN
BED...

Telegram Five

DEAR NO-ONE STOP I AM CERTAIN OF ONE THING ONLY STOP
AND THAT'S MY LOVE FOR THIS WORLD STOP IN MY DREAM I'M A
PRIVATE DETECTIVE RIPPED OUT OF A NOVEL AND DROPPED IN
THIS PLACE STOP I HAVE BEEN THINKING ABOUT STUFF STOP YOU
KNOW THE KIND OF STUFF IT'S HARD TO TALK ABOUT STOP HAVE
YOU NOTICED THE STRANGE CHANGES OF ONE'S BODY WITH
AGE? HAVE YOU NOTICED THAT? HAVE YOU NOTICED THE
POWER CUTS GETTING MORE FREQUENT? HAVE YOU EVER BEEN
SCARED?

Telegram Six

DEAR NO-ONE STOP WHEN I LOOK OUT OF THE WINDOW I CAN
SEE THE WHOLE CITY IN ALL ITS SPLENDOUR STOP WHAT A VIEW
STOP WHAT A VIEW STOP BUT WHERE ARE THE PEOPLE? IN MY
DREAM I'M FALLING DEEPER AND DEEPER INTO A BLACK HOLE
CALLED **THE NIGHT** STOP I'M FALLING AND I'M FALLING AND I'M
FALLING AND YOU'RE FALLING WITH ME STOP WE'RE FALLING
AND FALLING AND THERE'S NO END TO IT STOP DON'T KNOW IF
I'LL WRITE AGAIN I'M RUNNING OUT OF LUCK...

Tim Etchells, from *Club of No Regrets* (1993) (courtesy of the author).

that happens with any text. Described in that way I don't think our work's
any different to any other cultural artifact. Where I do think it's different is
that we try to bring to people's attention to their role in completing what's
happening. When in *Club of No Regrets* a saw is suddenly placed in Robin's
hand, you re-read the scene — that's it, it's a murder scene and Robin's the

one who's going to get Claire. Then a gun is put in Claire's hand and Claire comes for Robin with the saw and it's like — ah, she's gonna get him, and it's all switched round. Then the saw's taken off Robin and they go to kiss, and Claire's got the gun in her hand as they're about to kiss. So you're watching it change and you're very aware of your own part in realising that, of your own capacity for filling it out, for reading those things. I think the work is perhaps different from other cultural artifacts in that it stages and foregrounds your seeing, your experience of constructing things as they happen.

Actually, I stole that line or I've adapted it from something that James Turrel said. Turrel is a light sculptor, and he said this about one of his light pieces — that it was about seeing. It was a piece that he'd put up outside the Hayward Gallery in London, and as the day died, and so the neon insets began to burn more brightly, you made realisations about the way that you see. I think that's very true about this work as well. You're making realisations about how you watch, how you construct, what your visual and conceptual processes are doing when you look at something.

I've been thinking a lot about the way that people talk about our work and what it 'means', the way that people refer to characters and to what happens on stage. Well, obviously that's important, but there are key ways in which its wholly inadequate. In *Club of No Regrets*, especially, I think, you can make a kind of equation about what they do and how they do it and what the line of it is. Yet that describes the piece without telling you anything about it, because that's to defer to character and what happens on stage, when the piece is obviously, really, about what happens to you as a watcher. That's what it's about, it's about the process that you go through. A really important thing that we talk about in *Club of No Regrets*, in that sense, is that you almost reach a moment of narrative closure where Robin and Claire embrace. Richard and Cathy have stripped the room, and it looks like it's over. Then Terry calls for the dance routine, and the two fight their way out of the chairs. So you've had this huge architecture that leads to a point that's almost closed. Then you get a second architecture — and there's a gap between them. There is a relationship between the two, but there are all kinds of questions about what that relationship is. I think what happens is that it's been burned down to this embrace and this empty space around it and — just when you sort of understand — it goes, bang! It does something else and people come out of the show, usually, questioning it, in difficulty. And the reason — quite apart from the violence, energy and noise of those last few attempts to get out of the chairs — the real reason is that your brain is trying to read that last ten minutes against the hour and twenty-five minutes that went before it. It seems to me that it's rather like those

Warhol screenprints of Electric Chairs placed next to the colour-field paintings. Trying to cope with that does throw you back on yourself, on your own perceptual processes. I think that's what happens in *Club of No Regrets*. Just when you think it's closed and you've figured it, it does something else. You do just literally watch people coming out trying to compute that. A lot of people wish it would end at the embrace and I'm so glad it doesn't. I would hate it to. It seems really important to me that when it settles, you just have one final stirring of the mud and leave them with this rather incomputable equation.

ELIZABETH LECOMPTE
(THE WOOSTER GROUP)

Emerging out of Elizabeth LeCompte and Spalding Gray's development of the *Rhode Island Trilogy* (1975–1978) in collaboration with other members of The Performance Group, the Wooster Group was formally established in 1980 with The Performance Group's final dissolution. Since that time, members of the Wooster Group have worked collaboratively under the direction of LeCompte to compose highly original, rigorous and frequently complex performances. Beginning with the third play of their *Rhode Island Trilogy, Nyatt School* (1978), which was structured around six examinations of T. S. Eliot's *The Cocktail Party*, the group have included radical reworkings of well-known texts into productions incorporating performance fragments drawn from extremely diverse sources. *Route 1 and 9* (1981) set extracts from Thornton Wilder's *Our Town* against reconstructed blackface routines by the black vaudevillian Pigmeat Markham. *Frank Dell's Temptation of St Anthony* (1987) was the culmination of four years work by the Group and juxtaposed multiple texts against images and narrative lines drawn from Flaubert's *La Tentation de Saint Antoine*. More recently, *Brace Up!* (1991) brought together Chekhov's *Three Sisters* with the conventions of Noh theatre and popular Japanese television and film, while *Fish Story* (1993) addressed O'Neill's *The Emperor Jones*. Made up of a core membership — Jim Clayburgh, Willem Dafoe, Spalding Gray, Elizabeth LeCompte, Peyton Smith, Kate Valk and, until his death in 1994, Ron Vawter — the Group has a working structure intended to foster collaborations with other artists and performers, amongst whom have been Joan Jonas, Michael Kirby and Richard Foreman. Through its challenging and innovative nature, the Wooster Group's work has become a point around which much contemporary practice as well as performance theory and criticism positions itself. This interview was recorded in March 1993 at The Performing Garage, New York, and was part of a conversation including Marianne Weems, a Wooster Group Associate.

*　　　　*　　　　*

In developing Brace Up! *(1991) did you work with the Japanese material before addressing* Three Sisters?
    Yes.

Was this material linked to the notion of a Japanese theatre troupe?

I always use a framing device outside the material, so it's like an onion skin or a frame within a frame. In all the pieces there's some outside storyteller and there's a text within that story.

Do you see specific connections between the Japanese material and the Chekhov?

Well, I do after the fact, but it isn't something that informs the way we go about making the pieces. After the fact certain things become obvious, but they're never obvious to begin with. I didn't see any reason for them to be put together other than that I happen to be interested in the formal aspects of Japanese theatre and some of the Japanese pop culture stuff and that I happen to like Chekhov's writing. When I started working on *Route 1 and 9* (1981) I didn't have any idea that these routines from Pigmeat Markham would have anything to do with *Our Town*. I had no idea whatsoever that these two would go together. I was working on Pigmeat Markham material because I was interested in it formally, the way I'm interested in the Japanese material formally. Again, in a similar way, I was attracted to the writing, to Wilder's writing — specifically Wilder's writing as a sort of poetic text next to this popular material — 'poetic' in quotes — filled with sentimental meaning, but absolutely vacant of any *real* meaning taken apart from the characters. I then take these things as givens when we work. Of course, eventually — because I and the company are the catalysts for the two things coming together — I will see things.

You seem to be describing a process that allows very different kinds of material to inhabit the same space while, in some respects, remaining very much apart.

Yeah. Yeah, definitely. I think probably in *Brace Up!* they ended up coming too much together. I would really want something more disparate.

The emphasis you place on the formal qualities of the material seems to be in opposition to the kind of psychological basis of Wilder and Chekhov's texts.

I don't have a rejection of psychological motivation. I just have a rejection of psychological motivation existing in one form. I like to use the psychological motivation as a whole theatrical space. I can't imagine, in this day and age, not feeling the psychology in one way or another.

Were you interested in any way in the association between Chekhov's work and naturalism? Perhaps in opposition to the Japanese material?

You see, I don't know the history of the Chekhov. I hadn't, before I'd done this, seen a Chekhov play except in Dutch. I couldn't really tell what the psychology was. And the naturalism was –– well, I don't speak the language.

I don't have the history of that, I don't know what that is. I think I'm doing a naturalistic version of Chekhov.

One of the conventional things about naturalism is that it creates one unified world.
 Yeah. That's what I think I'm doing. Perhaps Stanislavski was not — he was fragmenting it all into different characters — to me it's all one thing.

Did you see any Noh theatre live?
 No. I did see some tapes in Japanese. I never saw it translated. I couldn't follow the content, but I could watch them come on and go off. That's very important. So, you know, I didn't read too much about what Noh was or what it's supposed to be. I just watched tapes in Japanese. So I think I was probably drawn to that structure, that physical architectonic structure. How they moved, how they dealt with entrances and exits.

Is it something you pursued in the piece particularly?
 Entrances and exits are extremely important. That's the defining thing, isn't it? In theatre. That's essential. It's the deepest, deepest place for me. But, I've said this before.

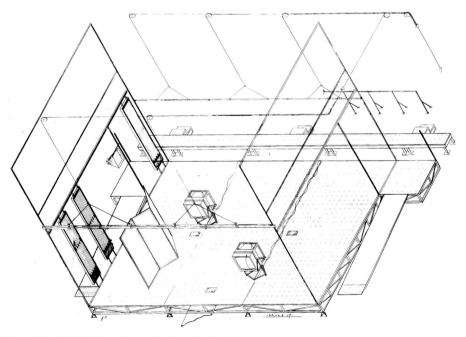

Figure 69 Jim Clayburgh, set design for the Wooster Group, *Brace Up!* (1991) (courtesy: The Wooster Group).

One of the things that interests me about the use of Noh is its emphasis upon continuity — and so its reflection upon its own history. This seems to be reflected in the Wooster Group's work. Performances seem to comment on previous productions, images are re-used, rehearsal procedures are remembered or re-presented. Were you interested in Noh's concern with its own history?
    I don't know. I mean, I'm not a Japanese theatre artist. I don't study Japanese theatre. I don't have any academic interest in Japanese theatre.

I'm just interested in what these appropriations might have to offer. Or what the juxtaposition of the Japanese material against the Chekhov might be doing.
    I think we were getting to that when I said 'entrances and exits'.

MW: The way that I look at it is that it's more like a contrapuntal reading. The two things go, and sometimes connect in the audience member's mind and sometimes don't. But there's no didactic, polemical —
Attempt.

MW: Connection being made. There's no attempt to connect them, really. I think there's a rhythmic attempt to make them relate, or perhaps to let them relate in the space.
Yes. To allow them to be in the space together, without this demand for meaning. 'Meaning' in quotes — that you're dealing with, very strongly.

Do you mean that I'm demanding meaning of you?
    Yes, absolutely. That's not what I'm about. My meaning is in the piece itself. I'm not going to now make meaning separately from that piece for you. Again, it's not a thing where I'm withholding that — I don't have it. It only happens for me in the space. In the moment of the theatrical act. Here I can just tell you the way I came up with those images, the way they are brought to the stage. Then, I could, if I wanted to, spin off and say, Oh, yes, isn't it funny how this image looks good, or it's good with that sound. I could even, after the fact, probably — if I were a writer — write a whole thing on the meaning of Japanese culture and Western language. About meaning and lack of meaning, about Western poetry and Eastern poetry. But I don't have much interest in it.

It may be that we don't have a language to talk with.
    It's possible.

Which is, on the one hand, a shame, on the other hand, it may be instructive.
    I think it is. I think it's probably very instructive looking at the work next to other people's work, too, to be honest, just by my inability to grapple

with whatever it is you're telling me. It has something to do with why the work is like it is.

It's important, from my point of view, because I don't intend to demand a meaning for the piece.
No, no. I know. Believe me, I'm not trying to be obfuscating. Maybe the language that you're using I don't use. Maybe you've talked to people who aren't as theatre-oriented as I am. That's why Joan Jonas came to work with us, because she wanted to make entrances and exits. She doesn't make them in her own work. I didn't come from theatre but from painting and film — which is, the cut, you know, entrances and exits again — when do you come into a scene and when do you leave it. It may be that.

And this is also connected with framing.
Well, of course. Again, I think what I'm saying to you is that form is extraordinarily important to me — certain kinds of theatrical form. And I'm always trying to see it in different ways. And of course I work to different theatre traditions — not only Japanese. I worked for a long time with vaudeville, American vaudeville. So —

And the focus upon form is a key to these very disparate elements coinciding in the same space.
Yes, absolutely. And anything can co-exist together — without, you know, losing its own uniqueness — without being absorbed and regurgitated. They are separate, and they can stay separate and at the same time inform each other — within the same work. At best, when the form is strong enough, that's what happens. If the form isn't strong enough, it's just chaos. That's the danger.

That kind of focus doesn't offer itself to any kind of question I might ask about meaning or theme, does it?
No. Again, you can talk to me about what's going on on the stage.

I'm interested in the emphasis you place on 'presence'. You've said that you use whatever methods you can to try and make — or allow — the actor to become as present as possible.
Yes.

Is this a formal quality in the work?
It can be. Usually that presence is something that I think is — kind of — always in conversation with the formal pattern. The formal pattern will tend to allow the performer to get lulled into feeling safe. Within this

structure that I've made, there are always holes that pop up — that's part of the form. So you have to be vigilant, all the time. Vigilant. Tremendously vigilant. And be aware of everything behind you and in front of you, of the entire structure. Or you might drown. Drowning, I mean — you know, stop you from breathing — to fill you up with water so you can't breath. I think the constant battle for me as a director is to find ways that an actor can be always present, always alive, always thinking this is the first and last moment that she's there — doing this thing — within a structure that is so strong and so sure.

Do you think about the audience in the making of work?

Yeah. I mean — it's like the audience is *there*. They're the air that you breathe. The audience is the other part of the exploration process for theatre. There is no theatre without audience, so there is no life without breath. It's that essential. But it's an involuntary thing, breathing. And my awareness of the audience is almost involuntary. Sometimes I'm conscious of it. Usually when they come in for the first time — it's like a pain in your chest. I become aware of them when things aren't working on the stage. When something's wrong, I become aware in a very conscious way. So then I work to become unaware of them in a way that I'm unaware of my breathing. It doesn't mean that I'm cutting them out. It's just that they should be part of the flow of the whole.

It strikes me that if you concentrate on these formal elements in a way that keeps the possibilities of the piece open, that keeps these things colliding or existing at the same moment, then — because there are many languages being held up at the same time — the work resists being read through a single language. I wonder if, as a consequence of this, the viewer might become more open to this 'presence'?

I know what you're saying — but I don't know. Again, I'm not always sure. It's no science. I was talking to a writer a while ago, who's a little older than me. He was saying how, you know, he now had become technically better. He could write more quickly. He knew when things weren't working. He'd acquired technique. And I had to realise when I was talking to him that I still don't know how to get that presence on the stage, that every time I go down for a new piece it's the same battle as it was for *Sakonnet Point* in 1975. That I had not gotten any clearer about how to get that presence, how to keep it, how to make the form balance with the —

Do you think it can succumb to technique?

Well, I don't know. I don't know. I wish I had the technique, because it's harder to do it.

Joe Chaikin tried to gear technique toward producing presence, didn't he?

Yes, he did. That's a good point. I hadn't thought about Chaikin in a long time. But it's also — I'll tell you what else. And this is where I'm different from the other people you've talked to, with the exception of John Cage. I think what keeps me unable to get that technique down so that I can, you know, produce more quickly, more easily and more fluidly what I need — again, I use *need* in a spiritual way — on the stage is that I'm always working with other people and other texts, not my own texts. You know, Ping Chong writes his own texts. He's controlling them all the time. Joan Jonas makes up her own actions. She doesn't go to a script. She's writing her own material. I'm not. I'm having to come up against a new person and new people downstairs every single piece. So I have to rediscover, in every piece, what makes the balance. Because people are so different. Actors are so different. I think that that's part of it. And it's that unique place — that I'm making a new thing out of old material. I'm not just redecorating an old script. I'm not just going to do Chekhov. I'm trying to — I'm trying to make it present for me. Which means literally reinventing. I mean — 'reinventing' it — it's an over-used word. I mean reinventing it from the ground up. From the way that the language resonates in the body on the stage — every way — to the way the psychology has to be — (CLAPS ONCE) — has to be crashed up against and fragmented and then reformed. So it's got a double problem. I'm reinventing something and I'm having to come up against material that I don't necessarily understand — my actors, a text — and that I don't know how to manipulate. And because I think on stage — I don't think separately, I don't sit down with the text and say, 'Ah, this means this — if I get Joan Jonas to do this on stage, then I'll get what I want from this text'. What I want from the text is what Joan Jonas and Chekhov give to me on the stage! Only on the stage. Not inside my head. So it makes it particularly difficult. I've got the worst of both worlds.

Does it not also mean that the work is difficult to talk about, in certain respects?

Well. It depends on what you mean by 'talk about'. I don't think it does. I just can't talk about it in literary terms, in the same way that most people talk about it. I've discovered more recently that theatre people — especially directors — don't talk in the same way that I do. They talk as if I'm writing. Yet I'm not a writer. I'm using other people's writing. The process is akin to that — the process of reinventing — it's akin to writing. I just have my characters, my words, my colleagues, all materialised on the stage. Writers can do it in their head. I can't. I have to take my head — I'm very literal, as you can see — I have to take my head and put it on the stage and move the little elements of ideas around the stage to see what it means. Maybe it's a little unusual.

So I'm really a classical director in the sense that — I do plays. You know. (Laughs). The most important thing in all of this is that — when I go downstairs I don't have any thematic ideas — I don't even have a theme. I don't have anything except the literal objects — some flowers, some images, some television sets, a chair, some costumes I like. In the last piece, something someone brought in by mistake. That's it. And then ideas come after the fact. It's a total reversal of most of the processes. And probably if I reversed it I'd do a lot more work and be a lot happier. (Laughs). On that note —

Thanks.

SELECT BIBLIOGRAPHY

This bibliography gives details of texts referred to in the main body of this book, as well as providing a brief guide to principal and primary source texts which include documentation of work or further bibliographical information.

Abramovic, M. and Ulay (1980) *Relation Work and Detour*, Amsterdam: Marina Abramovic and Ulay.
—— (1983) *Nightsea Crossing*, Amsterdam: Museum Fodor.
—— (1986) *Modus Vivendi*, Eindhoven: Stedelijk Van Abbemuseum.
Acconci, V. (1978) *Vito Acconci*, Luzern: Kunstmuseum Luzern.
—— (1982) *Recorded documentation by Vito Acconci of the exhibition and commission for San Diego State University* (audio cassette), San Diego: San Diego State University.
Acconci, V. and Wijers, L. (1979) *Vito Acconci Talks To Louwrien Wijers*, Velp: Kantoor Voor Cultuur Extracten.
Battcock, G. (1973) *The New Art* 2nd (revised) edn, New York: E. P. Dutton.
Battcock, G. and Nickas, R. (1984) *The Art of Performance: A Critical Anthology*, New York: E. P. Dutton.
Bethanien, K. (ed) (1983) *Performance: Another Dimension*, Berlin: Frolich and Kaufmann Gmbh.
Brisley, S. (1981) *Stuart Brisley*, London: Institute of Contemporary Arts.
—— (1981a) 'Conversations', *Audio Arts Magazine*, vol. 4 no. 4.
—— (1986) *The Georgiana Collection*, Glasgow: Third Eye Centre.
Bronson, A. A. and Gale, P. (eds) (1979) *Performance by Artists*, Toronto: Art Metropole.
Cage, J. (1967) *A Year from Monday*, Middletown, Conn: Wesleyan University Press.
—— (1968) *Silence: Lectures and Writings*, London: Marion Boyars.
—— (1973) *M*, Middletown, Conn.: Wesleyan University Press.
—— (1972) *Biology and History of the Future*, Edinburgh: Edinburgh University Press.
—— (1979) *Empty Words*, Middletown, Conn.: Wesleyan University Press.
—— (1986) *X*, Middletown, Conn.: Wesleyan University Press.
—— (1990) *I–VI*, Cambridge, Mass.: Harvard University Press.
—— (1993) *Composition in Retrospect*, Cambridge, Mass.: Exact Change.
Cage, J. and Charles, D. (1981) *For the Birds*, London: Marion Boyars.

Cage, J. and Knowles, A. (1969) *Notations*, New York: Something Else Press.

Cage J. and Kostalanetz R. (1988) *Conversing with Cage*, New York: Limelight Editions.

Champagne, L. (1981) 'Always Starting Anew: Elizabeth LeCompte' (interview), *The Drama Review*, vol. 25 no.3.

Chong, P. (1988) *Kind Ness* in *New Plays USA 4* edited by James Leverett and Gillian Richards, New York: Theatre Communications Group.

—— (1990) *Nuit Blanche: A Select View of Earthlings* in *Between Worlds: Contemporary Asian-American Plays* edited by Misha Berson, New York: Theatre Communications Group.

Cousin, G. (1994) 'An Interview with Mike Pearson of Brith Gof' in *British Live Art: Essays and Documentations* edited by Nick Kaye, *Contemporary Theatre Review*, vol. 2 no. 2.

Crimp, D. (ed) (1983) *Joan Jonas: Scripts and Descriptions*, Berekley: University of California.

Davy, K. (ed) (1976) *Richard Foreman: Plays and Manifestos*, New York: New York University.

Duchamp, M. (1973) 'The Creative Act' in *The New Art* 2nd (revised) edn, edited by G. Battcock, New York: E. P. Dutton.

Dupuy, J. (1980) *Collective Consciousness: Art Performances in the Seventies*, New York: Performing Arts Journal Publications.

Etchells, T. and Lowdon, R. (1994) '*Emmanuelle Enchanted*: Notes and Documents' in *British Live Art: Essays and Documentations* edited by Nick Kaye, *Contemporary Theatre Review*, vol. 2 no. 2.

Forced Entertainment (1994) '*The Red Room*', *Art and Design*, no. 38.

Foreman, R. (1985) *Reverberation Machines: The Later Plays and Essays*, New York: Station Hill Press.

—— (1991) *Love and Science: Selected Music-Theater Texts*, New York: Theatre Communications Group.

—— (1992) *Unbalancing Acts: Foundations for a Theatre*, New York: Pantheon Books.

Gray, S. and LeCompte, E. (1978) 'The Making of a Trilogy', *Performing Arts Journal*, vol. 3 no. 2.

—— (1978a) 'Play: *Rumstick Road*', *Performing Arts Journal*, vol. 3 no. 2.

Heiss, A. (1990) *Dennis Oppenheim: Selected Works 1967–90*, New York: Institute for Contemporary Art with Harry N. Abrams Inc.

Howell, A. (1983) *Notions of a Mirror*, London: Anvil Press.

—— (1986) *Why I may never see the Walls of China*, London: Anvil Press.

—— (1986a) *In the Company of Others*, London: Marion Boyars.

Howell, A. and Templeton, F. (1977) *Elements of Performance Art*, London: The Theatre of Mistakes.

Jonas, J. and White, R. (1979) 'Joan Jonas' (interview), *View*, vol. 2 no. 1.

King, E. A. (1988) *Barry Le Va: 1966–1988*, Pittsburgh: Carnegie Mellon University Press.

Kirby, M. (1965) *Happenings*, New York: E. P. Dutton.

—— (1969) *The Art of Time*, New York: E. P. Dutton.

—— (1978) *Photoanalysis: A Structuralist Play*, Seoul.

—— (1986) *First Signs of Decadence*, Schulenburg: I. E. Clark Publishers.

—— (1987) *A Formalist Theatre*, Philadelphia: University of Pennsylvania Press.

Kirby, M. and Schechner, R. (1986) 'An Interview with John Cage' in *The Drama Review: Thirty Years of Commentary on the Avant-Garde* edited by B. McNamara and J. Dolan, Ann Arbor: UMI Research Press.

Kirshner, J. R. (1980) *Vito Acconci: A Retrospective 1969 to 1980*, Chicago: The Museum of Contemporary Art, Chicago.

Kostalanetz, R. (ed) (1968) *The Theatre of Mixed Means* Dial Press: New York.

—— (ed) (1980) *Scenarios: Scripts to Perform*, New York: Assembling Press.

—— (ed) (1991) *John Cage: An Anthology* 2nd (revised) edn, New York: Da Capo Press.

Kultermann, U. (1971) *Art Events and Happenings*, London: Mathews Miller Dunbar.

LeCompte, E. (1985) 'The Wooster Group Dances', *The Drama Review*, vol. 29 no.2.

Le Va, B. (1978) *Barry Le Va: Four Consecutive Installations and Drawings 1967–1978*, New York: The New Museum.

Ligare, D. (1979) *Barry Le Va Drawings 1967–77*, Salinas, CA: Hartnell College Gallery.

Linker, K. (1994) *Vito Acconci*, New York: Rizzoli.

Loeffler, C. E. and Tong, D. (eds) (1980) *Performance Anthology: Source Book for a Decade of Californian Performance Art*, San Francisco: Contemporary Arts Press.

Marranca, B. (ed) (1977) *The Theatre of Images*, New York: Drama Book Specialists.

Maynard Smith, J. (1994) 'Station House Opera: *The Oracle*' in *British Live Art: Essays and Documentations* edited by Nick Kaye, *Contemporary Theatre Review*, vol. 2 no. 2.

Meyer, U. (1972) *Conceptual Art*, New York: E. P. Dutton.

Montano, L. (1981) *Art in Everyday Life*, Los Angeles: Astro Artz.

Monte, J. (1969) *Anti-Illusion: Procedures/Materials*, New York: Whitney Museum of American Art.

Oppenheim, D. (1990) *Dennis Oppenheim Retrospective 1970–1990*, Athens: Perides Museum of Contemporary Art.

Pearson, M. (1994) 'Theatre/Archaeology', *The Drama Review*, vol. 38 no.4.

Pontbraid, C. (1980) *Performance: Text(e)s and Documents*, Montreal: Parachute.

Rainer, Y. (1974) *Work 1961–73*, Nova Scotia and New York: Nova Scotia College of Art and Design and New York University.

Rogers, S. (1988) 'Showing the Wires: An Interview with Julian Maynard Smith', *Performance*, no. 56–57.

Savran, D. (1986) *Breaking the Rules: The Wooster Group*, New York: Theatre Communications Group.

Schechner, R. (ed) (1970) *The Performance Group: Dionysus in 69*, New York: Farrar, Strauss and Giroux.

—— (1973) *Environmental Theater*, New York: Hawthorn Books.

—— (1982) *The End of Humanism: Writings on Performance*, New York: Performing Arts Journal.

—— (1985) *Between Theatre and Anthropology*, Philadelphia: University of Pennsylvania Press.

—— (1988) *Performance Theory* 2nd (revised) edn, London and New York: Routledge.

—— (1993) *The Future of Ritual*, London and New York: Routledge.

Schmidt, P. (1992) 'The Sounds of *Brace Up!*: Translating the Music of Chekhov', *The Drama Review*, vol. 36 no.4.

Schneemann, C. (1979) *More Than Meat Joy*, Documentext: New York.

Sohm, H. (1970) *Happening and Fluxus*, Cologne: Koelnischer Kunstverein.

Spurlock, W. H. (1977) *Barry Le Va — Accumulated Vision: Extended Boundaries*, Dayton: Wright State University Galleries.

Spoerri, D. (1966) *An Anecdoted Topography of Chance*, New York: Something Else Press.

Templeton, F. (1990) *You — The City*, New York: Roof Books.

Tufnell, M. and Crickmay, C. (eds) (1990) *Body Space Image: Notes towards improvisation and performance*, London: Virago.

INDEX

Other titles in the Contemporary Theatre Studies series: